The Parental Figures and
the Representation of God

Religion and Society   21

GENERAL EDITORS
Leo Laeyendecker, *University of Leyden*
Jacques Waardenburg, *University of Utrecht*

MOUTON PUBLISHERS · THE HAGUE · PARIS · NEW YORK

The Parental Figures and the Representation of God

A Psychological and Cross-Cultural Study

ANTOINE VERGOTE and ALVARO TAMAYO

MOUTON PUBLISHERS · THE HAGUE · PARIS · NEW YORK

This title has been published jointly in Louvain Psychology Series Studia Psychologica by Leuven University Press.

Published with the support of the University Foundation of Belgium.

ISBN: 90-279-3059-7
Printed in Great Britain

Preface

This book is addressed to those who are interested in the human personality, in emotional development, and in the formation of the moral and religious conscience.

What does the mother–father polarity mean for the child and the adult? What is its function in the genesis of emotional relationships and in the establishment of ethical and religious attitudes? If it differs, how does it differ for the two sexes and in different cultures? Have the changes in society and in the relations between men and women altered the meaning of this parental polarity? If so, in what sense?

These are the questions that gave rise to the studies contained here. Though the literature on this subject is bountiful, empirical studies are rare.

We have tried to develop a new method that could furnish scientifically justified answers to these questions. And we think that our results can make a relevant contribution in this very complex area, an area that is often passionately controversial and that is of the highest importance for the future of humanity and religion.

We also believe that the data presented here are pertinent to the concerns of the behavorial scientist, the clinician, the theologian, and the educator.

Any scientific study is founded on hypotheses derived from previous observations and experience. Indeed, the questions themselves are an essential part of any study. The first chapter therefore explains at length the standpoint from which we approach the object of our research. The research instrument we designed is presented in the second chapter. It takes on its full significance in the light of the theoretical presuppositions of the first chapter. The following chapters consist of succinct accounts of the studies performed with that instrument on various population groups. The reader who is in a hurry or who is not familiar with this kind of research will profit in particular from the summary of the essential data given in the concluding chapter. This reader will certainly also appreciate the fact that the observations are integrated into a theoretical framework that illuminates the significance of the empirical data.

The study is based on only a few populations. It could, of course, be extended worldwide. The available means and collaborators in suitable circumstances have, along with some special interests, determined the population choice. We were thus not able to follow up some important variables such as the influence of various religions and environments like the Jewish and Islamic. This is left for others, or ourselves, to do in the future. Our first purpose was to see if there are fundamental and common factors in the parental images and, if this were the case, to determine the degree they contribute to the formation of the representation of God. The choice of some special populations (the religious and the psychologically deviant populations) was intended to provide a gauge of the possible influence of a particular life orientation or of exceptional psychic factors.

This project began in 1962 and has involved many researchers. We rely on the indulgence of our scientific colleagues with regard to the technical imperfections of the initial studies. In spite of these imperfections, we think their results are worthy of being summarized here. To the methodological gropings of the beginning, was sometimes added the difficulty of assembling suitable populations. And as our collaborators were often students doing graduate work on the master's degree level, their studies were, of necessity, limited. But without them, this project could not have been carried out. We are grateful to them, and are pleased to cite them by name in the bibliography.

Our particular gratitude goes to those who took on the task of synthesizing their own research and that of the other collaborators. Their names are cited at the head of the texts they authored. The final texts were prepared with the help of P. De Neuter, A. Vannesse, and L. Vercruysse. We should like to thank them. They patiently and carefully reread the many manuscripts to confirm the data and the conclusions. All this work would never have been finished in a reasonable length of time, however, if A. Tamayo had not agreed to consecrate the greater part of his sabbatical year to the critical revision and final editing of the text. It is only proper, therefore, that he be presented as coauthor.

The manuscripts for this book were originally written in French, Dutch, and English. P. Jones made some of the French translations and we were able to call upon the excellent translation and editorial services of Edward J. Haasl. Throughout this entire project, we have also been able to count on the devoted and intelligent help of M. Franssens who, in addition to the typing, took on the delicate and exacting task of proofreading.

If this study stimulates the interest of other investigators, gives rise to new studies, and forms the occasion for discussion and verification, our efforts will be amply rewarded.

A. VERGOTE
Louvain

Contents

PREFACE   V

1. THE PARENTAL FIGURES: SYMBOLIC FUNCTIONS
   AND MEDIUM FOR THE REPRESENTATION OF GOD
   by Antoine Vergote
   1 The Project   1
   2 Figure and Representation   3
   3 Symbolic Figures   5
   4 Symbolic Figures and Social Stereotypes   9
   5 Symbolic Figures and Their Functions   11
   6 The Symbolic Figures as Distinct from the Memory Images
     and the Affective Relationships   17
   7 The Parental Figures and the Representation of God   19

2. THE SEMANTIC DIFFERENTIAL PARENTAL SCALE
   by Alfred Vannesse and *Patrick de Neuter*   25
   1 Description of the SDPS   25
   2 Construction   27
   3 Versions   28
   4 Validity of the SDPS   31

3. MATERNAL AND PATERNAL DIMENSIONS IN THE
   PARENTAL AND DIVINE FIGURES *by Godelieve Vercruysse*
   and *Patrick de Neuter*   43
   1 Description of the Samples   43
     1.1 Belgian-Dutch Studies   43
     1.2 Belgian-French Studies   44
     1.3 American Study   46
     1.4 Italian Study   47
   2 Results   48
     2.1 Parental Figures   48
     2.2 The Representation of God as Related to the Parental Figures   57
   3 Conclusion   67

4. CULTURAL DIFFERENCES IN THE STRUCTURE AND
    SIGNIFICANCE OF THE PARENTAL FIGURES
    by Alvaro Tamayo   73
    1 Method   73
       1.1 Subjects   73
       1.2 Measuring Instrument   74
       1.3 Statistics   74
       1.4 Semantic Analysis   75
    2 Results   76
       2.1 Description of the Three Figures   76
       2.2 Symbolic Significance of the Parental Figures   82
    3 Discussion   95

5. DIFFERENTIAL PERSPECTIVES OF THE PARENTAL
    FIGURES AND THE REPRESENTATION OF GOD   99
    A The Influence of Age on the Parental Figures and the
       Representation of God *by Alvaro Tamayo* and *Suzanne Cooke* 99
    B The Influence of the Field of Study on the Parental Figures
       and the Representation of God *by Alvaro Tamayo*
       and *Albert Dugas*   103
    C The Influence of Belief Systems on the Parental Figures and
       the Representation of God *by Alvaro Tamayo*
       and *Léandre Desjardins*   108
    D Parental and Divine Figures of Christians and Hindus
       according to Belief System *by Léandre Desjardins*
       and *Alvaro Tamayo*   116
    E Belief in the Existence of God and the Representation of God
       by Dirk Hutsebaut   125
    F Parental Images and the Representation of God in Seminarians
       and Women Religious *by Alfred Vannesse* and *Therese Neff* 136

6. THE PARENTAL FIGURES AND THE REPRESENTATION
    OF GOD OF SCHIZOPHRENICS AND DELINQUENTS
    by Alvaro Tamayo and *Paul St.-Arnaud*   145
    1 Parent-Child Relationships of Schizophrenics and Delinquents 145
       1.1 Delinquents   146
       1.2 Schizophrenics   148
    2 Method   153
       2.1 Sample   153

2.2 The Measuring Instrument 154
3 Results 154
3.1 Relative Importance of the Figures 154
3.2 Similarity of the Figures 156
3.3 Factorial Structure of the Figures 157
4 Discussion 163

7. THE REPRESENTATION OF GOD AND PARENTAL
FIGURES AMONG NORTH AMERICAN STUDENTS
by Luiz Pasquali 169
1 Method 169
1.1 The SDPS II 169
1.2 Sample 172
2 Results and Discussion 172
2.1 The Factors 172
2.2 Factorial Structure of the Figures 175
2.3 Relational Structure of the Figures 177
2.4 Semantic Differences on the Basis of the Items 179
2.5 Semantic Distances on the Basis of the Factors 180

8. OVERVIEW AND THEORETICAL PERSPECTIVE
by Antoine Vergote 185
1 The Parental Figures 185
1.1 The Components of the Parental Figures 185
1.2 The Maternal Symbolic Figure 186
1.3 The Paternal Symbolic Figure 191
1.4 The Variations between the Groups 198
2 The Representation of God 204
2.1 The Fundamental Structure of the Representation of God
and Its Meaning 205
2.2 Differences between the Groups 209
2.3 The Father Figure: The Most Adequate Symbol of God? 215
2.4 Symbolization, That Which Animates the Paternal Metaphor 222

APPENDIX I : Some Developmental Characteristics of the Parental
Figures and the Representation of God
by Hervé Coster 227
APPENDIX II : The Paternal and Maternal Items in English,
French, Dutch, Spanish, and Italian 232

APPENDIX III : Sources of the Attributes used in Constructing
the SDPS   234

REFERENCES   239

AUTHOR INDEX   251

The Parental Figures: Symbolic Functions and Medium for the Representation of God

Parent–child relationships are highly individual and are involved in the relationship to God. But the individual experiences of the parents are contained in and formed by the general culture; the formation of the parental figures and the representation of the divine occur via discourse and behavior that are, in the cultural environment, symbolic. The purpose of this work is to study these figures and their relation to the representation of God.

In this chapter the general purpose of this work and its importance to psychology will be presented. In addition, the terminology needs to be explained, the method introduced, and the limits of the project set.

1 THE PROJECT

Compared to what anthropology has assembled, nonclinical psychology has little solid information to offer on the structure of parental roles (Lamb 1976). Cultural anthropology (Benedict 1953; Stephens 1963) and clinical psychology (Dolto 1971; Erikson 1963; Klein 1965; Masserman 1959; Rizzuto 1974; Winnicott 1965) have clearly demonstrated that parental figures are prime factors in the structure of personality — even in that of an adult. The study of the formation of these figures should not be confined, as often occurs, to the study of the child or of the patient still grapling with the problems of parental relationships. An adequate psychological analysis of humanity demands an appreciation of what cultural anthropology has accomplished. Thus, the meaning of the parental figures must be defined, and their roles in relation to other persons, to the world, and to the divine must be examined.

It has long been common knowledge among psychologists that there are certain parallels between the representation of God and parental figures (Bovet 1951; Freud 1927, 1943; Jones 1923; Jung 1961). These similarities have been interpreted as, among other things, conceptual expressions of religious experience (Girgensohn 1930; Van der Leeuw 1948), symbols motivated by some innate need (Allport 1953), and projections (Fromm 1952; Spiro and D'Andrade 1958). But what grounds are there for these theories? The hastiness of their elaboration accords well with their lack of foundation in observed fact. What constitutes the parental figures? Are they no more than the simple reflections of childhood experiences? And, for example, does the name 'father' mean the same thing when applied to the divine being as when applied to the human parent? Historically and anthropologically, the explanations offered by psychological theories often seem precariously hollow (Evans-Pritchard 1967).

The present study of the problem is empirically oriented. We shall try to derive, with the greatest possible precision, the components and structures of the parental figures and their relation to the contemporary perception of God — be it in terms of religious belief or in terms of doubt or denial. Without a clear understanding of these three great figures — mother, father, and God — it is impossible to devise an adequate psychological explanation of their interrelations.

The correspondence between parental figures and the representation of God, which is attested in the history of religions (Eliade 1958, 1976), necessarily implies fundamental psychological processes. Can these processes be delineated by means of a research instrument that focuses on the structures and components of these three concepts? Obviously, the results of this research are not sufficient in themselves to explain completely the recognized affinities and dissimilarities. But they do provide indications and pointers and any theory that fails to account for the observed data will have to be considered wanting.

2 FIGURE AND REPRESENTATION

To designate the distinctive qualities of parents and the fulfillment of functions with symbolic values by parents, the term 'paternal figure' was chosen. Of itself, the term 'figure' connotes a typical personality. Thus we speak of the great figures of history. We find the same connotations in the expression 'literary figures'. Some elements of the meaning of the expression 'parental figures' as it is used here are contained in the expression 'ballet or dance figures'. By this expression, then, we are specifically designating the typical significations and values that parents assume by their respective positions in the family configuration.

We prefer to speak of 'parental figures' rather than 'parental images' because the latter evokes, too directly, imaginative representations derived from visual perception. 'Image' suggests an internal representation that results from memories and that has been partially altered by the affectivity of the subject. One can thus submit the parental images to the test of reality. And in any event, 'image' does not connote the significations that parents assume by their roles in the family.

To designate the idea of God as it is formed in correspondence with the parental figures, the term 'representation of God' was chosen. 'Representation' expresses the rendering present to the spirit and to the emotions of an absent reality, and this by means of a figure. Thus religious symbols represent the divinity. As God is not directly present to one's mind, one always relates to God via figures, concepts, or symbols belonging to the human world. 'Representation of God' thus connotes two ideas: God must be rendered actively present to the mind, and this is done by means of that which is present to the mind from the experience of the realities of the human world.

For reasons of economy of style, 'figure of God' is often used for 'representation of God'. The reader is reminded, however, that the parental figures and the figure of God belong to different categories.

The terms 'figure' and 'representation' indicate that the present research is focused on the objective aspect of the relationships under consideration. One can envisage other approaches that would be directly concerned with the subjects and the internal undertones of their relationships, but they would inevitably omit certain types of essential relationships. By considering the objective poles of the relationships with the parents and with God, we believe that we can isolate the emotions, memories, and meanings that would not be revealed by a study that, by being focussed directly on the lived relationships, would depend more on introspection.

In examining the parental figures and the representation of God, however, we do not neglect the psychological point of view. What is intended is not the abstract meaning of the concepts of the mother, the father, and God, but what the mother, the father, and God are for the subjects. To obtain this, the instrument used in this research is composed of items expressing various components of the affective relations. This is also the reason why we have avoided using the term 'concept' with regard to the mother, the father, and God. Even though, in certain philosophical traditions (Kant 1964), 'concept' is defined to include experiential overtones, it generally denotes a representation raised to the level of abstract theory.

It would also be improper to use 'imago' to define the object of our research. Introduced by Jung (1947), it designates the 'unconscious prototype of personalities that electively orient the way in which the subject apprehends others'. An imaginary schema acquired through early relationships, it includes, besides memories of real relationships, that which is phantasmatic and, strictly speaking 'subconscious'. Since we do not wish to adopt Jungian psychology — in any case, it would be impossible to verify it with a semantic scale — we have dispensed with this term as well as with 'archetype', another term surrounded by dubious theories constructed on observations of an entirely different order than those with which we are concerned.

3 SYMBOLIC FIGURES

The very reality of the parental figures obliges us to go beyond the registration of memories recorded in images that simply reproduce previous relations. The parental figures, in fact, are not just real persons, endowed with particular personality traits, who survive in the imaginary and emotional world of those who participated in the family. Their significance is drawn primarily from their place and function within the family constellation. And this constellation receives its typical structure from the meanings and functions assigned to it by the culture as a whole. Therefore, we distinguish between memory images, which reproduce the traces of the past and are composed of intersubjective experiences, and symbol figures[1]. Let us explain.

3.1 *The Symbolic Order*

The expression, 'symbolic figure', indicates that the parental figures belong to the symbolic order: before evoking another reality — the divine, for example — parental figures are symbolic in and through their functions and differentiated qualities. 'Symbolic', therefore, is not taken here to imply isomorphism, the resemblance factor

1. It is in this respect that our study differs from others. Spiro and D'Andrade (1958), who see religion as a projective cultural system as did Kardiner and Linton (1939), stress that the similarity between the parental images and the God image is formed and transmitted by the religious tradition and is maintained by the 'private fantasies' of the individual. In our study, the parental figures are considered as personality structuring, relational poles in a system, and we investigate their correspondence with a structured religious relationship as this can be inferred from the representation of God. In their studies of the similarity between parental images and the God image, Strunk (1959), Godin and Hallez (1964), and Nelson (1971) investigate the representation of the real parents and their items also only reflect the affective preference for one of the parents. For these two reasons, in our opinion, these studies offer no insight into the parental images and therefore cannot clarify the similarity between them and the representation of God.

that causes the transfer of names, but rather the insertion of the parental figures into a structured order that, following contemporary anthropology (Lévi-Strauss 1949, 1969), we consider to be symbolic. The theoretical concept of a symbolic order is derived from the structural linguistics of F. de Saussure (1955), whose fundamental thesis is that a linguistic signifier is only indirectly connected with what is signified because of its integration into a system of signifiers that is characterized by differential oppositions. In this sense, language is a symbol system. Inspired by structural linguistics, anthropology (Geertz 1975) has set out to show that cultural facts, such as matrimonial rules, myths, religious rites and symbols, and economic relations, only reveal their meaning if they are considered in terms of the ordered ensemble. Hence, the specific relations between terms determine in some way the individual terms themselves. Relying upon psychological, sociological, and anthropological data, we consider parental figures to be symbolic realities.

3.2 *Sexuality and the Generations*

The disposition of life confers on the parents functions and qualities that compose a system that introduces the child into the cultural order, i.e., into the symbolic order. The parents not only share the experiences of the child after the manner of somewhat older traveling companions, they are what they are for the child because of their sexual differences and their procreative relationship. It is thus that the difference of generations is established. This double differentiation introduces very complex relationships between the members of the family, relationships that are determined by the very position the members occupy in it. In this way, parents and children are situated in the family as elements in a system. And, because the family system is an ensemble of signifying relations — a structured totality that composes a communication system — its functions are symbolic.

We are not, of course, postulating a stable ensemble of differential traits on the basis of an a priori principle. Our purpose is precisely to investigate these traits in various population groups. The instrument is therefore so designed that the items would express traits and functions that correspond to the structure of family relationships. Thus, a psychological and sociological hypothesis controlled the construction of this scientific instrument. This approach is by no means arbitrary: it is in response to the exigencies of the critical scientific attitude (Nagel 1968).

The parental figures are not differentiated on the basis of mutual exclusion: parents share a common humanity that is the essential foundation of their intersubjective relationships. We presume, therefore, that their differentiation is polar: their relational functions and qualities revolve around a common axis and maintain complementary distances from it. To bring out this difference of polarity, the measuring instrument of this research program was composed of differential items applied to each parental figure separately.

3.3   *Confirmation by Clinical Observations*

The qualities of the parental figures correspond to actual experience and thus reflect empirical facts. But they also belong to an 'order of things' that is symbolic. Should parental qualities and functions be deficient, then the child — and even the adult — will experience this lack as a distortion of the ensemble, which must obey specific laws to function humanly. Moreover, clinical psychology affirms (Dolto 1939, 1971) that these experiences of privation produce their effects precisely because they are perceived, more or less consciously, to be in conflict with accepted norms. Thus, the pathological effects of family aberrations prove that neither the presence nor the absence of parental functions is a matter of simple factual data. Their absence would have no effect if it did not constitute an active deficiency that disturbs the equilibrium of the system. The needs and desires of the child cause these absences to be experienced as privations. The needs correspond to the necessities

of life and belong to the natural order of things; the desires, however, are prompted by the presence of symbolic figures in cultural
discourse and in the significant relations within the culture. These
symbolic figures precede the individual, surround him, and make
him desire parents who correspond to what the symbolic figures
demand.

The family constellation, therefore, is organized, on the one
hand, according to the dispositions of life, which necessarily involve sexuality and the succession of generations, and on the other
hand, according to the significant relationships prescribed by the
cultural context as a whole. This configuration determines the role
of the parents whose very individuality sustains the symbolic values.

3.4   *Permanence and Relativity*

Anthropology has revealed considerable variety in the organization and attitudes that define the family structure (Corin 1972;
Radcliffe-Brown 1969). In doing so, it has emphasized all the more
the symbolic significance. Whatever may be the rules prescribed by
cultures for family relationships, they are always systematic: they
make up an ensemble of relationships and are not given in terms
of the individual, but in terms that are marked by specific differences. The great human realities — life and death, the dichotomy
of the sexes, morality, the origins of culture — are conceived and
transmitted in relation to the family structure. It is because the
family structure is part of the symbolic order making up the cultural ensemble that family relationships manifest the diversity of
form that characterizes all cultural phenomena. If they were merely
natural — only obeying an innate biological code or only answering
to basic needs — they would doubtless be stable and would recur
identically among groups separated by space and time.

Compared to some other civilizations studied by anthropology,
the contemporary Western family is characterized by two traits
that seem to be intimately related: its structure has been reduced
to the nuclear family, and the types of relationships that compose

it have undergone important changes (Ariès 1960). We believe that the reduction in the size of the family unit has opened a wide area for individual initiative, which explains, in part, why Western civilization is a 'hot civilization', one where values are rapidly changing. Sociological studies (Hauser 1963; Mitscherlich 1969) have emphasized the current crisis of the family and, particularly, of the paternal role. Nevertheless, observations on the state of the family in the West have few solid data to support them. That family relations are changing and that, in particular, the role of the father is being challenged, we do not deny. But are these changes destroying the specific references of the parental figures as clothed with symbolic significance? And does the questioning of the role of the father by a less authoritarian civilization lead to 'a fatherless society'?

4 SYMBOLIC FIGURES AND SOCIAL STEREOTYPES

The concept of stereotype comes from social psychology. A social stereotype is a static screen (Krech and Crutchfield 1948), constructed within the milieu, through which one views human beings. Antisemitism, anticlericalism, and animosity toward national groups are attitudes that cause a person to be perceived as though he/she had a mask on, a mask produced by the milieu. Hence, the stereotype is not a reflection of reality, even though a number of experiential elements may enter into its composition. It is an image that is, strictly speaking, imaginary. As such, it does fulfill a psychological function, though not the positive function of structuring a relationship. Rather, it diverts and displaces: groups designated by the social stereotype as enemies, for example, have often been cast in the role of scapegoat for political purposes. Psychology has shown that it is possible, in cases of intersubjective conflict, to project repressed affective representations onto people designated for this role by social stereotypes (Anzieu 1973; Rokeach 1960). Thus, the authoritarian father can represent that awesome power to which is imputed the responsibility for failure and feelings of guilt. Moreover, the intrapsychic and social laws governing its transmission, explain why it always presents a simplified image. It is composed of a very limited number of characteristics – the ones that serve the processes of diversion and displacement. A stereotype is therefore functional. Responding to unrecognized needs, it is essentially a failure to recognize the other.

And there is no doubt that parental figures are partially stereotyped, as is the case for the language and the ritual gestures in which one is educated. But if a stereotype designates a more or less stable relationship, it expresses an arguable value judgment. Thus generalized, it pronounces a negative judgment on any form of expression or on any relationship that is not a product of spontaneous creativity (Hameline 1972). Personally, we consider it falsely ideological to oppose creativity to formation that is culturally more or less stable and that is socially transmitted. Thus, we reserve 'stereotype' for the cliché that misrepresents reality for reasons of aggressivity toward, or defence against, others. Parental figures, far from distorting relations, have a structuring power for the development of the individual, as we will explain. Moreover, the fullness and the diversified composition of symbolic figures contrast with the oversimplified schematization characteristic of a stereotype.

As did C. Geertz (1975), we compare the function of the symbolic system in social life with the role of the genetic code in biological life. And since the interpretation of culture consists largely of the study of the influence of symbol systems on the community, so also must psychology investigate their formative contribution to the personality.

There is no doubt that idealized figures are very close to symbolic figures. Yet there is clear distinction between them. Observations have shown that idealization tends to blur the distinction between the parental figures (Godin and Hallez 1964), but when they are perceived symbolically, they are distinct. The inability of idealization to differentiate can be readily explained. Idealization is a magnification of the attributes of the admired object, an overestimation of the object of one's love with which one unconsciously identifies. Love is rich in idealizations because it is moved by powerful desires and parents are to some extent idealized by the child who assigns to them the imaginary fulfillment of desires that have yet to be tested by reality. This occurs also with adults who use idealization as a defence against guilt feelings resulting from long-term conflicts.

When we ask the subjects to envisage the symbolic figure and not the idealized figure, we have reason to believe they do so. Too many items on our scale do not correspond to desires that could provoke psychological exaltation of the parental figures. The attractiveness of other items of the affective order can produce an idealized figure, but an aggrandized ideal of these few qualities is certainly not alien to the symbolic figure. Indeed, our culture accords them positive value, and parents try to conform to them.

5 SYMBOLIC FIGURES AND THEIR FUNCTIONS

Our hypothesis is that the parental figures are symbolic mediators for the representation of God because they have psychological significance in themselves. The human being forms its relations with itself, with others, and with God via multiple intersubjective processes within the family constellation, the effects of which are determined by symbolic references. A change in society seems to have altered family relationships and brought about a new perception of the parental figures. Could not the advance of liberal democracy, the new conception of childhood, and the liberation of women have diminished if not erased the differences between maternal and paternal functions? The biology of procreation obviously requires two distinct and complementary functions. But once the child has been brought into the world, do not both the man and the woman share, in varying degrees, all of the educative and socializing functions? Normative authority, which may have been the paternal right and prerogative, resides today as much with the mother as with the father. The sexual differences no longer impose upon the parental partners tasks as distinct as was formerly the case. We are not prejudging the modern perception of parental figures, the purpose of this investigation being precisely to furnish solid data on the subject. The problem is, indeed, to find out if, notwithstanding the evolution of family and social customs, the child does not perceive the two parents as distinct from each other. By the construction of a measuring instrument and by its application, we want to test the hypothesis that the two parents give rise to specific symbolic figures and that, by virtue of the specific values that they represent, they contribute to the psychological, ethical, and religious formation of the human being.[2]

The literature of developmental psychology, cultural anthropology, and psychoanalysis, as well as general literature, furnished us with a long series of qualities and functions characterizing the mother and the father.[3] If one considers these characteristics within the dynamics of the family, they take on their psychological significance as functions of the process of becoming human.

We insist that we only hypothetically designate these characteristics as distinctive. Our first task consists of finding out if, for different populations, they are really and statistically discriminative. And, where they are, it is necessary then to examine the results given by their application to the symbolic parental figures. One of the essential questions this research is directed to is precisely if and in what manner the father and mother, in the complexity of their actual relationships, also assume each other's complementary characteristics.

Considering the terms with which the mother is described, the difficulty of distinguishing aspects that are truly differentiated in

2. Our study could be made more comprehensive by thorough comparative studies of subjects who were raised in various types of familial relationships or in nonfamilial groups. The existing studies (for example, Bettelheim 1969) do not deal with the specific symbolic parental images that derive from the interaction between cultural reference systems and personally experienced relational patterns. It is clear that only very complex studies that are based on, among other things, accurate individual observations and thorough knowledge of the cultural milieu can provide decisive answers in this area.

3. See the list in Appendix III.

the maternal dimension is striking. The qualities of the mother's personality seem to be from the very beginning linked to the qualities that typify her relation to the child, and that which she is for the child proceeds from the characteristics that qualify her in herself. This aspect of the maternal dimension is readily apparent when one compares it to the way in which the paternal dimension is qualified. Most of the paternal characteristics mentioned below are, by their very nature, not restricted to the relationship with the child; they could just as well designate a social role as a paternal function.

It is generally acknowledged that motherhood is characterized by values of the heart such as intimacy, tenderness, general concern, and warm receptivity. Joined to the child by the vital and affective bonds of physical generation, the mother seems to support all the values associated with intimacy. If the results of our research confirm this characterization, we shall have to take them into account in order to abstract its meaning for the formation of the religious factors of the human personality. And the confrontation of normal populations with those clinically identified as pathological can possibly help us to clarify the significance of the maternal figure in the process of becoming.

The figure of the father seems to be clearly characterized by its position in the familial constellation. Because the father is not attached to the infant by a primordial bioaffective bond, his presence does not represent values of the same vital and affective order as the maternal presence. It is not that the paternal bond is devoid of tenderness and intimacy. However indispensable these qualities may be to the efficacity of his presence, they do not specifically characterize that presence. The father, as a third party, is introduced progressively as a significant person for the infant's psychic development. It is even necessary that the father claim to be the father in exercising his specific qualities in his personal relationship with the child, whereas in the maternal dimension, the mother is mother by virtue of everything she is and does. Clinical experience, moreover, attests that if the father is physically present but does not assume his paternity, the child or adolescent will complain about not having a 'true father' (Michel 1954). In one way or another, the father must adopt his child. Civilizations that have recognized adoption to be equal to paternity by procreation, for example the Judaic and the Roman, doubtless understood that it is of the nature of the father to recognize the child by establishing himself as the father (Rouzic 1927). This specific position of the father can also be seen in the manner in which he is spoken of: the mother is described spontaneously in relation to the child, the paternal role not being necessarily implied, while the father is always considered in the context of the family structure.

The peculiar position of the father as the one who introduces himself as a third party in assuming his position and in actively recognizing his child results in his representing values that are the polar opposites of maternal values. Examining the characteristics by which his function is designated as *specific*, one notes that they indicate active insertion into the world of work, of ethics, of knowledge that masters and organizes things. In psychoanalytic terminology, one could say that the father preferentially assumes the reality principle, while the mother responds more specifically to the pleasure principle. From the perspective of developmental psychology, there is nothing very surprising here. In fact, intervening as a third person with regard to the mother as well as with regard to the child, the father, in a way, separates the child from his first affective bond. Parsons (1954) recognized this distinctive function of paternity and, for this reason, credited it with symbolic significance for the socialization of the child.

Let us describe the paternal figure in more detail. It is evident that, in the mother–father polarity, the function of authority dominates the paternal role. Many qualities contribute to this function: law, norm, rendering in some way the judgment to which the child defers. It does not seem that one can conceive of the father without recognizing this function in him, and, in this way it belongs to him as a right — not in the sense that a legal institution might confer this power on him, but as a function of authority that is inherent in the symbolic paternal figure prior to and independent of any legal regulation. Thus, one might imagine that this function will still characterize the father even where the father and the mother enjoy the same legal rights. And one might ask if this function will continue to define the symbolic status of the father even if, in fact, both parents exercise authority together and in common agreement.

Keeping in mind cultural changes and without anticipating our results, it is necessary that we arrive at an understanding of this classic figure of paternity and situate it among the familial vectors. Both the maternal and the paternal figures take on their significance from the point of view of the child, and not from the point of view of the adult. Now it would be difficult to dispute the bio-affective bond that primordially unites mother and child. As this bond is extended and expressed in the qualities that characterize the mother, the father is distinguished by a function that, in polarity with that of the mother, consists of the demands regarding that which the child must become. In this respect, the paternal function corresponds to the wish of the mother. Normally, therefore, the child does not perceive the two parental functions as being opposed to each other but rather as complementary.

The insertion of the father as a third party into the natural bond between the child and the mother certainly contributes to the attribution of authority to him as a specific function. He assumes his paternity by an initiative much like that taken in adoption, as we have pointed out. This initiative, which we term recognition by the father, implies that the father is perceived specifically as coming from without, constructing the bond between the family and society. In this way, the father represents, in particular, the cultural universe with its ethical laws and norms. The maternal values of tenderness are not repudiated, but their exclusivity is challenged.

Still other characteristics of the father were assembled from literature and taken into account in the construction of the instrument. Thus, the father is described by activity and force, for which there are many possible explanations. It could be that the perception of masculine physical force has affected the paternal figure in this sense. It is equally possible that the customary distinction between man's and woman's work has largely determined this polarity between force-activity and affective intimacy. In the latter case, one would expect to see these qualities disappear as constitutive elements of the symbolic differentiation between the parental figures. But one can suppose just as well that the maternal figure would not be profoundly modified as far as its symbolic status is concerned by a social context in which women exercised the same professions as men. Should such be the case, it could be that force and activity would continue to symbolize the paternal function for other than sociological reasons, for reasons that derive from the psychological differentiation within the symbol system of the family.

Obviously, we want to keep our study as open as possible. We are convinced that the family, as the domain of differentiated relationships, must be seen from the perspective of the person in becoming. In this sense, the family represents a specific institution in which the relationships are not the same as those that exist between adults in the society at large, even if changes in that society modify the intrafamilial relationships.

Can the actual influence of the father and mother on the psychological development of the child be inferred from the content of the symbolic parental figures? Although the method employed here does not provide direct proof, we are of the opinion that such an inference is legitimate — at least if it is accepted that the symbolic parental images are not merely superficial ideas but are deeply rooted in the affective and ethical orientations of the individual. Our primary interest here is to grasp the familial structure in which this influence operates. And precisely because parental behavior takes on its meaning in a complex field that is structured by means of the symbolic parental figures, the causal influences are never univocal. Just to observe what happens between parents and children is not enough, for such observation cannot discern the referential context. A clear example of this is the significance of deficiency in parental interaction with their children. This has an influence because it conflicts with the symbolic whole that constitutes the family. Attention must be therefore given to the particular family system when empirical observations are made.

But the symbolic family system as such cannot be derived by direct observation.

When we affirm the psychological significance of our study, we do not intend to imply that we are going to investigate directly the processes by which the influence of the parental figures is exercised. To Lamb's (1975) question, 'What are the effects of what?', our method can provide no answers. But we do hope to be able to give some indications based on our discoveries. Without an insight into the content of the symbolic parental figures, discussions about these psychological processes are necessarily replete with misunderstanding. For example, the complexity of indentification (Florence, 1978) is all too often misjudged for there is a tendency to reduce it to a simple psychological schema (for example, learning) and not to take the content of the parent–child relationship into account.

6   THE SYMBOLIC FIGURES AS DISTINCT FROM THE MEMORY IMAGES AND THE AFFECTIVE RELATIONSHIPS

Our working hypotheses are that the symbolic figures of the parents are distinct from the memory images and that the symbolic figures contribute the essential symbolic content to the representation of God. As we have already pointed out, certain spontaneous expressions suggest this fundamental distinction. The individual who says, 'I didn't have a real mother' or 'I didn't have a real father', is comparing the mother or the father he did have with the mother or father as they should have been to correspond to the specific functions as the family structure and the culture identify them. Children who do not have a father who acknowledges them demand one. And those who have lost their parents very early, even though they never knew them, like to hear people talk about them. As perceptive teachers and adoptive parents would say, they can still have their father or mother 'in their hearts'.

By memory image, therefore, we mean the mental representation that the subjects have of their real parents, with their particular personalities, their faults and individual qualities. The memory image includes the idea of the concrete manner in which the parents exercised their symbolic parental functions. By way of hypothesis, one can presume that, depending on the subjects, there is a variable distance between the memory images and the symbolic figures. It can be that the memory images are less differentiated than the symbolic figures to the extent that the parents acted in similar ways or that one of them substituted for some lack in the presence of the other. It is necessary, in any event, to investigate this variable distance between the memory images and the symbolic figures and correlate it with other data on the same subjects.

By virtue of this theoretical background, the present study differs from some studies that have set out to examine the relation between the parental images and the idea of God (Godin and Hallez 1964; Nelson and Jones 1957; Nelson 1971; Strunk 1959). These studies used the 'q-test for parent–deity concepts', which is composed of a series of statements expressing bonds of affective union, of tenderness, and of affectionate confidence. By the method of q-sorting, they had these statements applied to the mother, the father, and God. Quite apart from their results, which were not consistent, we believe that their choice of items did not permit, as they intended, the verification of Freud's theory that the idea of God is formed on the basis of the father image. Their items did not take into account two essential aspects of this theory. For Freud (1927, 1939a), the relationship to the father – and to God as father – is characterized by faith because paternity is on the symbolic level, and by law because the father is the one who imposes renunciation on behalf of spiritualization. Without limiting the present study to the Freudian theory on the bond between human and divine paternity, we would disagree with these authors because of our contention that the paternal function is characterized by other relational modes other than just by affective proximity. These other paternal characteristics were not included in the 'q-test for parent–deity concepts' and thus could not be measured by them.

7 THE PARENTAL FIGURES AND THE REPRESENTATION OF GOD

We also intend to determine the relation of the representation of God to the parental images. This, however, must be understood in its exact terms and within its limits. We do not examine religious attitudes by means of an attitude scale, nor do we try to investigate the degree or content of religious belief. However important such studies may be, the empirical psychology of religion would be too restricted if it were confined to the areas of attitude, motivation, and religious experience. While cultural anthropology, developmental psychology, and clinical psychology have demonstrated the preeminent importance of parental figures for personality formation, empirical psychology has neglected the crucial question of their significance for the religious relation as it is actualized in the representation of God.

Thus, as hypotheses of religious psychology, we suggest first that the representation of God is bound up with the symbolic parental figures, and second, that this representation implies living and specific relationships that belong to the psychological realm. Just what the psychological relation to God is, we hope to be able to derive, to a certain extent, from the results of our project. Thus, we do not proceed from such concepts as 'fulfillment of needs' or 'expression of an emotional experience', which have been dealt with so often (Allport 1953). These concepts are too vague and also contain theoretical preconceptions that, perhaps, misinterpret the reality. We also believe that the various meanings surrounding the term 'God' may not be conceived as conceptual constructs without psychological significance. We contend that there is an interaction between religion and personality: the concrete content of the representation of God is an expression of the psychic personality, but the representation of God has also a psychologically formative influence on the personality. Through this research, therefore, we are trying to understand the psychologically relevant meaning of the representation of God and to see if these data can be clarified in a psychological theory.

We are not trying to delineate an eternal and natural image of the divine as opposed to a cultural one. Most of our subjects belong to the Christian cultural and religious tradition, which postulates a God-who-is-father possessing particular traits, and they participate in family structures typical of their civilization. We can assume that their representation of God depends both on religious instruction and family relations. In view of the symbolic and cultural status of the parental figures, it is impossible to dissociate, in the representation of divine paternity, what comes from them from what comes from the religious tradition as such. But our study should be able to determine the meaning for our subjects of this term, which the Christian tradition has taught them to relate to God. It can be that this meaning does not correspond consistently with the Christian notion of divine paternity, and it can even be that, while addressing themselves to God with specifically Christian prayers, God is conceived more according to the symbolic figure of the mother than to that of the father. It is also necessary to determine precisely which paternal characteristics symbolize God for our subjects. From this data, one can hope to gain a better understanding of the psychological factors active in lived religion.

It is not even necessary that the subjects of such a study be believers. Unbelievers also possess a representation of God to which much cultural evidence bears witness. They also form their representation of the God of the believers on the basis of the symbolic parental figures. It would be extremely interesting to know precisely which symbolic parental characteristics are attributed to God by those who do not believe in God. Comparison with believers could shed light on the psychological reasons for the attitudes of belief and unbelief.

Without anticipating the results, we can already understand how there can be a specific bond between the symbolic function of the father and the representation of God. As trustee of a symbolic order acting through him and conferring status upon him, the father never completely fulfills the paternal role. It is even characteristic of the father not to derive his authority from himself. Should he exercise his function solely on the basis of his individual will, his presence becomes arbitrary and tyrannical. It is readily apparent, therefore, how a crisis can develop around the father figure in a society that restricts family ties to the nuclear family and organizes it purely horizontally. The paternal function requires that the father accept the role of representative of humanity: he is its delegate. Hence, various cultures have attributed the source and fullness of paternity to beings that transcend the common human situation — ancestors, kings, gods, God. Cultural anthropology has also shown that a number of peoples attribute a significant portion of the symbolic function of the father to a maternal uncle (Corin 1972; Leach 1961; Lévi-Strauss 1949, 1969; Malinowski 1924). The father is responsible to the maternal uncle who in turn exercises his authority as the representative of the ancestors who are the founders of the laws and customs.

It can be validly argued that the perception of the paternal symbol has inspired many peoples to conceive of their God as a paternal figure. This is not the place to outline the history of the representation of the divine being. We would, however, point out some facts from the history of religions that show that a certain understanding of divine paternity was common to markedly diverse belief and cult systems. It seems to be established that belief in a divine, celestial being was a universal phenomenon. To quote Mircea Eliade (1958: 38):

> What is quite beyond doubt is that there is an almost universal belief in a celestial divine being, who created the universe and guarantees the fecundity of the earth (by pouring rain down upon it). These beings are endowed with infinite foreknowledge and wisdom; moral laws and often tribal ritual as well were established by them during their brief visit to the earth; they watch to see that their laws are obeyed . . ..

And, further on,

> . . . what one may call the history of sky divinities is largely a history of notions of "force", of "creation", of "laws" and of "sovereignty".

Sometimes the divinity is called 'father'. The aborigines of Australia, for example, refer to the supreme being (or beings) not as Spirit or Great Spirit, but as 'fathers ours' (Eliade 1966–1967; 1967–1968).

Evolutionary prejudices — be they sociological or, properly speaking, philosophical and religious — lie at the failure to recognize the historicity and the terms of these archaic religious beliefs (Lang 1937).

Origin, legislator, judge of good and evil, height, founder of the clan, living at a distance — all these qualities and functions point to the representation of the father. That the name itself is not always attributed to the divine being accredited with paternal functions poses no difficulty. What is unique to the Christian tradition is the concentration of these diverse functions in the paternal name of God and the transmutation of the concept of father. Various figures have contributed to the emergence of divine paternity as the specific 'revelation' of Christianity (Pohier 1969; Ricoeur 1969). Most important is the historical initiative of the covenant, and then the recognition of Jesus as his son. Origin of life and law, judge and reconciler, founder of a new form of sonship by an act of recognition — such is the paternity of God in the Christian tradition, which was inaugurated by him who, in revealing himself as Son, proposed his God as Father. Having been so profoundly transformed by the Christian message, the paternity attributed to God ought to evoke particular connotations, and it is probable that its relation to human paternity is more than simple reflection.

Respecting the restricted area of reality that any science — and certainly any instrumental method — can deal with, we make no claim to explain theology by anthropology or, even less, by psychology alone. What is essential is to know how our subjects appropriate in themselves this representation of God and the mediatory role of the parental figures. For the mother can also represent values that the subjects find fully realized only in their representation of God. The mystical idea of the indwelling God, for example, could well correspond more to the mother figure than to the father figure. In any case, the paternal symbol within the family is only psychologically structuring in the context of the parental polarity. One may therefore wonder if a similar polarity occurs in the religious relationship and if this polarity can structure a religious dynamism. For this reason, it seems insufficient to ask simply whether the representation of God is mediated by the father figure or the mother figure. Such a division would fail to take into account the unity of the parental couple in which significance and symbolic function are always in terms of relations of complementarity and tension. Therefore, we must discern whether God is symbolized by the mother figure, the father figure, or by a combination of the two. And, if by a combination, what the modalities of the contributing elements are.

The Semantic Differential Parental Scale

In order to study the correspondence between each of the parental figures and the representation of God on the symbolic level, an instrument that could provide quantitative data was needed. The traditional semantic differential scale (Osgood et al. 1971) seemed to be appropriate. And, indeed such an instrument with its broadly formulated items in terms of good–bad, active–passive, or strong–weak, would measure the semantic similarity between the parental figures and the representation of God across a wide variety of scales. But the similarities that would possibly have been revealed would have been so general that they could not have satisfied the basic requirements of our project. For the fundamental purpose of our research is not to verify the existence of general similarities between the parental figures and the representation of God, but to see if there are specific similarities between the three figures, similarities based on specific maternal and paternal characteristics.

Thus, it was necessary to construct an appropriate measuring instrument that could provide quantitative data was needed. The it consist of a set of maternal and paternal attributes, the maternal attributes being more intensely attributed to the mother than to the father, and the paternal attributes being more intensely attributed to the father than to the mother. Such an instrument is the Semantic Differential Parental Scale (SDPS). In this chapter, the SDPS is described and its construction, translation, and validity are discussed.

1 DESCRIPTION OF THE SDPS

The SDPS is a semantic differential measure containing 36 items on a seven-point scale. Half of the items are maternal characteristics and half paternal. The items are distributed randomly. The subjects are asked to rate successively each parental figure and then the representation of God.

The SDPS is presented in a booklet containing the necessary instructions and the 36 items. The instructions state the general purpose of the SDPS, explain the functioning of the scales, introduce the figure to be rated stressing that it must be described at the symbolic level, and direct the subjects to give their first impressions in rating the figures.

The SDPS was originally constructed in Dutch (Pattyn and Custers 1964). It was translated into French by Bonami (1966) and then from the French into English (Tamayo and Pasquali 1967), Spanish (Tamayo 1970), and Italian (Bernardi 1972).[1]

The following are the English items of the SDPS:

Maternal items

The one who is most patient
Warmth
A warm-hearted refuge
Who takes loving care of me
Who will sympathize with the child's sorrows
Tenderness
Who is intimate
Who gives comfort
Who is always ready with open arms
Brings out which is delicate
Close to whom one feels at home
Self-giving love
Sensitive
Who welcomes me with open arms
Who is always waiting for me
Intuition
Who is all-embracing
Charming

---

1. The various language versions of the SDPS are given in Appendix II.

Paternal items

Strength
Power
Who gives the directions
Systematic mind
Who is the principle, the rule
Who takes the initiative
The one who has the knowledge
The authority
The one who acts
Who makes the decisions
Firmness
The judge
Dynamic
The one who maintains order
Who gives the law
Stern
Who examines things
Protection against danger

2 CONSTRUCTION

The first step in the construction of the **SDPS** was to assemble a set of attributes that representatively describe the mother and the father figures. This sample of attributes was drawn from numerous works of psychology, sociology, philosophy, phenomenology, religion and general culture written and published in Europe and America.[2] A preliminary sample of 226 qualities was assembled, 138 of which described the father, 58 described the mother, and 30 described both.

These qualities were then grouped into categories in function of their dictionary definitions, and their specific association to the father or to the mother was tested. First, 47 university students and faculty members, 28 men and 19 women, were asked to situate

2. The works from which the preliminary sample of attributes was drawn are listed in Appendix III.

each of the 226 qualities on a ten-point bipolar scale, the poles being the father and the mother. Thirty-six qualities were retained, 18 being significantly more applied to the mother than to the father figure and 18 being significantly more applied to the father than to the mother figure. Second, the discriminatory attribution of the two sets of qualities was evaluated with a group of 200 students, 96 male and 104 female. The subjects were asked to associate, on a seven-point scale, the 36 qualities to the father and mother figures and to their representation of God. The results confirmed the discriminatory value of the items. The maternal qualities were, indeed, attributed more to the mother and the paternal qualities more to the father.

3 VERSIONS

Several versions of the SDPS were constructed in order to transcend linguistic barriers in the study of the semantic similarities between the parental figures and the representation of God. The study of these similarities in different linguistic and cultural milieux allows at least the partial exploration of the general and specific principles controlling the symbolization of God via the parental figures. Two things must be considered: the translation procedure and the equivalence of the translated versions.

3.1 *Procedure*

The translation and adaptation of the SDPS into French, English, Spanish, and Italian comprised three stages for each version: literal translation of the items and of the instructions, clinical interviews, and empirical testing.

Literal translation   The translations of the items were made by teams varying from 6 to 11 members. The members of the teams were all proficient in both the source and target languages and were all university professors or graduate students. They were asked to give the closest translation possible of the source language. Working independently, they translated all the items. The accuracy of the translations presented was then verified using standard dictionaries of the target language. Some of the items were translated in exactly the same way by all the translators, while some not. In the latter case, the choice of the translation to be used was made in one of the following two stages of the selection process.

Clinical analysis   All expressions produced by the translators were then submitted to subjects, students for the most part, whose mother tongue was the target language. Individual interviews were conducted for the French version, collective interviews for the English and Spanish versions, and both individual and collective interviews for the Italian version.

The objective of these interviews was to verify the intelligibility of the translations, the actual meaning content, the manner in which they are associated with the parental figures, and their affective connotations. The interview conditions were standardized as much as possible, and the same procedure was followed for each of the 36 items. Most of the problems of the four different versions were resolved in this way, and it was possible to choose the most adequate formulation, that is; the one that was simultaneously the closest to the literal translation, the most saturated in the corresponding parental figure, and the most discriminating.

Empirical testing   The essential purpose of this stage was to verify statistically the formulation of the items, especially with regard to degree of saturation and discriminatory attribution. The conditions of administration and particularly the format of the scale were also tested. Thus, the scale was administered to samples of 40 to 80 subjects who were all university or secondary school students. Each group contained approximately the same number of males as females. The ages ranged from 16 to 25 years old with an average of about 21. The t-test was used to establish the discriminatory attribution of each item to the two parental figures.

The SDPS was administered collectively to each language group, the condition of administration being kept as identical as possible. Half of the subjects began with the paternal figure and the other half with the maternal. The results confirmed the saturation and discriminatory value of the items and showed that the instructions and format were adequate.

3.2   *Equivalence of the Versions*

The translation of linguistic measuring instruments poses difficult and occasionally insoluble problems. Thus the translation of the SDPS had to be done very carefully. But in spite of all the painstaking effort put into the process of translation, the equivalence of the different versions may still be questioned.

To assure equivalence, as close a correspondence of meaning and statistical results as possible was sought between the respective items in all the versions, i.e., equivalence of item content and of attribution of the items to the parental figures. As far as correspondence of meaning is concerned, the precautions taken to obtain exact translations are described above. Nevertheless, perfect correspondence between synonyms to two different languages does not, in general, exist; more often than not, corresponding words of two languages only share a semantic surface, the size of which can vary considerably. All translation involves this danger, and some degree of alteration of meaning is unavoidable. Therefore, perfect correspondence between the items in all versions of the SDPS is not claimed. What we have instead is functional correspondence, which is all that is linguistically possible, that guarantees the presence of the same content in all the versions.

It was also of fundamental importance to know if the content, equivalent in all versions, first, was suitable for the description of the parental figures and, second, could describe them differentially in all the languages. The statistical results provided the answer to these questions. As will be seen in more detail in the following section, the results concerning the discriminatory attribution of the items to the parental figures (Table 2.2) are virtually identical for all versions.

All versions of the SDPS are equivalent in two ways: in content and in attribution. Therefore, they all measure the same reality.

4 VALIDITY OF THE SDPS

For scientific purposes, the most important characteristic of a measuring instrument is its validity. In general, validity refers to the degree to which an instrument measures what it is supposed to measure (Lord and Novick 1968). The SDPS was designed to measure the degree in which the specific characteristics of each of the symbolic parental figures are present in the representation of God. Thus, the validity of the SDPS depends primarily on the adequacy with which the content of the maternal and paternal dimensions is represented in the item sample. Logically, three conditions have to be satisfied for the SDPS to be valid:

(1) The instructions must be able to elicit a measure of the parental figures on the symbolic level;
(2) The items must represent the fundamental characteristics of the father and the mother;
(3) Two series of items are necessary, one maternal and one paternal. Each maternal item must be more intensely attributed to the mother than to the father and inversely for the paternal items.

The empirical testing demonstrated that these three logical conditions were met for all versions of the SDPS.

4.1 *Adequacy of the Instructions*

The objective of our research program being to measure the semantic similarities between each of the symbolic parental figures and the representation of God, it was necessary to verify that the instructions given to the subjects to describe their parents on the

Table 2.1   *Mean intensity scores of the 36 items for the parental figures described on the symbolic and memory levels and the p-values between the differences*

	Mother			Father		
	Symbolic figure	Memory image	t(df=299)	Symbolic figure	Memory image	t(df=299)
Patient	5.95	5.27	6.54**	4.93	4.27	5.61**
Always there	5.75	5.68	0.64	4.13	4.20	0.68
Intuition	5.64	5.16	5.07**	4.12	3.85	2.54*
Who takes care	6.27	6.25	0.28	4.89	4.87	0.14
Who welcomes me	5.71	5.22	5.33**	4.53	4.09	4.05**
Tenderness	5.97	5.29	7.36**	3.91	3.45	4.62**
Who is always ready	5.19	5.45	2.50*	4.02	4.06	0.42
Who brings out which is delicate	5.53	4.92	6.06**	3.70	3.31	3.94**
Self-giving love	5.56	5.40	1.98*	4.56	4.46	0.96
Intimate	5.72	4.81	9.01**	3.91	3.31	5.76**
Sensitive	6.16	5.47	7.55**	4.72	4.32	3.64**
Sympathizes with the child's sorrows	6.36	5.86	5.53**	5.19	4.60	5.15**
Close to whom	5.75	5.00	7.11**	4.32	3.71	5.31**
Let you be a child	5.26	4.79	4.43**	4.34	3.92	3.23**
Always waiting	4.61	4.34	2.39*	3.65	3.45	1.79
Who gives comfort	5.50	5.01	5.08**	4.14	3.74	3.90**
All-embracing	5.16	4.96	2.06*	3.98	3.63	3.30**
Refuge	5.72	4.85	8.11**	4.43	3.53	8.32**

Maintains order	4.36	4.92	5.82**	5.35	4.86	4.92**
Who gives the law	2.78	3.41	6.19**	3.90	4.00	0.86
Initiative	4.76	4.78	0.14	5.82	4.62	11.27**
Strength	3.34	3.80	4.54***	5.48	5.00	5.14***
Guiding towards the future	5.40	5.53	1.32	5.92	5.38	5.37***
Who is the principle	3.91	4.00	0.81	4.41	4.25	1.50
Firmness	3.81	3.84	0.33	4.66	4.37	2.50*
Who makes the decisions	3.62	4.20	5.51**	4.91	4.61	2.58***
Dynamic	5.22	5.06	1.71	5.84	4.93	8.72***
Power	2.83	3.35	5.50**	4.59	4.36	2.14*
Systematic mind	4.39	4.44	0.51	5.75	5.13	6.51**
The judge	2.76	3.21	4.30**	3.75	3.71	0.31
Who gives the directions	3.57	4.19	5.90**	4.99	4.55	4.17***
Authority	3.76	4.18	3.83***	5.20	4.88	3.14***
The one who acts	4.75	5.03	2.97**	5.90	5.47	4.78**
Stern	3.33	3.57	2.30*	4.24	4.16	0.73
Who has the knowledge	4.25	4.25	0.00	5.42	5.04	4.03**
Who examines things	3.97	4.09	1.05	4.45	4.05	3.60**

* $p < 0.05$
** $p < 0.01$

symbolic level were actually effective. For this purpose, the SDPS was administered in two sessions to 300 university students. In one session they were instructed to describe their real parents, and in the other session to describe their parents on the symbolic level. Half of the subjects were instructed to describe their parental memory images in the first session and their symbolic parental figures in the second. The order of instructions was reversed for the other half.

Table 2.1 shows that there is a significant difference between the intensity of attribution of most of the items to the parental figures according to whether they were considered on the symbolic or memory image levels. Thirteen maternal items and fourteen paternal items of the eighteen in each series were attributed more to the symbolic figure of the father than to the memory image. Regarding the mother figure, fifteen maternal items were attributed to it with more intensity when it was described on the symbolic level than when it was described on the memory level. In addition, one maternal item (who is always ready with open arms) and ten paternal items were attributed with more intensity when they were described on the memory level than when they were described on the symbolic level.

Therefore, it is clear that, with the instructions given, the SDPS measures a reality that is other than a simple description of the real parents.

4.2 *Saturation of the Items*

The sources from which the items were collected allow the assumption that they are relevant to the parental figures. In fact, the items were chosen from among a large number of characteristics that have been found to express fundamental parental qualities attributed by numerous investigators from a wide range of disciplines in the human sciences.

Moreover, the empirical tests have shown that the items presented a satisfactory degree of saturation in the respective parental figures.

Table 2.2   *Distribution in percentages of attribution of maternal items to the mother and of paternal items to the father in function of the seven degrees of the scale*

Version	Items	Degrees of the scale							Total
		0	1	2	3	4	5	6	
French	Maternal to the mother	1.8	3.6	4.7	9.5	14.4	29	37	100%
	Paternal to the father	1.5	2	4.5	8.7	15.5	30.6	37.2	100%
English	Maternal to the mother	0.5	2.3	3.8	11.6	17.8	26.9	37.1	100%
	Paternal to the father	0.5	0.5	2.2	8.7	16.9	32.3	38.9	100%
Spanish	Maternal to the mother	0.4	2.1	3.3	11.1	20.1	24.9	38.1	100%
	Paternal to the father	0.4	1	1.6	11.9	16.2	30	38.9	100%
Italian	Maternal to the mother	1.1	2.4	4.7	10.1	16.8	24.3	40.6	100%
	Paternal to the father	3.6	4.8	6.1	13.2	18.9	26.7	26.7	100%

Table 2.2 presents, in percentages, the distribution of the intensity of attribution of the set of maternal items to the mother and of the set of paternal items to the father. It is to be noted that, for all samples, the figure corresponding to the set of items considered received more than 70 percent of the choices in the three higher degrees of the scale and, most often, less than 10 percent in the three lower degrees. Therefore, it seems logical to conclude that the items are relevant to their corresponding figure.

Furthermore, the parallelism of the scores shows that the saturation is almost identical for both maternal and paternal items.

4.3   *Discriminatory Attribution of the Items*

The discriminatory value of the items is satisfactory for all versions of the scale. The t-test demonstrates that the differences between the mean attribution scores of each of the maternal items to the mother figure and the father figure are significant beyond the 0.01 level in all the versions of the SDPS. The same level of significance was obtained for each of the paternal items when applied to the father and to the mother figures.

The discriminatory attribution of the items for the English version is illustrated in Figures 2.1 and 2.2. Each of the items is more intensely attributed to its corresponding figure than to the other parental figure. Figure 2.3 illustrates both the saturation and the discrimination of the items.

The factor analyses, which were worked out later, all confirmed the presence of the two fundamental parental dimensions in the items.

Validation of a measuring instrument is an unending process. Most instruments must be constantly checked to verify that they are behaving as they are supposed to (Nunnally 1967). This methodological rule applies particularly to the SDPS because of its very nature. The saturation and discriminatory attribution of the items of the SDPS cannot be considered as definitive and, even less, as universal. Characteristics proper to the parental figures can vary

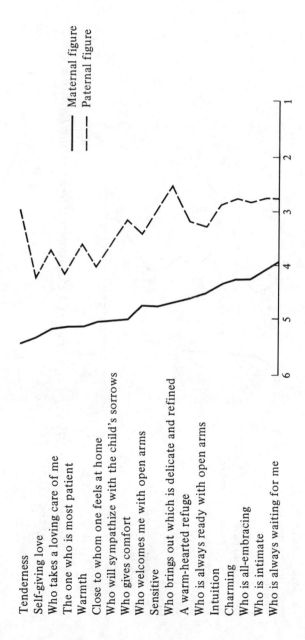

Figure 2.1 *Discrimination of the parental figures by the maternal items in the English version of the SDPS.*

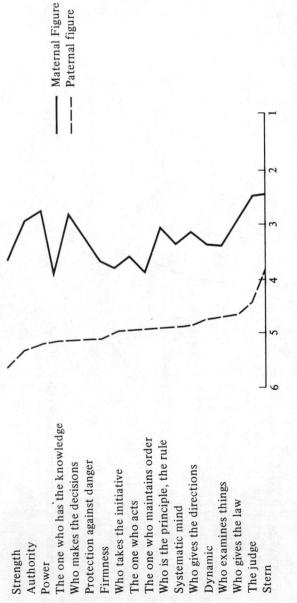

Figure 2.2 *Discrimination of the parental figures by the paternal items in the English version of the SDPS.*

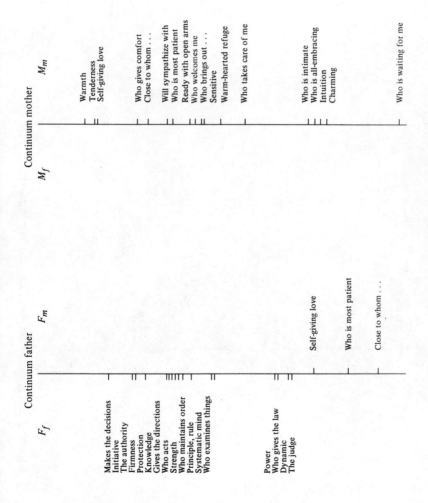

Figure 2.3   *Item saturation and discrimination (Continued overleaf)*

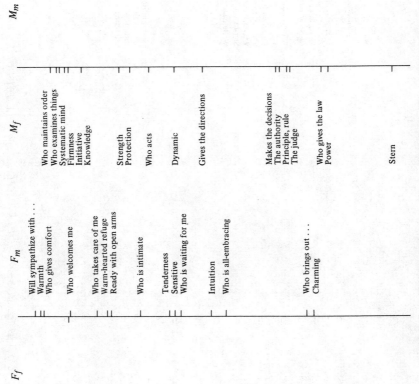

Figure 2.3 *Item saturation and discrimination*

considerably from one culture to another and even from one group to another within the same culture. Thus the saturation and the discriminatory attribution of the items must be previously verified each time the SDPS is used, and particularly when it is used with populations different from those for which these two requirements have been established.

Maternal and Paternal Dimensions in the Parental and Divine Figures

In this chapter, we describe the general results of the first applications of the versions of the SDPS after it was adapted to the various linguistic groups.

We are particularly concerned with the general orientation of the results, and we shall look for what constants emerge in the relationship between the parental figures and the representation of God. It is in reference to what is common to all groups that we shall be able to determine and interpret the specific differences between the various populations.

1 DESCRIPTION OF THE SAMPLES

The samples were taken from the following linguistic groups: Belgian-Dutch, Belgian-French, American-English, and Italian (see Table 3.1).

1.1 *Belgian-Dutch Studies*

Three studies conducted with Dutch-speaking Belgians are available.

The Belgian-Dutch 1 study (Pattyn and Custers 1964): the sample consisted of 200 subjects, 96 men and 104 women, with an average age of 21.6 and 20.0 years respectively. All the subjects were students in an advanced technical school.

The Belgian-Dutch 2 study (Van Mechelen 1968): the sample consisted of 165 subjects, 75 men and 90 women, also students in an advanced technical school. The average age was 22 years for males and 20 for females.

The subjects of both of these studies were largely practicing Roman Catholics (approximately 85 percent), and they confirmed belief in God either absolutely (approximately 55 percent) or with some reservations (35 percent).

The Belgian-Dutch 3 study (Schodts 1971; Olaerts 1971): the sample consisted of 300 university students, 181 male and 119 female; 157 were majoring in mathematics and 149 in Germanic philology; 177 were undergraduate students and 123 were graduate students. The average age of the undergraduate students was 19.0 years and of the graduate students, 22.6 years; 80 percent of the subjects acknowledged regular church attendance, but an average of only 65 percent confirmed belief in God either absolutely (23 percent) or with reservations (42 percent). Approximately 24 percent stated that they had doubts about the existence of God, and 11 percent stated that they were inclined not to, or did not, believe in God. Sunday church attendance was significantly higher among the women than among the men $[X^2(2) = 6.35, p < 0.05]$ and, though the difference in religious conviction was not significant, there were more nonbelievers among the men than among the women (6.2 percent as opposed to 0.9 percent). As regards the field of study, we note a higher degree of practice among the students in mathematics $[X^2(2) = 10.99, p < 0.01]$ than among the students in Germanic philology, as well as a higher level of belief $[X^2(2) = 7.25, p < 0.05]$. We noted no difference in religious practice between the undergraduate and graduate students, but there was one in religious conviction $[X^2(2) = 7.96, p < 0.05]$. The undergraduate students expressed significantly more doubt and less belief.

1.2 Belgian-French Studies

The Belgian-French 1 study (Bonami 1966) was based on a sample of 180 university students and adults. The group of students (N = 120) was equally divided over four subgroups (N = 30) in function of sex and field of study (philology and engineering for the men and pure sciences for the women). The average ages were 22.8 years for the men and 22.0 years for the women. All but one were

Table 3.1 *Sample characteristics*

Sample	Male subjects			Female subjects			Total number
	Secondary school	College and university	Adults	Secondary school	College and university	Adults	
Belgium-Dutch 1		$N = 96$ $m.a. = 21.6$ Higher technical education			$N = 104$ $m.a. = 20.0$ Higher technical education		200
Belgian-Dutch 2		$N = 75$ $m.a. = 22.0$ Higher technical education			$N = 90$ $m.a. = 20.0$ Higher technical education		165
Belgian-Dutch 3		$N = 181$ $m.a.: 1^{st}y = 19.0$ $4^{th}y = 22.6$ Philology and science			$N = 119$ $m.a.: 1^{st}y = 19.0$ $4^{th}y = 22.0$ Philology and science		300
Belgian-French 1		$N = 60$ $m.a. = 22.8$ Philology and engineering	$N = 60$ $m.a. = 37.5$ Philology and engineering		$N = 60$ $m.a. = 22.0$ Philology and science		180
Belgian-French 2	$N = 90$ $m.a. = 17.3$		$N = 40$ $m.a. = 47.1$			$N = 40$ $m.a. = 43.1$	170
American	$N = 30$ $m.a. = 17.0$	$N = 60$ $m.a. = 20.0$ Liberal arts and science		$N = 30$ $m.a. = 16.1$	$N = 60$ $m.a. = 20.0$ Liberal arts and science		180
Italian		$N = 70$ $m.a. = 22.0$ Classics and science $N = 32$ $m.a. = 26.8$ Theology			$N = 70$ $m.a. = 21.0$ Classics and science		140
							32

N = number
$m.a.$ = mean age

unmarried. An average of 90 percent attended church regularly: the group of engineering students had the lowest level of practice (77 percent) while the female subjects from the sciences had the highest level (97 percent). The group of adults consisted of 60 married male subjects with an average age of 37.5 years. These were 30 teachers with backgrounds in philology and 30 engineers.

The Belgian-French 2 study (Balestrieri 1974) was specifically intended to be a comparative inquiry into the influence of sex and age on the composition of the parental figures and the representation of God. The sample was composed of 170 subjects, 90 males from secondary school with an average age of 17.3 years and 40 married couples with an average age for the men of 47.1 years and for the women of 43.1 years. The average duration of the marriages was about 20 years. Eighty-nine percent of the adults acknowledged regular Sunday Mass attendance, as opposed to only 69 percent of the students. Both the young people and the adults were from the same socioeconomic level.

1.3 *American Study*

The American study (Tamayo and Pasquali 1967) was based on 180 subjects, 90 male and 90 female, who were students in Rochester, N.Y. There were two age groups: one of 60 high school students with an average age of 17 years, and the other of 120 college students with an average age of 20 years. The latter group consisted of 60 students in liberal arts and 60 from the sciences. In both groups, there were as many male as female subjects. All subjects were unmarried and from the middle socioeconomic status level. All were Roman.Catholic and 95 percent of the subjects declared that they believed in God absolutely; an average of 85 percent were weekly churchgoers. The group of male subjects from the liberal arts college were exceptional in that only 60 percent stated that they attended church weekly.

1.4 *Italian Study*

The Italian sample (Bernardi 1972) consisted of 140 Italian university students; 70 were majoring in arts (35 males and 35 females) and 70 in science (35 males and 35 females). The average age was 21.6. An average of 67 percent of the subjects acknowledged regular Sunday practice, this varied from 30 to 90 percent among the subgroups. Regular practice was significantly higher [$X^2(1) = 10.52$, $p < 0.01$] in the group of science students (80 percent) than in the groups of classics students (55 percent). There were no differences in function of sex.

1.5 *Conclusion*

In spite of the differences which exist between the populations from which the samples were taken, the following constants appear (Table 3.1):

(1) The subjects were predominantly students on the secondary or university level with an average age between 17 and 23 years, and adults with an average age between 35 and 47 years.

(2) Men and women are represented in roughly equal proportions. The women were generally somewhat younger than the men.

(3) In most of the studies, the fields of study were treated as an independent variable.

(4) With the exception of the adult groups (Belgian-French 1 and 2), virtually all the subjects were unmarried. All socioeconomic levels were represented, but the middle and upper classes predominated.

(5) Most of the subjects had Roman Catholicism as their religious background, and the greater majority (80 to 90 percent) affirmed weekly church attendance and belief in God. The percentage of nonbelievers and non-Catholics is always less than 10.

2 RESULTS

2.1 *Parental Figures*

The father and mother figures are not separate entities but receive
their full meaning in the triangular structure of parents and child.
For the sake of clarity, we shall briefly discuss the main aspects of
each parental figure separately before turning to a more comparative
and structural description. All tables are laid out so as to facilitate
this comparison.

Figure of the father   The paternal dimension is attributed more
strongly to the paternal figure than to the maternal $(F_f > F_m)$,
which is in line with the principles guiding the construction of the
scale. The maternal dimension, however, contributes significantly
to the father figure (see Table 3.2 for the mean intensity scores).
The mean intensity scores of the maternal dimension attributed to
the father are in all samples higher than the theoretical scale mean.
The mean attribution scores of the paternal dimension range from
4.03 to 4.82. Differences between both attribution scores, ranging
from 0.63 to 1.42 (Table 3.3), were not tested for significance except in the Belgian-Dutch 3 study where the difference of 0.73
proved to be significant $[t(299) = 9.27, p < 0.01]$.

The importance of maternal as well as paternal characteristics in
the symbolic figure of the father is also apparent when one considers the intensities with which individual items are attributed
(see Figure 3.1). When the paternal and maternal items are located
on a continuum according to their mean scores (Figure 3.1), there
is a partial overlap of both dimensions, and for several of the items
the overlap is considerable. This means that a number of maternal
items are attributed to the father with at least the same intensity as
some paternal ones, though on the average the paternal component
is more heavily stressed.

The father figure is essentially characterised by items that reflect
concrete action: (initiative, action, dynamism, firmness), guide
towards the future, authority and systematic mind. This holds,

Table 3.2 *Mean Intensity Scores[1] of paternal and maternal items in the three figures*

Samples	N	Father			Mother			God		
		Paternal items	Maternal items	Total items	Paternal items	Maternal items	Total items	Paternal items	Maternal items	Total items
Belgian-Dutch 1	200	4.56	3.30	3.93	2.81	4.86	3.83	3.71	3.97	3.84
Belgian-Dutch 2	165	4.60	3.18	3.89	2.92	4.82	3.87	3.47	3.73	3.60
Belgian-Dutch 3	300	4.03	3.30	3.66	2.93	4.66	3.79	3.18	3.40	3.29
Belgian-French 1	180	4.53	3.30	3.92	2.80	5.10	3.95	4.06	4.37	4.21
Belgian-French 2 adults	80	4.50	3.74	4.12	3.59	5.15	4.37	4.01	4.90	4.46
Belgian-French 2 students	90	4.23	3.60	3.91	2.89	4.63	3.76	3.84	4.61	4.23
Italian[2] students	140	4.21	3.17	3.66	2.33	4.54	3.43	4.16	4.98	4.59
American	180	4.82	3.42	4.12	3.08	4.87	3.98	4.81	4.52	4.67

1. The scale ranged from 0 to 6.
2. Medians have been calculated instead of means.

with only minor exceptions, for all the groups under consideration. Paternal items that appear less apt to characterize the symbolic figure of the father are those that belong to the realm of law and order — legislator and judge, power and stern. It should be noted, however, that these qualities are by no means denied with respect to the father, their average attribution being higher than the scale mean. On the other hand, the maternal items that express active and loving concern for the child are also attributed to the father figure with a high degree of intensity. He is described as someone who welcomes and who accepts the child, who makes it feel at home, who sympathizes with the child's sorrows, who takes care of it, and who is sensitive and patient. The items that primarily refer to the affective and more interior aspects of motherhood are rather weakly associated with the father figure. The correlations between the groups are high (Spearman-rhos higher than 0.60, with the exception of the correlations with Belgian-Dutch 1.

In summary, the symbolic figure of the father is constructed not only of qualities that are differentially more specific of fatherhood, but also of qualities that appear more descriptive of motherhood. The simultaneous qualification of the father as an authority who takes decisions and gives directions, who is — albeit to a lesser degree — the giver and guardian of the law on the one hand, and as someone close to whom one feels at home, who welcomes, and who sympathizes with the child's sorrows on the other, presents the father figure as complex and as composed of relational qualities that may be perceived as conflicting.

Figure of the mother   A clear distinction is observed in the intensity with which the maternal and the paternal items are attributed to the mother figure. The maternal items, taken globally, receive in all groups, high mean attribution scores, ranging from 4.54 to 5.15 (Table 3.2). The paternal items, however, are weakly associated with the symbolic figure of the mother. The greater discrimination between the two series of items within this figure as compared to the father figure is clearly visible in the differences for each sample between the mean maternal and paternal attribution scores (Table

Table 3.3 *Differences between the Mean Intensity Scores of the paternal and maternal dimensions within and between the three figures*[1]

Samples	N	1 $F_f - F_m$	2 $M_m - M_f$	3 $G_f - G_m$	4 $F_f - M_m$	5 $F_m - M_f$	6 $F_f - M_f$	7 $F_m - M_m$	8 $F_f - G_f$	9 $F_m - G_m$	10 $M_m - G_m$	11 $M_f - G_f$
Belgian-Dutch 1	200	1.26	2.05	−0.26	−0.30	0.49	1.75	−1.56	0.85	−0.67	0.89	−0.90
Belgian-Dutch 2	165	1.42	1.90	−0.26	−0.22	0.26	1.68	−1.64	1.13	−0.55	1.09	−0.55
Belgian-Dutch 3[2]	300	0.73	1.73	−0.22	−0.63	0.37	1.10	−1.36	0.85	−0.10	1.26	−0.25
Belgian-French 1	180	1.23	2.30	−0.31	−0.57	0.50	1.73	−1.80	0.47	−1.07	0.73	−1.26
Belgian-French 2 adults	80	0.76	1.56	−0.89	−0.65	0.15	0.91	−1.41	0.49	−1.16	0.25	−0.42
Belgian-French 2 students	90	0.63	1.74	−0.77	−0.40	0.71	1.34	−1.03	0.39	−1.01	0.02	−0.95
Italian students	140	1.04	2.21	−0.82	−0.33	0.84	1.88	−1.37	0.05	−1.81	−0.44	−1.83
American	180	1.40	1.79	+0.29	−0.05	0.34	1.74	−1.45	0.01	−1.10	0.35	−1.73

1. Col. 1, 2, 3   : differences within each figure
   4, 5, 6, 7   : differences between the parental figures in the same and different dimensions
   8, 9, 10, 11 : differences between each parental figure and God in both dimensions.
2. Differences were tested for significance using the t-test for paired observations. All differences are significant at the 0.01 level (df. 299) with the exception of $F_m - G_m$ (col. 9).
   No significance tests were applied in the other studies.

3.3). The smallest difference is 1.5 scale units, which is larger than the largest difference in the father figure. Regarding the location of the individual maternal and paternal items along the maternal continuum, there is little or no overlap of the series of items (see Figure 3.1).

The mother figure is most strongly characterized by tenderness, patience, acceptance, and sympathetic concern. The aspect of active motherly care is stressed more in the Belgian-Dutch samples than in the others, and considerably more than in the American and Italian samples where relatively higher emphasis is placed on self-giving love and who gives comfort. The following items are relatively less attributed to the mother figure: always waiting, all-embracing,[3] intuition (except in the Belgian-Dutch and Italian groups), always present (except in the Belgian-Dutch 3 group), and lets one be a child. These items, however, still obtain mean scores between 3.5 and 4.5, i.e., in the high intermediate range. As we have already mentioned, the paternal attribution scores are generally lower than the maternal ones. The paternal items that are relatively the most important, i.e., those scored in the intermediate scale range, are the ones implying concrete action, dynamism, and initiative. Items like legislator, judge, power, and stern present very low attribution scores. The agreement between the groups as to the relative importance of the paternal qualities is very high, and is, in fact, higher than for the maternal series. The greatest discrepancies are observed between the Belgian-Dutch and the American groups. It is our opinion that the lesser similarity between the groups for the maternal as compared to the paternal series is not a simple accident of translation. The maternal figure shows less semantic differentiation in its specific characteristics, which seem to be rooted in a basic attitude of affection towards the child. Being less differentiated, the maternal items are more

---

3. One might think that the lower attribution score of this item is due to the prefix 'all'. This is not the case. Indeed, the attribution score is no higher in the Dutch and French samples where the corresponding items are 'omringt mij' and 'qui m'entoure'.

interchangeable than the paternal ones which refer to more distinct functions, and this lessens the statistical agreement between the samples. Of more importance, it seems to us, is that the items that describe maternal characteristics and functions appear to have emotional connotations that could be culture specific. The resulting shifts in meaning from one version to the other with their effect on intergroup agreement thus reflect genuine differences between the various groups.

In summary, the symbolic figure of the mother appears to be mostly characterized by the maternal items, and most strongly by those which are a direct expression of the affective mother–child relationship. As a whole, the paternal dimension is rather weakly represented in the symbolic mother figure; items that are of some importance are those that imply action and initiative.

Father and mother as parental structures   Comparing the symbolic figures of the father and the mother as they have been defined by our subjects in terms of paternal and maternal items, we can make some general observations. Both figures appear equally well-defined by the combined paternal and maternal dimensions and this to a comparable degree in all groups. There is no systematic trend in the direction of the differences between the mean total scores for the father (F_t) and for the mother (M_t), and the differences never exceed 0.25 scale units (Table 3.2). But the proportion of the paternal and maternal dimensions in the total attribution score is less balanced within the mother figure than within the father figure. The father, integrating the maternal component to a relatively large degree in addition to his specific characteristics, appears thus more complex than the mother. Within the mother figure, both dimensions are more distinctly present, with high attribution scores for the specific qualities (maternal items) and low for the nonspecific qualities (paternal items). For the mother figure, the differences between the mean maternal and the mean paternal attribution scores $(M_m - M_f)$ range from 1.56 to 2.30 and are all larger than the same differences for the father figure $(F_f - F_m)$, which range from 0.63 to 1.42 (Table 3.3), thus indicating the greater specificity of the mother symbol. This greater specificity is reflected not only in the lesser attribution of paternal items to the mother figure than of maternal items to the father figure ($M_f < F_m$) but also in the stronger emphasis on the maternal dimension in the mother figure than on the paternal dimension in the father figure ($M_m > F_f$). These differences, $F_m - M_f$ being positive and $F_f - M_m$ negative, are the same for all groups though not always of the same magnitude. Where they have been tested for significance (Belgian-Dutch 3 sample) both differences are significant at the 0.01 level. In the American group the difference $F_f - M_m$ was almost nil, which is mainly due to a stronger attribution of paternal items to the father by the American sample than by the other samples. The adult subgroup of the Belgian-French 2 group emphasizes the paternal dimension in the mother more strongly than the other groups (Tables 3.2 and 3.3).

The above observations $M_f < F_m$ and $M_m > F_f$ lead to the conclusion that the maternal dimension appears more highly valued than the paternal one. Within the father figure, it may represent affective support for the exercise of the paternal functions. This is also congruent with the parental figures as they were drawn from literature, where the father appeared more a harmony of contrasts than a simple melody.

Let us now consider both figures in terms of the individual items in order to explain the similarities and dissimilarities between them. We have seen that, when the items are ranked according to their mean attributions to the father and to the mother, there is more overlap between the maternal and paternal items in the father figure than in the mother figure (See Figure 3.1). From these rankings it is also evident that the number of nonspecific items (maternal items for the father figure and paternal items for the mother figure) with an intensity equal to or greater than the theoretical scale mean is higher for the father figure than for the mother figure. This, of course, is also implied by mean maternal and paternal attribution scores.

In spite of the differences in the degree of integration of the characteristics, do the items maintain the same order of importance when they are attributed to the father and to the mother? And are there any meaningful differences between the parental dimensions? Table 3.4 presents the correlations between the 18 paternal and 18 maternal items attributed to the father, to the mother, and to God. The correlations, which are either rank correlations or product moment correlations, are based on the mean item scores. At this point we are only interested in the correlations between the parental figures, i.e., $F_f - M_f$ and $F_m - M_m$.

The correlations between the figures of the father and of the mother for the paternal dimension are all significant to at least the 0.05 level of significance, with the exception of the female subgroup in the Belgian-French 2 study.[4] They are also significant for the maternal dimension, the only exception being the Belgian-Dutch 1 group with a correlation of 0.34 (Spearman-rho). This means that, despite a difference in saturation, the items, paternal as well as maternal, maintain to a significant degree the same order of importance when they are attributed to the father as when they are attributed to the mother. The Spearman-rho coefficients between the mean overall ranking of the items attributed to the father and to the mother are 0.76 (df 16, $p < 0.01$) for the paternal dimension and 0.66 (df 16, $p < 0.01$) for the maternal dimension.

Insofar as the mother figure integrates *paternal* characteristics, it is quite similar to the father figure. Most important are those items that refer to concrete action, initiative, and dynamism, and to the parent as guiding stimulus towards the future. Relatively more important (higher in rank) in the mother figure than in the father figure are the one who maintains order and who examines. Relatively less important in the mother figure than in the father figure are authority and strength. These items pertain here more clearly to the law and order aspect than in the father figure.

The *maternal* items are also attributed to both parental figures in a highly similar constellation. Most ascribed are those items that express acceptance, sympathetic concern, patience, self-giving love, and active care. The most striking difference, and this very consist-

---

4. Coefficients for the combined adult group are not available.

ently over all the subject groups, is the importance of tenderness. Whereas tenderness is highly valued in the mother figure (highest mean rank over the samples), it is almost rejected for the father. The father should be sensitive (position 4.5 on the mean rank scale) but not tender (position 15). Nor is the father conceived of as someone who brings out what is delicate (lowest mean rank). We certainly do not intend to imply that the items preserve exactly the same meanings when they are associated with the figure of the father as when they are associated with the figure of the mother. For example, it is possible that such paternal items as initiative and order take on different meanings when they are applied to the mother.

The association between both parental figures is given by the distance score (Osgood 1971). Table 3.5 presents the significances of the differences between the distance scores. The distances between the parental figures are either larger for the paternal dimension than for the maternal dimension (FM_f superior to FM_m at the $p < 0.01$ level) or they are not significantly different. In no case is the distance FM_f smaller than the distance FM_m. From this we may conclude that the parental figures are generally more discriminated by the paternal than by the maternal dimension.

Summary From the comparison of both parental figures and their structural relationship the following conclusions may be drawn.

(1) The figure of the father is less differentiated with regard to both parental dimensions than the figure of the mother. The subjects attribute, on the one hand, the paternal items to the father figure less intensely than the maternal items to the mother figure, and, on the other hand, the maternal items to the father figure more intensely than the paternal items to the mother figure.

(2) Despite differences in the intensity of attribution, the paternal as well as the maternal items maintain their same order of importance when ascribed to each of the figures. The *paternal* items that appear to characterize most aptly the parental figures are the ones that differentially define the father as dynamic and ready to take initiative and to act, as systematic in his thinking, as

firm, and as guide for the future, and this in opposition to the items representing law and order. The *maternal* items that seem to characterize most aptly the parental figures are those which express acceptance, sympathetic concern, and a solicitude that is patient and ready to give. The mother, in contrast to the father, is also strongly qualified by tenderness.

(3) Using the distance score as a combined measure of the differences in item attribution and profile covariation, it is found that the paternal dimension differentiates the parental figures more strongly than does the maternal dimension.

(4) The above observation and the higher attribution of maternal items in general leads to the conclusion of their higher positive valence for our subjects.

(5) Differences between the groups considered here are generally small and are differences in degree rather than in structure.

2.2 *The Representation of God as Related to the Parental Figures.*

In this section we are mainly concerned with two questions: first, to what extent does the representation of God integrate the parental dimensions, and second, what is the saturation of the various items? We shall also consider in detail the similarities and dissimilarities between the parental figures as symbols for the representation of God.

Parental dimensions in the representation of God   From Table 3.2 it is obvious that both the paternal and the maternal dimensions are relevant to the representation of God. The subjects ascribe them both to God to a higher than average degree. And in all groups, except the American group, the maternal dimension is more strongly emphasized than the paternal one ($G_m > G_f$). The consistency of the direction of the difference between both dimensions over the samples and the statistical significance of a difference as small as 0.22 in the Belgian-Dutch 3 sample [$t(299) = 3.50$,

$p < 0.01$] supports the conclusion that the predominance of the maternal aspect in the representation of God is not purely a matter of chance (Table 3.3). As for the higher stress that the American subjects place on a paternal God, further research is necessary to determine whether this is a genuine deviation from the other groups and thus would represent a real cultural difference.

Another difference is the less intense attribution of the items to the representation of God by the Belgian-Dutch groups (Table 3.2). These are also the only groups for which the mean total scores for God (G_t) are not higher than the ones for the father (F_t) and for the mother (M_t). From an inspection of the item attribution scores it appears that these groups tend to be more reserved in their ascription. Since it occurs only for the representation of God, it is hypothesized that differences in religiosity will most likely be associated with this type of response. The data regarding the religiosity of our subjects do not permit a definitive answer. However, the Belgian-Dutch 3 group, on the self-rating scale of 'belief in God', has the lowest percentage of 'absolute believers' and the highest percentage of 'believers with occasional or frequent doubts'. The effect of religiosity will be further discussed in Chapter 5.

The representation of God integrates both parental dimensions to a relatively high degree and thus appears to be even more complex than the father figure. This complexity is reflected in the mean attribution scores and their differences (Tables 3.2 and 3.3) as well as in the individual item scores. The representation of God receives, on the one hand, an intermediate position in each of the dimensions: the representation of God is thus less maternal than the mother figure (except in the Italian group where G_m is higher than M_m) but more maternal than the father figure $(M_m > G_m > F_m)$; but, on the other hand, it is less paternal than the father figure and more paternal than the mother figure $(F_f > G_f > M_f)$.

Let us now consider the individual items and their relevance for the representation of God. As a rule, both the maternal and paternal items are about equally distributed over the continuum. In the *paternal* dimension God is defined mostly in terms of power and strength, knowledge, and justice. The authority that is ascribed to God has clearly a different form than that attributed to the father. The authority of the father is associated with action and initiative rather than with law and justice. An item which appears very prominently in the representation of God, but which in its very strong meaning was only present in the Dutch version, is *onwankelbaar* (firm as a rock, in French: *inébranlable*). This item received the highest rank for the representation of God and only intermediate ranks for the father, while its translation, 'firmness', defined the father more strongly than God. The items that are least relevant to God are: stern, who takes the initiative, who makes the decisions, who examines things, and the one who maintains order.

The *maternal* items most strongly stressed in the representation of God are those that express unconditional love and acceptance rather than those that reflect active concern and solicitude or those that refer to a more immediate affective bond. God is described as the one who is always there when needed, who is always waiting for me, who welcomes me with open arms, who is self-giving love, most patient, and a warm-hearted refuge.

The agreement between the samples is higher for the paternal dimension (Spearman-rho is significant to at least the 0.05 level except between Belgian-Dutch 1 and American) than for the maternal dimension. The lesser degree of similarity between the Belgian-Dutch and American samples, though, does not affect the essentials of the representation of God as described above.

We may conclude that generally the characteristics and functions that describe the parental figures in a differential way enter into the composition of the representation of God.

However, a striking difference is already apparent. While the paternal and the maternal items kept the same order of importance when they were attributed to the parental figures, this is not so when they are attributed to God (Table 3.4). Let us consider the *paternal* dimension first. In none of the samples are the correlations between the mean attribution of the items to the father and to God significant. The correlations between the mother figure and the representation of God are also insignificant, except in the

Table 3.4 *Correlations between the figures for the paternal and maternal dimensions*[1]

Samples	N	$F_f M_f$	$F_f G_f$	$M_f G_f$	$F_m M_m$	$F_m G_m$	$M_m G_m$	Coefficient
Belgian-Dutch 1	200	0.58*	0.39	0.04	0.34	0.48*	0.13	Spearman-rho
Belgian-Dutch 2	165	0.75***	0.13	−0.06	0.55*	0.51*	0.13	Spearman-rho
Belgian-Dutch 3	300	0.82***	0.13	−0.08	0.59***	0.39	0.14	Spearman-rho
Belgian-French 1	180	0.49*	0.16	−0.50*	0.76***	0.54*	0.44	Pearson
Belgian-French 2[2]								
adult males	40	0.66**	−0.02	−0.02	0.47**	0.32	0.32	Kendall-tau
adult females	40	0.28	0.30	−0.24	0.42*	0.20	0.26	Kendall-tau
students	90	0.48***	−0.24	−0.03	0.63***	0.33	0.16	Kendall-tau
Italian								
students	140	0.87**	−0.03	−0.07	0.49*	0.54*	0.02	Pearson
American	180	0.55*	0.10	−0.01	0.63***	0.69**	0.37	Pearson
Mean ranks over the samples		0.76**	0.05	−0.25	0.66**	0.30	0.07	Spearman-rho

1. $df: N − 2 = 16$, where N is the number of items in each dimension.
2. The correlation coefficients for the total adult sample (Belgian-French 2) are not available.
   * $p < 0.05$
   ** $p < 0.01$

Belgian-Dutch 1 sample, where the negative correlation is significant ($r = -0.50, p < 0.05$). We shall come back to this later. Thus, it may be concluded that there is no relationship between the order of importance of the paternal items in the parental figures and in the representation of God. Further inspection of the attribution of the individual items to the three figures yields some interesting observations. We have seen that, taken globally, the paternal dimension is more intensely attributed to the father than to God. This, however, does not hold for all items, and the exceptions appear strikingly consistent over the samples. The representation of God is more intensely qualified, in absolute scores, as judge, legislator, power, and knowledge than the father figure. It integrates the items referring to concrete action (initiative, dynamic, the one who acts, and who examines things) not only less than the father figure but, in most samples, also less than the mother figure, or at most to an equal degree. The exception for dynamic in the American sample (God figure higher than the father and mother figures) appears idiosyncratic and has not been confirmed in later studies with American subjects. Differences between the representation of God and the parental figures appear not only in intensity of attribution but also in the relative importance of the items within the figures. The items ascribed with more intensity to God than to the father are those that are least important in the father, whereas the ones with lower attribution scores for God belong to those that are most saturated in the father figure and also in the paternal dimension of the mother figure. This inverse relationship, however, does not affect the entire range of items and is thus not strong enough to produce significant negative correlations, with the exception of the Belgian-French 1 sample, where the correlation between M_f and G_f is significantly negative.

The correlations presented in Table 3.4, indicate that the parental figures, from the point of view of the *maternal* dimension, are not associated with God in a similar way. The maternal items do not preserve the same order of relevance when they are attributed to the mother and to God (M_m G_m), all correlations being insignificant. But the correlations F_m G_m are significant to the 0.05

level of confidence in five of the seven studies considered here; the only exceptions are the Belgian-Dutch 3 and the Belgian-French 2 groups.

Which terms now are most responsible for the lack of correlation between the maternal profiles for mother and God? The representation of God is, on the one hand, defined relatively less than the mother figure (rank difference greater than five) by tenderness, close to whom one feels at home, who takes a loving care of me, and who will sympathize with the child's sorrows, and, on the other hand, defined relatively more than the mother figure by the items who is always there when needed, who is always waiting for me, and intuition.

There is a significant correlation between the maternal profiles for the father and God figures, which means that the items keep the same order of importance to a significant degree when they are attributed to these two figures. The covariance, however, is not perfect and the greatest rank differences between both profiles coincide with the ones observed in the case of the mother and God figures, with the exception of tenderness and intuition, which both have a low degree of importance in the father and God figures.

We have thus been able to determine that the divine figure is, in its complexity, closer to that of the father. In addition, the maternal items are attributed to the representation of God to a higher degree than the paternal ones except by the American group.

Affinity and distance between the representation of God and the parental figures   On the basis of the distance scores let us now try to construct a more integrated view of the relations between the figures of the father, the mother, and God. Table 3.5 summarizes the results of the statistical testing applied to the differences between the various distances within the groups.

Considering the total item distance scores, the representation of God tends to be closer to the figure of the father than to that of the mother. This difference ($FG_t < MG_t$) is significant to at least the 0.05 level in the three Belgian-Dutch and the American samples.

Table 3.5   *Comparison of the mean distance scores between the figures*[1]

Samples Distances	Belgian- Dutch 1	Belgian- Dutch 2	Belgian- Dutch 3	Belgian- French 1	Belgian French 2 adults	Belgian- French 2 students	American
FM_t–FG_t	*SUP*	.	*INF*	SUP	.	INF	.
FM_t–MG_t	.	.	*INF*	.	.	.	*INF*
FG_t–MG_t	*INF*	INF	INF	.	.	.	*INF*
FM_f–FG_f	*SUP*	.	*INF*	*SUP*	.	.	*SUP*
FM_f–MG_f	.	*INF*	*INF*	*INF*	*INF*	*INF*	*INF*
FG_f–MG_f	*INF*	.	.	*INF*	*INF*	*INF*	*INF*
FM_m–FG_m	.	.	*INF*	.	.	*INF*	*INF*
FM_m–MG_m	.	.	*INF*	*SUP*	*SUP*	.	.
FG_m–MG_m	.	.	*INF*	*SUP*	*SUP*	*SUP*	*SUP*
FM_f–FM_m	*SUP*	.	.	*SUP*	.	*SUP*	*SUP*
FG_f–FG_m	.	*SUP*	*SUP*	.	.	.	*INF*
MG_f–MG_m	*SUP*	*SUP*	.	*SUP*	*SUP*	*SUP*	*SUP*
FG_f–MG_m	.	*SUP*	.	*SUP*	*SUP*	*SUP*	INF
FG_m–MG_f	*INF*	*INF*	*INF*	*INF*	.	.	*INF*

1. Differences were tested for significance by Fisher's t-test for paired observations ($df =$ sample size $-$ 1).

SUP and *SUP*: the distance mentioned first is superior to the second one at the 0.05 respectively 0.01 level of significance.

INF and *INF*: the distance mentioned first is inferior to the second one at the 0.05 respectively 0.01 level of significance.

The first distance is equivalent to the second, i.e., the difference is not significant.

It is in the same direction, but not significantly so, in Belgian-French 1, and in the opposite direction, again not significantly, in Belgian-French 2. There is no consistency between the samples with regard to the distance between the parental figures when compared to the distance between each of them and God. The parental distance (FM_t) is the smallest in Belgian-Dutch 3 and Belgian-French 2 but the difference reaches significance ($p < 0.01$) only in Belgian-Dutch 3. The same distance is the largest in Belgian-

Dutch 1 and Belgian-French 1. In both studies the father figure is closer to the representation of God than to the mother figure ($FG_t < FM_t$). Lastly, in the Belgian-Dutch 2 study and in the American study, the distance between the parental figures is larger than the father–God distance (not significant) and smaller than the mother–God distance (significant in the American study).

The consistent finding, then, that there is a greater proximity between the figures of the father and of God seems to indicate that the father figure is a more adequate symbol for God than is the mother figure.

What is the specific contribution of each of the parental dimensions to this general finding? An analysis of the distances involved in these dimensions will help clarify this question.

From the perspective of the *paternal* dimension, the distance between the mother and God figures is always larger than that between the father and God figures ($MG_f > FG_f$), and the distance between the mother and father figures is significantly shorter than the distance between the mother and God figures ($FM_f < MG_f$). As for the figure of the father in its relation to the figures of the mother and of God, the findings are less consistent. The father figure proves to be significantly more distant from that of the mother than from that of God ($FM_f > FG_f$; $p < 0.01$) in the Belgian-Dutch 1, Belgian-French 1, and American studies. In the other studies the relationship is inverted, namely $FM_f < FG_f$, but this difference reaches significance only in the Belgian-Dutch 3 sample ($p < 0.01$). The data for the paternal dimension may thus be summarized in the following expression:

$$FG_f \lesseqgtr FM_f < MG_f.$$

From the point of view of the *maternal* items, the representation of God is more often closer to the figure of the mother than to that of the father, i.e., $MG_m < FG_m$. This difference is significant in the Belgian-French [$t(179) = 4.94$, $p < 0.01$] and American groups [$t(179) = 8.07$, $p < 0.01$]. This is not the case for the Belgian-Dutch groups. The same difference is found in Belgian-Dutch 1 but it is not significant; the representation of God is closer to the father than to the mother figure ($FG_m < MG_m$) in Belgian-Dutch 3 ($p < 0.01$) and Belgian-Dutch 2 (not significant). It is worth mentioning that, in the Belgian-Dutch samples 1 and 2, the distances in the maternal dimension are more similar to each other than in the other groups. This is due primarily to a larger distance MG_m as compared to the same distance in the other groups. The deviation from the other samples is most pronounced in Belgian-Dutch 3 where the difference between the mother and God figures is significantly larger than the other maternal distances. In terms of the mean intensity scores the Belgian-Dutch samples showed a greater difference between the attribution of maternal items to God and to the mother than the other groups, and more particularly so when compared with the difference between the father and God figures (Tables 3.2 and 3.3).

With the exception of the Belgian-Dutch 3 group, the distance between the parental figures is larger than that between the mother and God figures ($FM_m > MG_m$), although the difference is significant only in Belgian-Dutch 1 and 2. And lastly, the figure of the father is, from the point of view of the maternal dimension, either significantly closer to the mother than to God or about equidistant. The following expression summarizes the data for the maternal dimension (excluding the Belgian-Dutch 3 group):

$$MG_m < FM_m \leqslant FG_m.$$

The greater proximity between the father and God figures does not occur when maternal items are involved. The representation of God is manifestly closer to the father figure when the figures are considered from the point of view of the paternal items and closer to the mother figure when the figures are considered from the point of view of the maternal items ($FG_f < MG_f$ and $MG_m < FG_m$). This, however, does not imply that the representation of God is also closer to each of the parental figures in their specific dimensions than in their nonspecific dimensions. From a comparison of the distances between the figures from the perspective of the maternal and the paternal dimensions, we see that the mother is closer to God for the maternal than for the paternal component ($MG_m < MG_f$, $p < 0.01$). As for the father figure we observe a clear breakdown of the relation in function of the different groups. In the Belgian-Dutch samples, the figure of the father was more removed from the representation of God for the paternal than for the maternal dimension ($FG_f > FG_m$), while in the Belgian-French groups the relation is inverted though not significantly so. In the American sample, finally, it is the distance in the paternal dimension that is significantly smaller ($FG_f < FG_m$).

Our last comparison concerns the distances between the representation of God and each of the parental figures in their specific and nonspecific items. For the specific items, the father tends to be further from God for the paternal dimension than the mother for the maternal dimension ($FG_f > MG_m$). In Belgian-Dutch 1 and 3 the difference is in the same direction but not significant. In the American group, however, the inverse relation ($FG_f < MG_m$) is found [$t(179) = 2.31, p < 0.05$].

For the nonspecific items, however, the distance between the father and God figures for the maternal dimension is, in all samples, less than the distance between the mother and God figures for the paternal series ($FG_m < MG_f$, $p < 0.01$; except in Belgian-French 2 where the same difference is not significant).

The findings with regard to the distance scores may be summarized as follows. First, the representation of God is in all samples most removed from the mother in the paternal dimension. MG_f is uniformly the largest distance, though it is not always significantly different from the others. Second, with regard to the sequence of the other distances between the parental figures and God, the following sequences schematically summarize the results:

Belgian-Dutch groups : $FG_m \leqslant MG_m \leqslant FG_f \leqslant MG_f$

Belgian-French groups : $MG_m < FG_f = FG_m \leqslant MG_f$

American group   : $FG_f < MG_m < FG_m < MG_f$

Third, the parental figures always take an intermediate position between the father–God and the mother–God distances. Only in Belgian-Dutch 3 is there a marked proximity between the parental figures as compared to the other distances ($FM_f = FM_m < FG_m$, $p < 0.01$). The parental figures are generally closer to each other in the maternal dimension than in the paternal. Fourth, more often than not the distances are smaller when the maternal dimension is involved than when the paternal dimension is involved.

3 CONCLUSION

After having set out the results in a rather analytic way, we shall now integrate the various data into a more comprehensive view of the symbolic parental figures and the symbolization of God through them. We shall take into account what appears consistent among the different groups considered, as well as what has been found to vary among them.

(1) Our first general observation is that the maternal items as compared to the paternal ones have higher positive valence and are more inclusive. Indeed, not only is the mother figure more strongly saturated with the maternal items than the father figure with the paternal ones, but also the father figure is more strongly maternal than the mother figure is paternal. Likewise, the maternal component is also of more importance in God than the paternal one. Moreover, the maternal dimension tends to produce smaller distances between the figures than the paternal one. This is especially so when the distance between the figures of the mother and of God for the maternal dimension is compared with the same distance for the paternal dimension, and when the maternal and paternal distances between both parental figures are compared with each other. Likewise, the mother is closer to God from the maternal perspective than the father is from the paternal perspective and she is further from God from the paternal perspective than the father is from the maternal perspective.

(2) From this it can be concluded that the father, as a rule,

achieves a higher integration of parental functions and characteristics than the mother, who is more distinctly defined by the maternal dimension. The paternal component presupposes the more
affective substructure represented by the maternal qualities.

(3) Although the representation of God is less saturated than
the father figure in the paternal items and also less than the mother
figure in the maternal ones, it realizes a more complete synthesis
of both components. Thus in its complexity the father figure is a
more adequate symbol for God than the mother figure. That the
mother is less suited to signify God is mainly a consequence of the
manner and the degree with which the maternal figure integrates
the *paternal* dimension. This results in uniformly high distance
scores between the figures of the mother and of God for the
paternal component and affects the total score so as to provoke
a significantly larger distance between the figures of the mother
and God than between the figures of the father and God.

(4) That the father figure is the more adequate symbol for God,
however, by no means implies direct similarity between them.
From the correlations between the mean attributions of the items
to the three figures, it is obvious that the representation of God is
structured by the paternal items quite independently of the parental figures. From the maternal perspective, however, the representation of God appears more similar to the father figure than
to the mother figure. Both these observations are in contrast with
the correlations obtained for the parental figures, which correlations are highly significant from both perspectives and this despite
major differences in intensity of attribution.

Within the series of *paternal* items one can discern two rather
distinct sets of qualities. The first set, which is most characteristic
of God and least of the father and of the mother, qualifies God as
authority in the realm of law and justice: he has knowledge and
power, he is giver and guardian of the law. The other set, which
is relatively more important in the parental figures than in God,
contains the qualities that imply action and initiative. The father
also has authority and knowledge, but in the field of decision
making and concrete action.

As for the *maternal* dimension, the difference in saturation of the items between the figures of the mother and of God concerns primarily the items that express the immediate affective bond between mother and child. God is also described relatively less than both the mother and the father in terms of care and solicitude. The mother is preeminently viewed as someone who is tender, warm, and patient; she shows sympathy for and takes care of the child's needs; she is accepting and makes the child feel close and at home. God, on the other hand, is most strongly characterized as someone who is ever-present and waiting; he is self-giving love, most patient and, as such, a safe refuge in human distress.

Thus, God is viewed as lawgiver and judge, as representing ethical exigencies and, though powerful and firm, as being patient and loving, as just but not stern.

(5) It has become clear that the parental dimensions are differentially important in the symbolization of God through the parental figures. The distance scores clarify this further and reveal at the same time some important differences in this symbolization process.

(a) The American group is distinguished from the other groups by a greater emphasis on the paternal dimension. Not only is this dimension more strongly present in the representation of God than the maternal one, but it also equals in intensity its presence in the father figure. Consequently, unlike in the other groups, the father and God are more closely connected with each other via the paternal dimension than via the maternal dimension. The father is also closer to God via the paternal dimension than the mother is via the maternal dimension. The difference between the American group and the other groups is primarily a matter of intensity of integration of the paternal items relative to the maternal items, and not so much one of mode of integration.

(b) In both Belgian-French studies, as opposed to the Belgian-Dutch and American ones, the mother is as close to God as to the father. Most characteristic here is that God is closer to the mother on the maternal dimension than to the father in the paternal one.

This somewhat greater similarity seems to prevail over the difference in intensity of attribution of the items.

The father figure is about as close to the representation of God from the maternal perspective as from the paternal perspective. In the maternal dimension, the emphasis lies on the similarity of structure of the items, whereas for the paternal dimension it lies rather on the similarity of intensity of attribution of the items despite structural independence.

(c) In the Belgian-Dutch groups, finally, both parental figures symbolize God more from the maternal perspective than from the paternal. This group, in comparison to the others, tends to attribute the items, paternal and maternal alike, less intensively to the representation of God. This reduces the differences in intensity of attribution of the items between the representation of God and the parental figure measured by the nonspecific items. Thus, the father appears a better symbol for God in the *maternal* than in the paternal dimension. And this is a matter of greater similarity in the constellation of the items as well as in the degree of their attribution. The father figure is even closer to the representation of God in the maternal dimension than is the mother figure (Belgian-Dutch 3), or is at the same distance. But the father figure is further from the representation of God in the paternal dimension than the mother figure in the maternal dimension (Belgian-Dutch 2), or at about the same distance. In the Belgian-Dutch groups, too, the greatest distance is the one between the mother and God figures for the paternal dimension. However, only in one, Belgian-Dutch 1, is this distance significantly greater than the distance between father and God figures for the paternal component.

(6) The parental figures, considered from the perspective of both the maternal and the paternal dimensions, present a high degree of structural similarity, and this quite consistently for all groups. As for the distance scores, the father and mother figures are either closer to each other for the maternal than for the paternal dimension, or at the same distance for both. Comparison of the distances between the parental figures with those between the representation of God and each parental figure reveals the following:

in general, the parental figure measured by its specific items is either closer to the representation of God than to the other parental figure or equidistant from both. But the parental figure measured by its noncorresponding items is either further from the representation of God than from the other parental figure or at equal distance from both.

Therefore, both parental figures symbolize God. When God is called Father it is because his representation includes specific paternal items that are not attributed in a significant degree to the mother. Moreover, the representation of God includes the maternal items also in a way that is more similar to the manner in which the father figure integrates them. But the representation of God approaches the mother figure with regard to the degree of saturation in maternal items that are more strongly emphasized in the representation of God than are the paternal items, for the American group.

Cultural Differences in the Structure and Significance of the Parental Figures

The studies presented in the last chapter all show that there is a semantic similarity between the parental figures and the representation of God, and they suggest that cultural environment could have an effect on the perception of the divine and parental figures and on the semantic relationships between them. This seems quite probable, given that the figures of the mother, father, and God, insofar as they are cultural manifestations, are subject to the influence of local spiritual constructs, which are themselves tributaries of specific historical trajectories, and are conditioned by strictly circumscribed traditions.

The purpose of the research reported in this chapter is to examine possible cultural variations in the structures of the mother, father, and God figures, and in the symbolic significance of the parental figures. By structure of the figures is meant the proportion and manner in which the maternal and paternal dimensions are integrated within each figure. By symbolic significance of the parental figures is meant the semantic similarity between each of the parental figures and the representation of God.

1 METHOD

1.1 *Subjects*

The sample was composed of 360 subjects from six different countries Belgium: Zaire, Colombia, Indonesia, the Philippines, and the United States of America. Each cultural group was composed of 60 subjects and was divided into two equal subgroups according to sex. All of the subjects were university students majoring in psychology or educational sciences, unmarried, Roman Catholic, and from the middle socioeconomic level. The average age was 22 years 5 months.

1.2　*Measuring Instrument*

The measuring instrument used was the SDPS in its French, English, and Spanish versions. It was administered in the different countries by psychologists, most of them university professors, who had agreed to collaborate in this study and who were thoroughly aware of the conditions required so that the procedure could be standardized as much as possible. The SDPS was administered collectively and the tester was restricted to requesting the collaboration of the subjects in an intercultural study in the area of psychology. For this a standardized formula was used.

1.3　*Statistics*

Factor analysis　The intercorrelations of the 36 items of the SDPS were calculated within each cultural group for the mother, father, and God figures. The 18 correlation matrices were independently factorized by the principal factor solutions. The factors thus obtained were first subjected to orthogonal rotation by the Varimax method and then to oblique rotation by the Oblimin method ($g = 0.5$). The number of factors was limited to four, which accounted for more than 55 percent of the observed variance in the three figures and in all the cultural groups. The existing congruence between the 72 factors resulting from the 18 different factor analyses was established by the Phi-coefficient method proposed by Tucker (1951). A Phi-coefficient equal to or higher than 0.9398 indicates a perfect congruence between the compared factors, and a Phi-coefficient equal to or less than 0.4597 defines a total absence of congruence (Harman 1960: 259). Phi-coefficients between 0.7000 and 0.9398 are considered here as defining semi-congruence.

Distance scores and significance tests   The semantic distances between the three figures were calculated for each subject with the formula proposed by Osgood (1971). The calculations were made on three different levels: first, by plotting all of the items (the mother–father, mother–God, and father–God distances), second, by separately plotting the series of maternal (m) and paternal (f) items (the distances $M_m - F_m$, $M_m - G_m$, $F_m - G_m$, $M_f - F_f$, $M_f - G_f$, $F_f - G_f$), and third, by plotting alternatively the set of items significantly loaded in each of the factors common to the mother, the father, and God figures for the six cultural groups. The means and standard deviations of the distance scores were calculated for each group and subgroup. The Student t-test and the Snédécor F-test were used to establish the significant differences between, repectively, the means and the standard deviations.

1.4   *Semantic Analysis*

All items of the SDPS were subjected to semantic analysis that was designed to determine their degree of univocity when associated with the mother, the father, and God respectively. This semantic analysis was done using group discussion. The leader introduced each of the items in turn for discussion by the participants. The leader's task was limited to making sure that the group discussed the stimulus item and to facilitate the discussion without intervening in the content of the discussion. The meetings were conducted by a team of nine graduate students in psychology who were properly prepared for the task. Two stages of preparation were provided, one theoretical and one practical. In the first stage, four orientation sessions were given regarding the SDPS, the studies already done with this instrument, and the group discussion method. In the second stage, each discussion leader conducted two supervised group meetings in order to master the technique. For the semantic analysis proper, each discussion leader directed eight sessions, each with a different group. The groups always consisted of five male and female subjects. The discussions were recorded on tape. The total number of subjects came to 360, all of them French-speaking Belgians.

2   RESULTS

2.1   *Description of the Three Figures*

Semantic structure   By semantic structure is meant here the specific meaning of the items when associated to each of the three figures. Semantic analysis revealed that the items are not associated in a perfectly univocal manner to the mother, the father, and to God. The maternal items have a literal, immediate, and concrete meaning when associated with the mother, a symbolic meaning when associated with the father, and both literal and symbolic meanings when associated with God. Moreover, they most often take on another meaning specific to God. For example, the item, who is always waiting for me, was understood by the subjects in the sense of immediate and affective physical presence when assigned to the mother; it was taken in the sense of symbolic presence when assigned to the father, i.e., as a model and point of reference, but when attributed to God, it was associated with the immediate presence of the Divinity in the personal believer–God relationship, or with symbolic presence insofar as it reflected a model of sanctity to be imitated, or, finally, with transpersonal presence insofar as it is a cultural construct.

The paternal items have a direct and immediate meaning when they are attributed to the father and a mediated meaning when applied to the mother. In other words, in the latter case they imply an essential reference to the father. For example, when applied to the mother, the item, who gives the law, does not signify that the law is given by the mother, but that she reflects, by her words and behavior, the prohibitions and judgements of the father. In the same way, the authority, sternness, initiative, decisions, and so on of the mother appear as maternal versions of these same qualities of the father. It must be stressed that this mediated meaning of the paternal items attributed to the mother does not appear when the maternal items are attributed to the father. And when applied to God, the paternal items always have the direct and immediate meaning specific to their association to the father, but they never have the mediated meaning specific to their application to the mother. In certain cases, they even go beyond the specific paternal meaning and take on a meaning proper to God.

Factorial structure   The factors isolated by factor analysis are considered here as the elements of the structure of the figures. The factors that are congruent (Phi $\geqslant$ 0.9398) for all six cultural groups are called nuclear factors. All other factors semicongruent for (0.7000 $\leqslant$ Phi < 0.9398), or specific to (Phi < 0.4597), one or more groups are called peripheral factors. The nuclear factors are considered as the core of the figure, a core that is present no matter which culture is considered. A factor is called maternal or paternal according to whether the significantly loaded items in it are maternal or paternal. The maternal factors are designated by an upper case M followed by a subscript identifying the factor, thus M_1, M_2, M_3 and so on. Upper case F and G and numerical subscripts are used to represent the factors of the paternal and divine figures. The individual factors are named after the set of items that are the most heavily loaded in the individual factor and that are found in the results obtained from all the groups and for all the figures to which the individual factor is congruent (Table 4.1).

Maternal figure   The maternal figure (see Figure 4.1) has two nuclear factors: availability and law, the first being maternal, the second paternal. There are three maternal and three paternal peripheral factors in the mother figure. The maternal peripheral factors are feminity (Belgian and Colombian groups), protection (Zairian and Filipino groups), and intuition (specific to the Indonesian group). The paternal peripheral factors of the mother figure are power (specific to the Filipino group), order (specific to the Colombian subjects), and authority (specific to the American sample). For the content of the factors, see Table 4.1.

Table 4.1   *Content of the nuclear and peripheral factors*

Nuclear factors	
Availability	*Law*
Always ready . . .	Who gives the law
Always waiting for me	Judge
Self-giving love	Who is the principle . . .
Who welcomes me	Authority
Tenderness	Who gives directions
Close to whom one feels at home	Who makes decisions
All-embracing	Power

Peripheral factors		
Dynamism	*Power*	*Order*
Dynamic	Power	Maintains order
Gives directions	Strength	Stern
Who acts	Firmness	Strength
Takes the initiative	Knowledge	Who acts
	Feminity	*Protection*
	Sensitive	Protection against dangers
	Who is intimate	All-embracing
	Brings out which is delicate	Always waiting for me
	Tenderness	Gives comfort
Knowledge	*Authority*	*Intuition*
Knowledge	Authority	Intuition
Systematic mind	Firmness	Charming
Who examines things	Stern	Warmth

Paternal figure   The core of the paternal figure, as that of the maternal figure, is constituted by the factors availability and law (see Figure 4.2). In addition to the factor availability, there is another maternal factor, protection, which is peripheral and which occurs in the Belgian and Filipino groups. The paternal peripheral factors are dynamism, knowledge, authority, and order. The first is

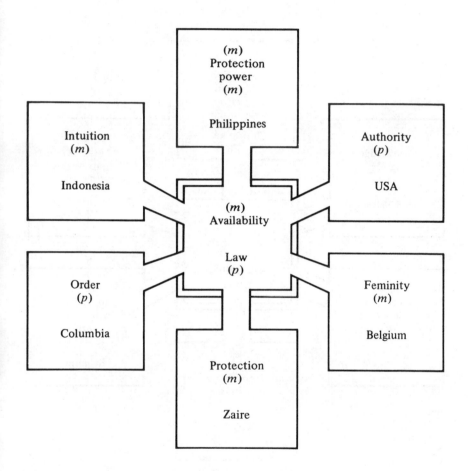

Figure 4.1   *Figure of the mother*

shared by the American, Colombian, Filipino, and Belgian samples, the second by the Zairian and Indonesian samples, and the third and fourth are specific for the American and Colombian groups.

Representation of God   The core of the representation of God is formed by the factors availability and law (see Figure 4.3). The

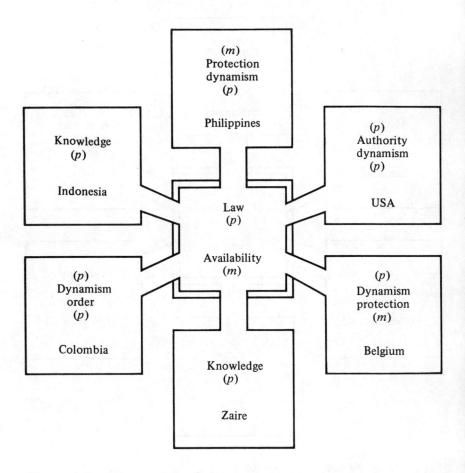

Figure 4.2   *Figure of the father*

maternal peripheral factors are protection and feminity. The first appears in the Zairian sample and is congruent with the factor of the same name found in the maternal figure (Phi = 0.9507194). The second is from the Belgian subjects and is congruent with the feminity factor met in the maternal figure of the same group

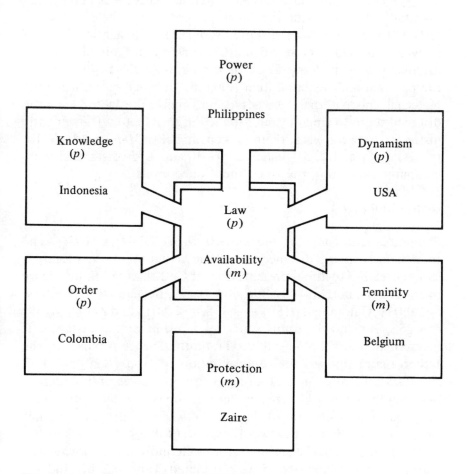

Figure 4.3   *Representation of God*

(Phi = 0.9659432). The paternal peripheral factors of the representation of God are order, power, knowledge, and dynamism, which are specific to the Colombian, Filipino, Indonesian, and American samples respectively.

2.2   *Symbolic Significance of the Parental Figures*

The symbolic significance of the parental figures was determined essentially by means of the distance scores and the significance tests between the mean distance scores. The semantic distances between the figures were calculated: first, the total item semantic distance scores, in terms of all of the items of the SDPS; second, the paternal and maternal item semantic distance scores using the maternal and paternal item sets; and finally, the factor semantic distance scores, using the items loaded in each factor. The semantic distances between each figure taken in pairs (*M–F* and *M–G* distances, *F–G* and *F–M* distances, *G–M* and *G–F* distances) were compared on each of the above mentioned levels.

General approach

Symbolic significance of the mother figure (F–M *vs* M–G)   The total item semantic distance scores show that the mother figure is situated closer to the representation of God than the father figure in the American [$t(59) = 2.396, p < 0.05$], Belgian [$t(59 = 5.620, p < 0.01$], Colombian [$t(59) = 4.858, p < 0.01$] and Zairian [$t(59) = 4.258, p < 0.01$] groups. This relationship of the distances is inverted in the Filipino group: the mother figure is closer to the father figure than to the representation of God [$t(59) = 2.396, p < 0.05$]. Finally, for the Indonesian group, the semantic distances between the maternal figure and each of the two other figures seem to be equivalent since the differences between the distances are not significant in either of the two directions (Table 4.2, a_1).

The results from the cultural groups are more uniform when the maternal item distance scores are considered (Table 4.2, b_1). Indeed, except for the Filipino group, the mother is situated semantically closer to God than to the father in all the groups [$t(59), p < 0.01$].

The paternal item distance scores show that the semantic relations vary according to the cultural milieu (Table 4.2, c_1). For the American and Zairian subjects, the semantic relations of the mother figure with the father and the God figures are not significant in either of the two directions. For the Belgian group, the mother figure is semantically closer to the representation of God than to the father figure [$t(59) = 3.209, p < 0.01$], and the inverse is the case for the Colombian [$t(59) = 3.236, p < 0.01$], Indonesian [$t(59) = 5.652, p < 0.01$], and Filipino [$t(59) = 4.344, p < 0.01$] groups.

The availability factor distance scores (Table 4.2, d_1) show that the mother figure is, without exception, significantly closer to the representation of God than to the father figure. In terms of the law factor semantic distances, the mother figure is closer to the father figure than to the representation of God in the American [$t(59) = 6.274, p < 0.01$], Colombian [$t(59) = 10.137, p < 0.01$], Filipino [$t(59) = 3.112, p < 0.01$], and Indonesian [$t(59) = 3.943, p < 0.01$] groups, and closer to the representation of God than to the father figure in the Belgian [$t(59) = 4.003, p < 0.01$] and Zairian [$t(59) = 2.220, p < 0.05$] groups.

In summary, the symbolic significance of the maternal figure is uniform for the different cultural groups when the figures are examined from the perspective of the maternal items and, more particularly, of the availability factor. On the other hand, the variability between the groups is obvious when the figures are seen from the perspectives of the paternal items and of the law factor. Thus, it can be affirmed that the symbolic significance of the mother figure is both invariable and variable in all the cultural milieux considered, depending on the perspective from which it is considered. Invariability appears when the symbolic significance is considered using the specific dimensions of the mother figure (maternal items and the availability factor) and variability when it is considered using the nonspecific dimensions of the mother figure (paternal items and the law factor).

Symbolic significance of the father figure (M–F *vs* F–G) The total item semantic distances between the figures (Table 4.2, a_2) show that the father figure is significantly closer to the representation of God than to the mother figure. This is true for all of the cultural communities except the Filipinos with whom this relationship is not significant. Uniformity, however, is not found in the maternal distance scores (Table 4.2, b_2). With the American and Colombian subjects, the difference between the maternal semantic distances is not significant. Therefore, for these two groups, the distances between the father figure and the two other figures are equivalent. For the two Asian groups, the father figure is closer to the mother figure than to the representation of God [$t(59), p < 0.05$], while for the Belgian [$t(59) = 5.290, p < 0.01$] and Zairian [$t(59) = 7.593, p < 0.01$] groups, the father figure is closer to the representation of God than to the mother figure. The paternal semantic distances (Table 4.2, c_2), show that the father figure is always closer to the representation of God than to the mother figure. This result is the same for all six cultural communities [$t(59), p < 0.01$], and the sex variable has no influence on it (Table 4.4).

From the perspective of the availability factor (Table 4.2, d_2), the father figure is closer to the representation of God than to the mother figure in the Colombian [$t(59) = 2.885, p < 0.01$] and the Zairian [$t(59) = 3.732, p < 0.01$] groups, and closer to the mother figure than to the representation of God in the Filipino group [$t(59) = 2.185, p < 0.05$]. In the American, Belgian, and Indonesian groups, the distances between the father figure and the other two figures seem to be equivalent since the differences between them are not significant.

From the perspective of the law factor (Table 4.2, e_2), the father figure, without exception, is everywhere closer to the representation of God than to the mother figure [$t(59), p < 0.01$].

In summary, the symbolic significance of the paternal figure is invariable in all six cultural groups when it is seen from the perspective of the specific dimensions of the father (paternal items and the law factor), and variable when it is considered from the perspective of its nonspecific dimensions (maternal items and availability factor). Consequently, it seems that, in this regard, the symbolic significance of the father figure is equivalent to that of the mother figure. In both cases, the symbolic significance presents partial uniformity and partial variability, the former when the figures are considered from the perspective of their specific

Table 4.2 *Probability levels of the differences between the mean distance scores within each cultural group. Test used: Student t-test*

Distances compared	Belgium	Zaire	Colombia	Indonesia	Philippines	USA
(a) 1 FM-MG	SUP	SUP	SUP		INF	SUP
2 FM-FG	SUP	SUP	SUP	SUP	·	SUP
3 MG-FG	·	SUP	·	SUP	SUP	·
(b) 1 FM-MG	SUP	SUP	SUP	SUP	·	SUP
2 FM-FG	SUP	SUP	·	INF	INF	·
3 MG-FG	INF	INF	INF	INF	INF	INF
(c) 1 FM-MG	SUP	·	INF	INF	INF	·
2 FM-FG	SUP	SUP	SUP	SUP	SUP	SUP
3 MG-FG	SUP	SUP	SUP	SUP	SUP	SUP
(d) 1 FM-MG	SUP	SUP	SUP	SUP	SUP	SUP
2 FM-FG	·	SUP	SUP	·	INF	·
3 MG-FG	INF	INF	INF	INF	INF	INF
(e) 1 FM-MG	SUP	SUP	INF	INF	INF	INF
2 FM-FG	SUP	SUP	SUP	SUP	SUP	SUP
3 MG-FG	SUP	SUP	SUP	SUP	SUP	SUP

a = item set
b = maternal items
c = paternal items
d = availability factor
e = law factor
  · The first distance is equivalent to the second, i.e., the difference is not significant
INF The first distance is inferior to the second ($p < 0.05$)
INF The first distance is inferior to the second ($p < 0.01$)
SUP The first distance is superior to the second ($p < 0.05$)
SUP The first distance is superior to the second ($p < 0.01$)

dimensions, and the latter when they are seen from the perspective of their nonspecific dimensions. Thus, for what is specific to each parental figure, the symbolic significance is uniform and invariable in all of the cultural structures, and for what is nonspecific, the symbolic meaning is dependent on the cultural context.

The semantic relations of the representation of God (M–G *vs* G–F)
Analysis of the total item semantic distances shows that the representation of God is semantically closer to the father figure than to the mother figure in the Indonesian [$t(59) = 3.211, p < 0.01$], Filipino [$t(59) = 3.168, p < 0.01$], and Zairian [$t(59) = 3.313, p < 0.01$] groups. For the American, Belgian, and Colombian subjects, the representation of God seems to be situated at an equivalent distance from both parents as the differences between the mother–God and father–God distances are not significant. It must be stressed that, from the cultural perspective, the total figure of God is never significantly closer to the mother figure than to the father figure (Table 4.2, a_3).

The maternal distance scores (Table 4.2, b_3), show that the representation of God is closer to the mother figure than to the father figure for all six cultural communities [$t(59), p < 0.01$]. From the perspective of the paternal dimension (Table 4.2, c_3), the representation of God is closer to the father figure than to the mother figure and this also for all six cultural groups [$t(59), p < 0.01$].

From the perspective of the availability factor (Table 4.2, d_3), the representation of God is more maternal than paternal in all the cultural groups [$t(59), p < 0.01$].

In terms of the law factor (Table 4.2, e_3), God is significantly more paternal than maternal in all the cultural groups [$t(59), p < 0.01$].

In summary, the representation of God, considered from the specific dimensions of the father figure (paternal items and the law factor) is always closer to the father figure than to the mother figure; considered from the perspective of the dimensions specific to the mother (maternal items and the availability factor), it is always closer to the mother figure than to the father figure. Therefore, in terms of the specific parental dimensions, the representation of God has a semantical similarity with each parental figure, a similarity that is fundamental and uniform in all six cultural groups.

This uniformity disappears as soon as the representation of God is considered as a whole, that is, as a synthesis of the maternal and paternal dimensions. The importance accorded to each parental dimension varies in function of the culture: the representation of God can be more paternal than maternal, or equally paternal as maternal, or even more maternal than paternal. The last possibility was not observed in the course of the present study.

Differential approach

The objective of this section is to examine certain intergroup and sexual differences in the representation of God.

Intergroup differences   Table 4.3 shows the levels of significance of the differences between the semantic distances of the groups compared. Analysis of the semantic relations between the parental figures indicates, that the distance between them is significantly smaller for the two Asian groups than for the other cultural groups. For the Belgian and Zairian subjects, however, this distance is generally greater than for the other samples. This is true for the figures when analyzed in terms of the entire item set, in terms of the paternal and maternal dimensions, and in terms of the two nuclear factors.

The mother–God distance has fewer significant differences than does the mother–father distance. The total item semantic distances and the maternal item semantic distances indicate that for the Indonesians and the Filipinos the mother–father distance is significantly shorter than it is for the Belgians and the Zairians. On the basis of the paternal items and the nuclear factors, the mother–God distance is virtually the same for all the groups (see Table 4.3).

The father–God semantic distance in the Indonesian and Filipino communities is shorter than in the other cultural groups. This is

Table 4.3 Probability levels of the differences between the mean distance scores, the cultural groups being compared to one another. Test used: Student t-test

	Total figures			Maternal items			Paternal items			Availability			Law		
	M-F	M-G	F-G	M-F	M-G	F-G	M-F	M-G	F-G	M-F	M-G	F-G	M-F	M-G	F-G
Belgium –															
Zaire	·	·	SUP	·	·	·	·	·	SUP	·	·	·	·	·	SUP
Colombia	SUP	·	SUP	SUP	SUP	·	SUP	·	SUP	SUP	·	SUP	SUP	·	SUP
Indonesia	SUP	SUP	SUP	SUP	SUP	SUP	SUP	·	SUP	SUP	SUP	SUP	SUP	·	SUP
Philippines	SUP	SUP	·	SUP	SUP	SUP	·	·	·	SUP	·	·	·	INF	SUP
USA	SUP	·		SUP	SUP		SUP	·	SUP	SUP	·	·	·	·	SUP
Zaire –															
Colombia	SUP	SUP	·	SUP	SUP	·	SUP	SUP	SUP	SUP	·	·	SUP	·	SUP
Indonesia	SUP	SUP	SUP	SUP	SUP	SUP	SUP	SUP	SUP	SUP	SUP	SUP	SUP	·	·
Philippines	SUP	SUP	SUP	SUP	SUP	SUP	SUP	SUP	SUP	SUP	·	SUP	SUP	SUP	·
USA	SUP	SUP	·	SUP	SUP	·	·	·	·	SUP	·	·	SUP	·	SUP
Colombia –															
Indonesia	SUP	SUP	SUP	SUP	·	SUP	SUP	·	·	SUP	SUP	SUP	·	·	·
Philippines	SUP	·	SUP	SUP	·	SUP	SUP	SUP	·	SUP	SUP	SUP	·	INF	·
USA	·	·	·	·	·	·	·	·	·	SUP	·	·	INF	INF	SUP
Indonesia –															
Philippines	·	·	·	·	INF	·	INF	·	·	·	·	·	INF	INF	·
USA	INF	·	INF	INF	·	INF	INF	·	INF	·	INF	INF	INF	INF	·
Philippines –															
USA	INF	·	INF	INF	·	INF	INF	INF	INF	INF	·	INF	INF	INF	SUP

M-F = mother–father distance
M-G = mother–God distance
F-G = father–God distance
INF, INF, SUP, SUP as in Table 4.1. For example: SUP for the total figures, M-F, in the Belgian Colombian comparison means that the distance scores between the total figures of the father and the mother are higher for the Belgians than for the Colombians and that this difference is significant.

true from the perspective of the total item set of the maternal and paternal dimensions, and of the availability factor. In function of the law factor, the American group has the smallest father–God distance, and the Belgian group the largest.

In summary, the Asian groups have the smallest semantic distances between the figures. For them, the symbolic significance of the father is clearly more emphasized than in the other groups. The polarity between the parental figures is less for them and the distance between the mother figure and the representation of God tends to be the largest. The Belgian and the Zairian groups, on the other hand, have the largest differences between the parental figures and, in particular, the greatest degree of differentiation between the parental figures.

Sexual differences Table 4.4 shows that, for the American, Colombian, Indonesian, and Filipino groups, the sex of the subjects makes no difference in the representation of God. This is true for all levels on which the figures have been considered, i.e., from the perspectives of the entire item set, of the maternal and paternal dimensions, and of the availability and law factors.

In the Zairian group, sex seems to have an influence on the representation of God (Table 4.5). The total item semantic distances show that for the males, God is closer to the father than to the mother $[t(29) = 4.573, p < 0.01]$, while for the females, the difference between the mother–God and father–God distances is not significant.

Important nuances appear when the figures are considered more analytically. For the males, God is closer to the father than to the mother when the figures are considered from the perspective of the dimensions specific to the father, i.e., the paternal items $[t(29) = 5.622, p < 0.01]$, the law factor $[t(29) = 5.349, p < 0.01]$, and the knowledge factor $[t(29) = 3.624, p < 0.01]$. When the figures are considered from the perspective of the dimensions specific to the mother, the distances between the representation of God and each parental figure are equivalent since the differences are not significant (Table 4.5).

Table 4.4   Probability levels of the differences between the mean distance scores for males and females within each cultural group

Distances compared	Belgium Males	Belgium Females	Zaire Males	Zaire Females	Colombia Males	Colombia Females	Indonesia Males	Indonesia Females	Philippines Males	Philippines Females	USA Males	USA Females
(a) 1 *FM–MG*	SUP	SUP	·	SUP	SUP	SUP	·	·	INF	·	SUP	·
2 *FM–FG*	SUP	SUP	SUP	SUP	·	SUP	·	·	·	·	SUP	SUP
3 *MG–FG*	SUP	SUP	SUP	·	·	·	SUP	·	SUP	SUP	·	·
(b) 1 FM_m–MG_m	SUP	SUP	·	SUP	SUP	SUP	SUP	SUP	·	·	SUP	SUP
2 FM_m–FG_m	·	SUP	SUP	SUP	·	·	INF	·	INF	INF	·	INF
3 MG_m–FG_m	·	INF	·	INF	INF	INF	INF	INF	INF	INF	INF	INF
(c) 1 FM_f–MG_f	·	SUP	·	·	·	INF	INF	INF	INF	INF	·	SUP
2 FM_f–FG_f	SUP	SUP	SUP	SUP	SUP	SUP	SUP	SUP	SUP	SUP	SUP	SUP
3 MG_f–FG_f	SUP	·	SUP	SUP	SUP	SUP	SUP	SUP	SUP	SUP	SUP	SUP
(d) Availability 1 *FM–MG*	SUP	SUP	SUP	SUP	SUP	SUP	SUP	SUP	SUP	SUP	SUP	SUP
2 *FM–FG*	·	·	SUP	SUP	SUP	·	·	·	·	INF	·	INF
3 *MG–FG*	INF	INF	·	INF	INF	INF	INF	INF	INF	INF	INF	INF
(e) Law 1 *FM–MG*	SUP	SUP	·	·	INF	INF	INF	INF	INF	·	INF	INF
2 *FM–FG*	SUP	SUP	SUP	SUP	SUP	SUP	SUP	SUP	SUP	SUP	SUP	SUP
3 *MG–FG*	SUP	·	SUP	SUP	SUP	SUP	SUP	SUP	SUP	SUP	SUP	SUP

·   The first distance cited is equivalent to the second
INF   The first distance cited is inferior to the second ($p < 0.05$)
INF   The first distance cited is inferior to the second ($p < 0.01$)
SUP   The first distance cited is superior to the second ($p < 0.05$)
SUP   The first distance cited is superior to the second ($p < 0.01$)

Table 4.5 *Mean distance scores and p-values (Student t-test for males and females in the Zairian group*

Items or factors		*M–G*	*F–G*	*M–G* vs *F–G*	
TOTAL	Males	16.73	13.26	4.573	$p < 0.01$
	Females	15.59	15.37	0.310	n.s.
Maternal items	Males	10.73	9.78	1.390	n.s.
	Females	8.31	12.31	4.637	$p < 0.01$
Paternal items	Males	12.54	8.57	5.622	$p < 0.01$
	Females	12.93	8.74	5.912	$p < 0.01$
Availability	Males	5.43	5.81	0.546	n.s.
	Females	3.27	7.87	5.499	$p < 0.01$
Protection	Males	6.84	6.49	0.662	n.s.
	Females	5.67	7.36	2.395	$p < 0.05$
Knowledge	Males	6.75	5.36	3.624	$p < 0.01$
	Females	6.63	6.22	1.034	n.s.
Law	Males	8.11	4.72	5.349	$p < 0.01$
	Females	8.43	4.93	4.778	$p < 0.01$

n.s. = not significant

For the females, however, God is closer to the mother than to the father if the figures are considered from the perspective of the dimensions specific to the mother, i.e., the maternal items [$t(29) = 4.637, p < 0.01$], the availability factor [$t(29) = 5.499, p < 0.01$], and the protection factor [$t(29) = 2.395, p < 0.05$]. On the other hand, God is closer to the father than to the mother when the figures are considered from the perspective of the paternal items [$t(29) = 5.912$, $p < 0.01$] and the law factor [$t(29) = 4.778$, $p < 0.01$].

In summary, for the Zairians, both male and female, God is more paternal than maternal when the dimensions specific to the father are used as criteria of comparison between the figures. The influence of sex on the representation of God appears when the dimensions specific to the mother are taken into account. It seems, therefore, that the mother symbolizes God differentially and the father symbolizes God uniformly.

With the Belgian group, the sex of the subjects also influences the representation of God. Table 4.6 gives some of the differences. Considering the figures from the perspective of the entire item set, one notices that for the males, God is closer to the father than to the mother [$t(29) = 2.079, p < 0.05$], and for the females, God is closer to the mother than to the father [$t(29) = 2.167, p < 0.05$]. For the females, God is also more maternal than paternal when the figures are examined from the perspective of the maternal items [$t(29) = 4.339, p < 0.01$] while for the males, God is more paternal than maternal when the figures are studied from the point of view of the paternal items [$t(29) = 3.673, p < 0.01$].

Table 4.6 also shows that the mother–God distance on all three levels is equivalent for both males and females, while the father–God distance is always shorter for the males than for the females. Thus, the figure of the mother seems to mediate the representation of God uniformly both for the males and the females. The figure of the father, however, symbolizes God differentially for both males and females.

Analysis of the distances between the figures that were calculated using the factors (Table 4.4) adds some nuances to this observation.

Table 4.6   *Mean distance scores and p-values (Student t-test) for males and females in the Belgian group*

Items		M–G	F–G	M–G vs	F–G
Total	Males	14.98	13.05	2.079	$p < 0.05$
	Females	14.99	16.53	2.167	$p < 0.05$
Maternal items	Males	8.99	9.68	0.779	n.s.
	Females	8.68	12.36	4.339	$p < 0.01$
Paternal items	Males	11.55	8.51	3.673	$p < 0.01$
	Females	11.83	10.56	1.328	n.s.

n.s. = not significant

From the perspective of the availability factor, the representation of God is closer to the mother figure than to the father figure for the males [$t(29) = 3.062, p < 0.01$] as well as for the females [$t(29) = 5.841, p < 0.01$]. The two other maternal factors, feminity and protection, differentiate the sexes more in the semantic relation of the figures. For the males, the differences between the mother–God and the father–God distances are not significant, while for the females, God is nearer to the mother from both the perspectives of the feminity factor [$t(29) = 3.234, p < 0.01$] and of the protection factor [$t(29) = 2.294, p < 0.05$].

In function of the paternal factors (dynamism and law), the relation of the semantic distances between the figures is the inverse of the preceding. Indeed, for the females, God is about equidistant between the two parental figures, while for the males, God is closer to the father than to the mother both from the perspectives of the dynamism factor [$t(29) = 4.888, p < 0.01$] and from that of the law factor [$t(29) = 3.292, p < 0.01$].

In summary, for the Belgian group the representation of God depends on the sex of the subjects. But this dependence is not total. As far as the factor availability is concerned, the representation of God is not sexually determined. The representation of God is sexually determined, however, with regard to the feminity and protection factors for the females, and the law and dynamism factors for the males.

The father figure symbolizes God always differentially, while the mother figure symbolizes God uniformly from the perspective of the availability factor, and differentially from the perspective of the feminity and protection factors.

Factorial approach

Comparison of the availability factor semantic distances with the distances calculated on the basis of each of all the other factors (Table 4.7), shows that the availability factor influences the mother–God distance uniformly for all six cultural groups but not the father–God distance. Indeed, for all the groups the mother–God

Table 4.7　*Probability levels of the differences between the M-F, M-G, and F-G distances, comparing the availability factor with all the others*

Countries	M-F distance				M-G distance				F-G distance			
	F_1-F_2	F_1-F_3	F_1-F_4	F_1-F_5	F_1-F_2	F_1-F_3	F_1-F_4	F_1-F_5	F_1-F_2	F_1-F_3	F_1-F_4	F_1-F_5
Belgium	INF	·	INF	INF	INF	INF	INF	INF	·	·	SUP	SUP
Zaire	·	INF	SUP		INF	INF	INF	INF	·	SUP	SUP	SUP
Colombia	INF	·	·	SUP	INF	INF	INF	INF	·	SUP	SUP	SUP
Indonesia	·	INF	INF	INF	INF	INF	INF	INF	INF	·	·	
Philippines	·	INF	INF	INF	INF	INF	INF	INF	·	SUP	SUP	SUP
USA	INF	INF	INF	INF	INF	INF	INF	INF	SUP	·	SUP	SUP

·　The distance between the figures is equal for the two factors (i.e., the difference is not significant)
INF　The distance between the figures is inferior for the first factor in relation to the others　$(p < 0.05)$
INF　The distance between the figures is inferior for the first factor in relation to the others　$(p < 0.01)$
SUP　The distance between the figures is superior for the first factor in relation to the others　$(p < 0.05)$
SUP　The distance between the figures is superior for the first factor in relation to the others　$(p < 0.01)$

The factors are the following for each country:

	Belgium	*Zaire*	*Colombia*	*Indonesia*	*Philippines*	*USA*
F_1	Availability	Availability	Availability	Availability	Availability	Availability
F_2	Feminity	Protection	Feminity	Intuition	Protection	Authority
F_3	Protection	Knowledge	Order	Knowledge	Dynamism	Dynamism
F_4	Dynamism	Law	Dynamism	Law	Power	Law
F_5	Law		Law		Law	Law

distance is significantly shorter in function of this factor than in function of all the other factors [$t(59)$, $p < 0.01$]. The availability factor thus determines the most striking semantic similarity between the mother and God figures. For the father–God distance, however, the results are not uniform.

Comparison of the distances between the figures from the perspective of the law factor with the distances from the perspective of all the other factors, shows that the results are also uniform for the mother–God distance but not for the father–God distance. There is no consistent pattern in the variation of the father–God distance among the groups nor in terms of the perspective used. But for the mother–God distance, there is a striking uniformity in all the cultural groups. The mother–God distance is always greater from the perspective of the law factor than from the perspective of any other factor.

It thus seems that the symbolic power of the mother is maximal from the perspective of the availability factor since this factor always produces the shortest distance between the mother and God figures, and minimal from the perspective of the law factor as this factor produces the greatest distances between the two figures for all the cultural groups.

3 DISCUSSION

(1) Structurally, the mother, father, and God figures can be presented as composed of nuclear factorial components (availability and law) and peripheral factorial components (feminity, protection, power, intuition, dynamism, knowledge, order). The peripheral factors essentially express the values emphasized in the figures by the various cultural groups. It may be supposed that these factors are fundamentally bound to local traditions and spiritual constructs, thus manifesting characteristic differences in the manner of experiencing the figures within each culture. On the other hand, the nuclear factors, which show a more marked autonomy relative to cultural structures, constitute a stable core,

a common denominator for the figures across the different cultural milieux.

The limitations of these results must, however, be stressed. They have to be taken more in the sense of directions and indications, than in the sense of certain and definitive conclusions. Because the factor analyses were calculated with very small groups (N = 60), the correlation matrices cannot be considered stable enough to allow reliable factor extraction. Consequently, interpretation of the factorial structures must be approached very prudently.

(2) From the perspective of the nuclear factors, the results obtained for the mother–God distance are perfectly uniform for all six cultural groups. This is not the case for the father–God distance. The symbolic power of the maternal figure is maximal from the perspective of the availability factor. It is because of the mother's total availability as response to the desires and needs of the child, that the mother figure best symbolizes the representation of God. But from the perspective of the law factor, the mother only symbolizes it in a very limited way. This observation can be clarified by considering two other results obtained in the study. First, semantic analysis of the items shows that the law-related items are not attributed in the same manner to God as to the mother: they are associated directly with the representation of God and only mediately with the mother figure (cf. p. 76). Second, the intensity scores of the law factor are low for the mother and high for God. It thus seems that the mother is not experienced directly as law, as restriction of desire, though God is experienced directly as law in a radical manner. In the representation of God, the two dimensions characteristic of paternal law appear: prohibition and demands, on the one hand, and the reference to happiness to be achieved, to a life of perfection, on the other. It seems that on the semantic surfaces of the mother and God figures, there is a sector, defined by the law factor, in which the overlapping is not distinct. This phenomenon is present in all the groups.

Interestingly, there is no similar phenomenon occurring between the father figure and the representation of God in relation to any of the factors examined in the course of this study.

(3) The symbolic significance of the parental figures is present in all of the cultural groups. This capacity to symbolize God is particularly clear when the figures are considered from the perspective of their specific characteristics. In this case, symbolization occurs uniformly in all the cultural groups. God is invariably closer to the father than to the mother from the perspective of the paternal dimensions, and closer to the mother than to the father from the perspective of the maternal dimensions. When the figures are considered as a whole, significant cultural differences emerge: for the American and Colombian groups, God is as paternal as maternal; for the Indonesian and Filipino groups, God is more paternal than maternal; for the Belgian group, God is more maternal than paternal for the females with the inverse being the case for the males; and, finally, for the Zairian group, God is more paternal than maternal for the males, and equally paternal as maternal for the females.

The symbolic function of the parental figures studied here is limited to the semantic similarity between the parental figures and the representation of God. The developmental sequence of the representation of God must still be studied to establish the contribution of each parental figure to its genesis and development.

Differential Perspectives of the Parental Figures and the Representation of God

Some of the elements of the human situation, such as sex and age, are imposed by the very nature of things; others, such as profession and affiliation with political, religious, and social groups proceed from choices more or less freely made. Imposed or chosen, these situations condition, to varying degrees, each person's manner of being in the world. Their specific impact on the individual has been and is the object of countless psychological studies. The objective of this chapter is to consider the effects of a very small number of these variables on the symbolic parental figures and the representation of God. The variables discussed here are age, field of study, belief systems, and religious affiliation. In the preceding chapter, the impact of culture on the structure of the parental and divine figures was presented, and in the following chapter, the influence of schizophrenia and delinquency will be explored.*

A THE INFLUENCE OF AGE ON THE PARENTAL FIGURES AND THE REPRESENTATION OF GOD by *Alvaro Tamayo and Suzanne Cooke*

1 INTRODUCTION

The transformations occurring in the parental and God figures from childhood through old age have yet to be studied systematically. Exploratory research in this area was done by Bonami (1966) with a sample composed of young adults (average age, 22 years) and

---

* Sections two and three of this chapter have already been published in the *Journal of Psychology* 92 (1976), 131–140 and 97 (1977), 79–84. They have been revised and are included here with permission of the editor.

adults (average age, 37 years 6 months). His results revealed no significant differences between the two groups. Tamayo and Pasquali (1967) found the representation of God to be more maternal for postadolescents (average age, 20 years) than for adolescents (average age, 16 years 6 months). The object of the present study is to examine the parental and divine figures of the elderly in comparison with postadolescents.

2 METHOD

2.1 *Instrument*

The French version of the SDPS was used.

2.2 *Sample*

The sample was composed of 160 subjects, of which 80 were elderly with an average age of 69 years and 80 were postadolescents with an average age of 20 years. All were French-speaking Roman Catholic Canadians from the middle socioeconomic level.

2.3 *Statistical Analyses*

Three factor analyses were calculated for the group of elderly persons. The intercorrelation matrices were factorized by the principal factor solution and the factors thus obtained were subjected to orthogonal rotation by the Varimax method. The degrees of congruence between the factors thus isolated were established by means of the Tucker Phi-coefficient (1951).

Three distance scores (Osgood 1971) were calculated for each subject (M–F, M–G, and F–G). The distance scores were compared by analysis of the variance using $2 \times 2 \times 3$ split-plot $p\, r.q$ factorial design (Kirk 1968) with p = sex, r = age, and q = semantic relations (mother–father vs mother–God, mother–father vs father–God and mother–God vs father–God).

3 RESULTS AND DISCUSSION

Table 5.1 gives the loading coefficients of the factors obtained for the three figures. The mother figure is composed of three factors: availability (46 percent), direction (20.8 percent), and sternness (8.6 percent). The factors of the father figure are law (42.3 percent), receptivity (18.6 percent), and intimacy (7.7 percent). The representation of God also has three factors: presence (69.1 percent), initiative (13.6 percent), and power (8.5 percent).

In the other studies reported in this chapter as well as those of the preceding chapter, the fundamental factor of the representation of God is availability, which factor comprises most of the maternal items. For the elderly persons, the fundamental factor in the representation of God is presence, which is made up of fewer maternal items. These items express the idea of a presence that calms, that shares weaknesses and sufferings, and that is patient and intimate. The dimensions of acceptance and receptivity, both included in the availability factor of the representation of God in the other samples, are absent here.

Analysis of variance showed that the semantic relation (i.e., MF–MG, MF–FG, MG–FG) had a significant effect [$F(2) = 20.90$, $p < 0.01$]. The age variable also had a significant effect [$F(1) = 16.24$, $p < 0.01$]. Finally, the interaction between semantic relations, sex, and age was also significant [$F(2) = 3.23, p < 0.05$].

Concerning the significant effect of semantic relations, the Tukey q-test showed that the mother–father distance was shorter than the mother–God ($p < 0.01$) and the father–God ($p < 0.01$) distances. Regarding the significant effect of the age variable, the Tukey q-test showed that the three semantic distances were shorter for the elderly persons than for the postadolescents.

The only difference between the two groups is expressed in the closer relation of the three figures for the aged. For both groups, the representation of God offers equivalent semantic similarity with each of the parental figures.

Table 5.1   *Factor coefficients and percentages of variance for each factor of the mother, father and God figures*

Items	Mother F_1	Mother F_2	Mother F_3	Father F_1	Father F_2	Father F_3	God F_1	God F_2	God F_3
Who is always ready with open arms	0.88				0.68				
Who gives comfort	0.84						0.63		
Self-giving love	0.83				0.67				
Who welcomes me with open arms	0.81				0.82		0.83		
Who is always there when needed[1]	0.77				0.60				
Who is always waiting for me	0.74								
Who takes loving care of me	0.72								
Who will sympathize with the child's sorrows	0.71						0.72		
Sensitive	0.63						0.72		
The one who is most patient							0.62		
Who is intimate						0.75		0.61	
Intuition			0.77						
Who gives law				0.77					
The one who maintains order				0.72					
Who gives the directions		0.64		0.66					
Authority				0.63			0.62		
Who is the principle, the rule				0.64					0.62
Who takes the initiative		0.64						0.81	
Who makes the decisions		0.62							
The one who has the knowledge								0.65	
The one who acts							0.74		
Power									0.67
Stern			0.75						
Strength			0.67						0.65
Percentage of variance	40.6	20.6	8.6	42.3	18.6	7.9	49.1	13.6	7.9

1. This item does not occur in the English version of the scale.

Thus, initial examination of the effect of age on the parental and divine figures seems to indicate that there are no important transformations beyond postadolescence. The possible changes taking place during the first stages of human development and, more concretely, the entire genetic process of the modeling of the representation of God on the parental figures are still to be investigated.

B   THE INFLUENCE OF THE FIELD OF STUDY ON THE
    PARENTAL FIGURES AND THE REPRESENTATION
    OF GOD *by Alvaro Tamayo and Albert Dugas*

1 INTRODUCTION

Empirical research into the influence of the field of study on the perception of the parental figures and the representation of God has included both the arts and the sciences. Many recent studies have focused on the effect of these two academic orientations on various dimensions of the personality and on cognitive structures (Kirkland 1974 and 1976; Barton and Cattell 1972; Smithers and Child 1974; Hudson 1966; Goldman et al. 1973; Simon and Ward 1974; Kline 1971; George et al. 1972).

   The purpose of the present research was to study the influence of such variables as field of study (arts students vs science students), level of studies (undergraduate vs graduate students), and sex on the conceptual representation of the mother, the father, and God.

2 METHOD

2.1 *Instrument*

The instrument of measure used was the French version of the SDPS, constructed in Belgium. Its validity for the French Canadian population was tested with a sample of 200 subjects. The discriminability of the maternal and paternal items was carefully verified. The t-test showed that all maternal items were significantly more often applied to the mother than to the father, and all paternal items more often applied to the father than to the mother.

2.2 Subjects

The subjects were 351 university students recruited from the liberal arts (69 males, 83 females), science (87 males, 40 females), and graduate student (52 males, 20 females) populations. All of them were French Canadians. The average age was 21 years, 1 month.

3 RESULTS

Table 5.2 presents the factors obtained for each of the three figures. The principal factor solution was used for the extraction of factors and the Varimax criterion for rotation. The congruence between the factors obtained from the three different analyses was calculated with the use of Tucker's Phi-coefficient (Tucker, 1951). Coefficients of congruence are reported in Table 5.3. It appears clear that M_1, F_2, and G_1, on the one hand, and M_2, F_1, and G_2, on the other hand, are, respectively perfectly congruent. The first set (M_1, F_2, and G_1) suggests the idea of receptivity, and the second (M_2, F_1, and G_2) the idea of law. For the mother and God figures, receptivity was the first and most important factor (percentage of variance 63.3 and 78.9, respectively), and law a secondary factor (percentage of variance 26.2 and 16.3, respectively). For the father figure an inverse order was found (56.3 for the law factor and 34.5 for the receptivity factor). Thus, there was more similarity in factorial structure between the mother and God figures than between the father and God figures. The analysis of variance, comparing the subjects on the basis of the distance scores, revealed that the semantic relations (i.e., *MF* vs *MG*, *MF* vs *FG*, and *MG* vs *FG*) had a signifi-

Table 5.2 *Factor coefficients and percentage of variance accounted for by each factor of the mother, father, and God figures*

Items	Mother		Father		God	
	M_1	M_2	F_1	F_2	G_1	G_2
Who will sympathize with the child's sorrows	0.77				0.72	
Who welcomes me with open arms	0.74				0.83	
Sensitive	0.74			0.64	0.67	
Tenderness	0.73				0.69	
Who is always there when needed [1]	0.71				0.75	
Who takes loving care of me	0.70				0.64	
Who gives comfort	0.70			0.67	0.77	
Close to whom one feels at home	0.69				0.80	
Who is always ready with open arms	0.69				0.79	
Who brings out which is delicate	0.68					
The one who is most patient	0.64				0.78	
Who is always waiting for me					0.72	
Self-giving love					0.68	
Who is all-embracing					0.65	
Who is intimate					0.64	
A warm-hearted refuge					0.63	
Who gives the law		0.75	0.81			0.76
Who is the principle, the rule		0.63	0.67			0.67
Judge		0.62				0.66
Who makes the decisions			0.70			0.63
Who gives the directions			0.67			0.61
The one who maintains order			0.65			
Strength			0.63			
Stern			0.62			0.62
Power			0.62			
Authority						0.71
Percentage of variance	63.3	26.2	56.3	34.5	78.9	16.3

1. This item does not occur in the English version of the scale.

cant effect [$F(2) = 53.480$, $p < 0.001$]. There was also an interaction effect between the field of study of the respondent and the semantic relations [$F(4) = 6.033$, $p < 0.01$]. Finally, there was an interaction effect between the sex of the respondent and the semantic relations [$F(2) = 4.015$, $p < 0.05$].

Concerning the effect of the semantic relations, Tukey's q-test

Table 5.3   *Significant coefficients of congruence between the mother, father, and God factors*

Factor	Coefficient
M_1 vs F_2	0.97683
M_1 vs G_1	0.95311
F_2 vs G_1	0.94006
M_2 vs F_1	0.96968
M_2 vs G_2	0.94623
F_1 vs G_2	0.94456

revealed that the mother–father distance score was smaller than either the mother–God or the father–God distance ($p < 0.001$), and the mother–God distance smaller than the father–God distance score ($p < 0.01$). The interaction effect between the field of study and the semantic relations showed, first, that for the arts students the mother–God distance was smaller than the father–God distance score ($p < 0.01$); second, that the mother–God and father–God distances were smaller for both groups of undergraduate students (arts and science) than for the graduate students ($p < 0.01$); and finally, that the mother–father distance was smaller for the graduate and arts students than for the science students ($p < 0.01$).

The interaction effect between sex and the semantic relation revealed that for both males and females the mother–God distance was smaller than the father–God distance ($p < 0.01$), and that the mother–father distance was smaller for the females than for the males ($p < 0.01$).

4 DISCUSSION

There are three main points: (a) the sex variable had an influence on the parental figures but not on the representation of God; (b) the field of studies and the level of studies affected the representation of God; (c) the God figure seems to be modeled more on the mother figure than on the father figure.

Concerning the influence of sex on the representation of the parental figures, the results of the present research confirm those obtained in previous investigations. The females in all the cultures studied seemed to perceive the parents in a less contrasted way than do the males.

The effect of the field of studies on the representation of God was previously studied in Belgium (Bonami 1964; Schodts 1971; Olaerts 1971), in the USA (Tamayo and Pasquali 1967), and in Italy (Bernardi 1972), but in all cases with negative results. This contrasts with the findings of the present study. In fact, intellectual professional training seemed clearly associated with differences in the representation of God. For the arts students the representation of God was more maternal than paternal, while for the science and graduate students it was equally modeled on both parental figures. This discrepancy suggests that when there is an influence due to the field of studies, this influence could be the result of the cultural environment.

The semantic similarity between the representation of God and both parental figures was larger for the undergraduates than for the graduate students. One wonders if this could indicate that, as individuals obtain higher intellectual development or higher professional training, the similarity between the representation of God and the parental figures decreases.

The mother figure appears to be the most adequate symbol for the representation of God. This was true for the entire sample without distinction of sex. In fact, the divine figure presented a more definite similarity to the mother than to the father on the basis of factorial structure and semantic distance scores. In all previous studies the representation of God was either more paternal than maternal or equally symbolized by both parental figures. Tamayo showed that the extent and the pattern of the symbolization of the God figure by the parental figures are largely determined by the cultural environment (cf. Chapter 4). The present results not only confirm this finding but also indicate that either the father or the mother can become the most adequate symbol of the God figure. One may conclude that even if the father figure is more consistently and more frequently used as the most adequate symbol of God, this cannot be considered as an exclusive privilege. The mother figure can assume also the function of being the most adequate symbol of God, depending on the cultural background of the subjects.

C   THE INFLUENCE OF BELIEF SYSTEMS ON THE PARENTAL FIGURES AND THE REPRESENTATION OF GOD *by Alvaro Tamayo and Léandre Desjardins*

1   INTRODUCTION

Is the perception of the parental and divine figures influenced by the psychological structure of the individual? According to Harvey and Beverly (1961: 25):

perceiving, thinking, judging and related activities are profoundly affected by — perhaps even wholly dependent upon — a pre-established system of ordering on conceptual placement. . . . And yet this very dependence on a system of categories leads to a kind of conceptual closedness, reflected in a functional blindness to alternative evaluations that are not embodied in the conceptual framework employed at the moment.

Stimuli and significant events are differentiated, structured, and integrated by the individual in a way that is compatible with his needs and ideals. Moreover, this organizing and structuring of the different situations that are encountered seem to be fundamentally characterized, first, by stability or the tendency to be repetitive in the face of new stimuli, and, second, by resistance to change.

Harvey (1970: 68) calls this predisposition of the individual to structure significant situations in a specific manner a 'belief system', which he defines as follows: 'A belief system represents a set of predispositions to perceive, feel toward and respond to ego-involving stimuli and events in a consistent way'. The belief system of an individual includes the totality of his bonds with the world and of his definitions of the world. It has been argued that the belief system constitutes the very core of the self (Harvey 1963; Harvey et al. 1961).

Belief content and structure are the two dimensions used to differentiate the systems. The structural dimension consists of the ways used by the individual to integrate, organize, and discriminate information, concepts, and values. The content dimension refers to the values and realities that are fundamental to a particular structural level.

The structural dimension has two poles: abstractness and concreteness.

Concreteness-Abstractness refers to a superordinate conceptual dimension encompassing such more molecular organizational properties as the degree of differentiation, articulation, integration, and centrality of the cognitive elements. Being more generic and qualitative, variation in concreteness-abstractness rests upon differences in patterning or organization and not in differences in algebraic quantity of these subordinate characteristics. Different syndromes of interpretive, affective, and behavioral tendencies accompany or underlie concrete and abstract functioning (Harvey 1967: 205).

Concrete individuals, as opposed to abstract individuals, are characterized by a need for structure and order (Harvey et al. 1966), a greater dependence on authoritative criteria as guidelines for action and belief (Harvey 1964; Harvey and Beverly 1961), an incapacity to tolerate incertitude and ambiguity (Harvey 1966), a tendency to dogmatism and categorization (Hoffmeister 1965), a resistance to novelty and change (Harvey 1966), a greater tendency to make more polarized evaluations (White and Harvey 1965), a greater tendency to form and to generalize impressions of others on the basis of very incomplete information (Ware and Harvey 1967), a marked lack of sensitivity to subtle and minimal cues (Harvey 1966), an orientation and a tendency towards overvaluing superficial characteristics to the detriment of the substance of information or of an activity (Harvey et al. 1966), and a simpler cognitive structure with little capacity for discrimination and integration (Harvey 1966). Abstract individuals are characterized by inverse degrees of these tendencies and qualities.

All these dimensions and many others interact in multiple ways, and it is possible to identify different belief systems by observing the interaction of the belief content with the belief structure. Harvey (1967, 1970) has identified four: systems I and II corresponding to the concrete pole, and systems III and IV corresponding to the abstract pole.

Harvey (1967) developed an objective scale, the Conceptual Systems Test (CST), that measures the belief systems. The CST is composed of these seven factors: divine faith control, need for simplicity-consistency, need for structure-order, distrust of social authority, friendship absolutism, moral absolutism, and general pessimism.

In operational terms, therefore, the present study was directed to the relationships between the type of mediational system that links the divine figure to the parental figures and the degree of concreteness-abstractness of the individual. We surmised that the divine figure of concrete individuals would have more resemblance to the father than the mother figure, and that these concrete subjects would show a clear preference for paternal values (authority, law, order, rules), since these values meet their need for structure and order as well as their intolerance of uncertainties. Abstract subjects, on the other hand, through their ability to live with ambiguities and with lack of structure, as well as through their higher success in integration of complex phenomena, would have, as a representation of God, a mixture of both parental figures.

2 METHOD

2.1 *Instruments*

The CST was used to group the subjects according to their degree of concreteness-abstractness, and the English version of the SDPS was used to assess the parental figures and the representation of God.

2.2 *Sample*

The sample was composed of 390 undergraduate university students (English-speaking Canadians). On the basis of the results of the CST, the sample was divided into two groups: concrete subjects (Systems I and II), which consisted of 157 students, 66 males and 91 females, and abstract subjects (Systems III and IV), which consisted of 203 students, 85 males and 118 females.

2.3 *Statistical Procedures*

Factors were extracted for each of the three figures (the mother figure, the father figure, and the divine figure) and for each group (concretes, abstracts, and total) with use of the principal factor solution for the extraction of factors and the Varimax criterion for rotation. Tucker's Phi-coefficient was used to determine the degree of congruence between the factors obtained from the different analyses (Tucker 1951).

The semantic differences between the three figures were calculated for each subject using all 36 items of the SDPS. Three distance scores resulted: mother–father, mother–God, and father–God. The subjects were compared, on the basis of the distance scores, by analysis of variance using a $2 \times 2 \times 3$ split-plot $p \: r.q$ factorial design where p = systems, r = sex, and q = semantic relations. All significant results were further analyzed with the use of the Tukey's q-test.

3 RESULTS AND DISCUSSION

The loading coefficients of each of the factors obtained for the three figures are given on Table 5.4.

Each parental figure is composed of two factors that in each case account for more than 80 percent of the variance. Factor M_1 of the mother figure and factor F_2 of the father figure are congruent

(Phi = 0.98913) and are both labeled tenderness. The factors M_2 and F_1, both labeled authority, are also congruent (Phi = 0.97653). The representation of God is composed of three factors of which the first, availability (G_1), accounts for 81.6 percent of the total variance. The two other factors are firmness (G_2) and authority (G_3) and they account for 9.9 and 5.5 percent of the variance respectively.

Table 5.4   *Factor coefficients and percentage of variance accounted for by each factor of the mother, father, and God figures*

Items	Mother M_1	Mother M_2	Father F_1	Father F_2	God G_1	God G_2	God G_3
Tenderness	0.81			0.79	0.73		
Warmth	0.83			0.74	0.62		
Who gives comfort	0.89			0.79	0.76		
A warm-hearted refuge	0.80			0.78	0.70		
Always ready with open arms	0.75			0.76	0.81		
Who will sympathize	0.74			0.69	0.68		
Who takes loving care of me	0.74			0.73	0.67		
Close to whom one feels at home	0.72			0.65	0.68		
Who welcomes me with open arms	0.70			0.75	0.80		
The one who is most patient	0.62						
Who is intimate				0.66			
Self-giving love				0.66	0.64		
Who is always waiting for me					0.76		
Who is all-embracing					0.70		
Authority		0.78	0.84				0.73
Who is the principle, the rule		0.78	0.79				0.68
Judge		0.72	0.75				0.66
Who gives the law		0.70	0.82				
Who gives the directions		0.65	0.75				
Who makes the decisions		0.72	0.82			0.68	
Power			0.73				
The one who maintains order			0.77			0.61	
Firmness			0.71			0.70	
Stern						0.67	
The one who acts						0.67	
Who takes the initiative						0.66	
Percentage of variance	53.2	29.5	47.1	37.2	81.6	9.9	5.5

It is interesting to note the parallelism in the factorial structure of the parental figures. The only difference between the two figures consists in that, for the mother figure, the tenderness factor (53.2 percent of the total variance) seems to be more fundamental than authority (29.5 percent), while, for the father figure, authority (47.1 percent) seems to be more important than tenderness (37.2 percent).

It is equally important to stress the similarity between the factorial structure of the parental figures and that of the representation of God. As can be seen on Table 5.5, there is semicongruence ($0.7000 \leqslant Phi \leqslant 0.9398$) between the fundamental factor of the representation of God, availability, and the tenderness factor, which is congruent for the two parental figures, and also between the authority factor of the parental figures and the firmness and authority factors of the representation of God.

Table 5.5   *Phi-coefficients for the factors of the parental figures and the representation of God*

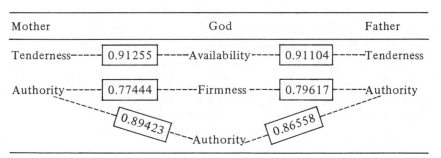

Mother	God	Father
Tenderness---- 0.91255	----Availability---- 0.91104	----Tenderness
Authority---- 0.77444	------Firmness ---- 0.79617	----Authority
0.89423	---Authority--- 0.86558	

While parents are mainly perceived as showing tenderness and warmth, God is seen as showing availability, dedication, hospitality, together with parental tenderness and warmth. Table 5.4 illustrates the distinction between the parental and divine authority. Divine authority is perceived as being normative, encompassing the idea of the standard in authority, while parental authority also contains the ideas of disciplinary authority, of command, and of decision making.

As already mentioned, factor analyses were calculated for each of the two groups. The results were fundamentally the same as those presented on Table 5.4; this shows that the factorial structures of the three figures are essentially the same for the abstract as for the concrete groups.

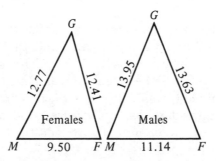

Figure 5.1   *Semantic distances between the three figures according to sex*

Regarding the semantic distances between the three figures, analysis of the variance showed that sex $[F(1) = 13.615, p < 0.001]$ and semantic relations $[F(2) = 101.748, p < 0.001]$ had a significant effect. A significant interaction was also found between the semantic relations and the belief system $[F(2) = 3.535, p < 0.05]$.

The effects due to the sex of the respondent are illustrated in Figure 5.1. The mother–father and parent–God distance scores were larger for the males than for the females.

Figure 5.2 indicates that the mother–father distance score was smaller than either the mother–God or the father–God distance score and that the latter two were equivalent. The interaction effect between the belief system and the semantic relations revealed that the abstract subjects had a higher father–God distance score than the concrete subjects (see Figure 5.3).

The expectations of the present investigation were that abstract individuals would have, as a divine figure, a mixture of both parental figures with a possible accent on the mother figure. The factorial structure of the representation of God corroborated this

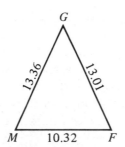

Significance level following Tukey's q-test for the total sample is as follows:
$MF < MG$ ($p < 0.01$); $MF < FG$ ($p < 0.01$); $MG = FG$ (not significant).

Figure 5.2 *Semantic distances between the three figures*

hypothesis. It was composed of a fundamental factor, availability (a maternal factor) and two secondary factors, authority and firmness (both paternal factors). It was also expected that the representation of God of abstract individuals would be equidistant from both parental figures. The results also supported this hypothesis.

Expectations regarding the figures given by concrete individuals were partially confirmed. Their divine figure was expected to be closer (in terms of the distance score) to that of the father than

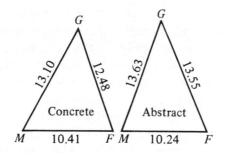

Significance level following Tukey's q-test is as follows:
$MF_{concrete} = MF_{abstract}$ (n.s.); $MG_{concrete} = MG_{abstract}$ (n.s.);
$FG_{concrete} < FG_{abstract}$ ($p < 0.05$).

Figure 5.3 *Semantic distances between the three figures for concrete and abstract samples*

to that of the mother and structured according to such values as authority, law, order, and command. As expected, the results showed that the paternal characteristic of their representation of God was significantly more important than it was for the abtracts. However, it remained almost equidistant from the two parental figures within their own group, as it was for the abstracts, and it was structured according to the same set of factors that the abstracts used.

D   PARENTAL AND DIVINE FIGURES OF CHRISTIANS AND HINDUS ACCORDING TO BELIEF SYSTEM *by Léandre Desjardins and Alvaro Tamayo*

1 INTRODUCTION

Psychology has recently shown an increasing interest in the study of religious behavior. Some studies in this area have looked beyond opinions and beliefs to the experiential aspects of religion, thus dealing with personality variables. These studies are concerned with the dynamic structure of personality — perceptions, motivations, feelings — as it is revealed in religious attitudes, beliefs, and behavior.

In monotheist religions, paternity is an essential attribute of divinity. Freud perceived this association and attempted to discover historical and psychological factors capable of explaining it. The results discussed in the preceding chapters revealed that both parental figures present specific similarities with the representation of God. The relative importance of each of the two parental figures in the structure of the representation of God is influenced by culture, age, field of study, and belief system. The main purpose of the present investigation was to study the influence of the religious affiliation on the parental and divine figures. It is also intended to reexplore the influence of belief systems and sex. Adherence to two major religions that present significant cultural and theological contrasts, namely, Christianity and Hinduism, was chosen for this study. The subjects were drawn from populations residing in traditional Christian and Hindu cultures with the risk of not being able to discern the specific effects of religious affiliation from those caused by the culture. The choice of two samples from a homogeneous cultural milieu would, obviously, have led to better isolation of the religious affiliation variable, but this would have given rise to another methodological problem also difficult to overcome: the impact of acculturation on the lived religion of the individual.

2 METHOD

2.1 *Measures*

The English version of the SDPS and the CST. The subjects were asked to describe the divinity instead of the representation of God.

2.2 *Subjects*

Altogether, 251 university students participated in the project. Of these, 116 were Christians from Canada (36 men and 80 women) and 135 were Hindus from India (66 men and 69 women). Of the total, 91 were classified as concretes and 111 as abstracts.

2.3 *Statistics*

Three distance scores were calculated for each subject: mother–father, mother–God, and father–God. The analysis of variance performed with these scores had four dimensions: religious affiliation (two categories), sex (two categories), belief system (two categories), and semantic relations (three categories). The statistical formula used was that suggested by Kirk (1968) and labeled a split-plot p $r.q$ 9 factorial design.

Finally, 6 factor analyses were calculated, one for each figure (father, mother, and divinity) for each group (Hindus and

Christians). The Phi-coefficient was used to determine the degree of congruence between the different factors obtained (Tucker 1951).

3 RESULTS AND DISCUSSION

The analysis of the variance showed significant effects due to belief systems $[F(1) = 4.914, p < 0.05]$, religion $[F(1) = 6.111, p < 0.05]$, and semantic relations $[F(2) = 33.655, p < 0.01]$.

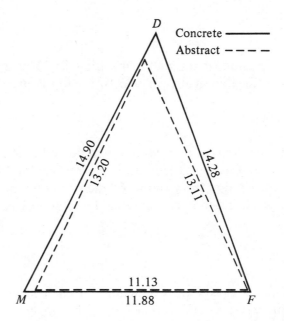

Figure 5.4   *Semantic distances between the three figures according to personality*

Figure 5.4 illustrates the effects due to the belief systems. The mother–divinity and father–divinity distances are significantly larger for the concretes than for the abstracts ($p < 0.01$).

The effect due to religion reveals that all three distance scores are greater in the Hindu group than they are in the Christian group (see Figure 5.5). This first indication of a religious difference suggests more differentiated roles and figures for the mother, the father, and divinity in the Hindu group.

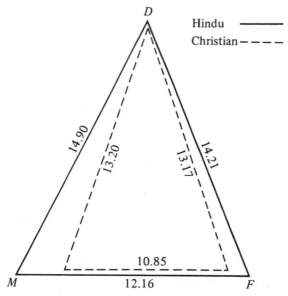

Figure 5.5   *Semantic distances between the three figures according to religion*

There were no interaction effects, however, between religion and the semantic relations. The mother–divinity distance score was equivalent to the father–divinity distance score for both groups. There were also no differences between the mother–divinity distance scores and the father–divinity distance scores of the two groups respectively. This suggests that the representation of God was equally mediated by both parental figures in the two groups. More specifically, the psychological notion of divinity was equally mediated by both parental figures in each of the two groups in

Table 5.6   Factor coefficients and percentage of variance for the Christians

	Mother		Father			Divinity		
	M_1	M_2	F_1	F_2	F_3	D_1	D_2	D_3
Tenderness	0.89		0.83			0.66		
Who gives comfort	0.88		0.79				0.60	
Who is always ready	0.84		0.82			0.67		
Who will sympathize	0.82		0.78			0.64		
Who welcomes me	0.76		0.79			0.80		
Close to whom one feels at home	0.74		0.73			0.68		
Who takes a loving care of me	0.71		0.78					
Who is intimate	0.66		0.67			0.67		
Sensitive	0.64		0.70			0.65		
Who is all-embracing	0.63		0.68			0.64		
Warmth	0.60		0.70					
Who brings out which is delicate	0.60		0.72			0.63		
Self-giving love			0.80			0.64		
A warm-hearted refuge			0.67					
Who is always waiting for me			0.61			0.70		
The one who is most patient							0.78	
The authority		0.83		0.83			0.63	
Who makes the decisions		0.77		0.76				0.66
The one who maintains order		0.77		0.73	0.67			
Firmness		0.76		0.75			0.65	
Who is the principle, the rule		0.76		0.67				0.68
Who gives the directions		0.70		0.76				
Who gives the law		0.68						0.71
Who takes the initiative		0.66		0.76				
The judge		0.66						
Stern		0.65						0.60
Power		0.65		0.60			0.81	0.67
Who has the knowledge		0.65					0.77	
Dynamic		0.64						
The one who acts		0.61						
Strength					0.63		0.82	
Percentage of variance	40.8	37.3	43.8	35.5	6.4	83.9	6.7	5.8

spite of theological, philosophical, and historical differences between Christians and Hindus regarding the divinity.

Tables 5.6 and 5.7 present the factors extracted for the three figures of the Christian and Hindu samples respectively. These factors account for more than 78 percent of the variance in the Christian sample and more than 65 percent in the Hindu sample.

Figure 5.6 schematically illustrates:
(1) the name given to each factor for each figure and in each of the two groups;
(2) the percentage of variance accounted for by each factor;
(3) the degrees of congruence and semicongruence between factors.

For the Christian group, the mother figure is composed of two main factors: tenderness and authority. The first of these factors is maternal and the second paternal. That is, those items that have significant factor loading are all maternal items in the case of tenderness and all paternal items in the case of authority.

The same two factors (tenderness and authority) compose the father figure and both are congruent with the respective factors of the mother figure. Another factor, firmness, is also involved in the definition of the father figure.

The first factor of the divine figure, availability, is maternal and explains most of the variance (84 percent). The two minor factors, strength and law, are paternal. Availability and law are semicongruent[1] with the two factors common to both paternal figures, tenderness and authority, respectively.

For the Hindus, the mother figure has four factors: warmth, acceptance, force, and judge. The first two are maternal and the last two paternal. Warmth is semicongruent with tenderness of the mother figure of the Christian group.

The father figure of the Hindus also has four factors: receptivity, principle, initiative, and power. The first is maternal and the last three are paternal. Receptivity is semicongruent with acceptance of the mother figure. Receptivity and principle are respectively

---

1. For the notion of semicongruence see Chapter 4, p. 74.

Table 5.7   *Factor coefficients and percentage of variance for the Hindus*

	Mother				Father				Divinity	
	M_1	M_2	M_3	M_4	F_1	F_2	F_3	F_4	D_1	D_2
Tenderness	0.63									
Who gives comfort										0.61
Who is always ready										0.62
Who welcomes me		0.66								0.79
Close to whom one feels at home					0.60					
Who takes a loving care of me										0.64
Who is intimate										0.65
Warmth	0.69									
Self-giving love		0.63			0.62					
A warm-hearted refuge	0.64									
Who is always waiting for me		0.73			0.66					0.66
The authority			0.71			0.60			0.81	
Who makes the decisions							0.60		0.62	
The one who maintains order									0.72	
Firmness										
Who is the principle, the rule						0.70				
Who gives the law						0.72			0.76	
The judge				0.66						
Stern						0.63		0.71	0.61	
Power			0.72							
Percentage of variance	32.3	19.2	12.0	7.1	25.6	20.6	10.4	8.3	72.3	12.3

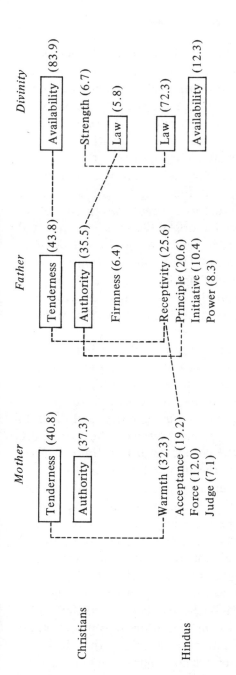

The factors enclosed in boxes are congruent (Phi ≥ 0.9398) when they are of the same name (Tenderness — Tenderness; Law — Law; Authority — Authority; Availability — Availability).
The factors linked by dotted lines are semicongruent (0.7000 < Phi < 0.9398).
The numbers in parentheses indicate the percentage of variance accounted for by the factor.

Figure 5.6   *Schematic description of the factorial structure of the three figures in the two religious groups (factors, congruence, and percentage of variance)*

semicongruent with tenderness and authority of the father figure of the Christian group.

Two factors compose the representation of the divine figure for the Hindus: law and availability, which are respectively congruent with law and availability of the divine figure of the Christian group.

Comparison of the two groups yields three observations. First of all, the father and mother figures are highly similar in the Christian sample. These two figures are actually composed of common factors, tenderness and authority, and the percentage of variance explained by each one of these factors is practically identical. In contrast, there are no common factors between the father and mother figures of the Hindus, each figure being factorially very distinct from the other in this sample. Thus, the common structure of the two parental figures of the Christian sample is clearly different from that of the Hindu sample, where this structure is not found and where the mother and father figures are differentially structured.

Second, although there is practically no similarity between the parental figures of the Christian group and those of the Hindu group, their respective divine figures appear to be highly similar. The divine figure of the Christians and the divine figure of the Hindus have two factors in common: availability and law. In addition, the third factor of the divine figure of the Christians, strength, is semicongruent with the law factor of the Hindu sample. The apparent similarity between the divine figures of Christians and Hindus is clarified by the differences in the amount of variance explained by each factor. In the Christian sample, availability accounts for 84 percent of the variance and law, 5.8 percent. The inverse proportions, law, 72.3 percent and availability, 12.3 percent, are found in the Hindu sample. Therefore, it would seem that Christians perceive divinity through affective values such as availability, proximity, and tenderness, while Hindus do so through more organizational values such as authority, law, and order.

Third, the factorial structure of the divine figure is more similar to the factorial structure of the parental figures for the Christians than it is for the Hindus. While there is no congruence between the factors of the divine figure and those of the parental figures of the Hindus, the two common factors of the parental figures of the Christians are semicongruent with the two most important factors of the divine figure in that group. This suggests that divinity adequately represents the values attached to parental figures among the Christians, while, conversely, among the Hindus, divinity represents values that are secondary to the description of the parental figures.

E   BELIEF IN THE EXISTENCE OF GOD AND THE REPRESENTATION OF GOD
by Dirk Hutsebaut

1 INTRODUCTION

The main purpose of this study is to determine whether and how the intensity of attribution of the items of the SDPS vary in function of belief in the existence of God and also whether and how the rank order of the items changes in function of this same variable. This report is based on a larger project (Hutsebaut 1976) in which some of the subjects were given the SDPS along with other testing instruments. Because of the quantity of the other test materials, the SDPS item series was only applied to the representation of God.

The importance of the belief variable has been stressed by Spilka, Armatas, and Nussbaum (1964). In their study, the scores of 64 qualities attributed to God were subjected to factor analysis, and the factor structure of a very religious sample (frequency of church attendance, strong agreement with Catholic theological doctrine, participation in Catholic religious activities) was compared with that of a heterogeneous sample (some degree of religiosity and church participation). By means of a congruence index, these authors concluded that clear differences existed in the representation of God of the two samples.

2 METHOD

2.1 *Instrument*

The instrument used was the Dutch version of the SDPS.

2.2 *Sample*

The sample consisted of 133 adults with an average age of 37 years. There were 71 men and 62 women. The structure of this group's belief in God is given in Table 5.8. We analyzed only the first three groups, a total of 130 subjects. The vast majority of these subjects attended mass every Sunday (90.3 percent).

Table 5.8 *Structure of belief in God*

	Men	%	Women	%	Total	%
Absolute belief in the existence of God	34	47.9	20	32.3	54	40.6
Belief in the existence of God but with questions	25	35.2	34	54.8	59	44.4
Doubt in the existence of God	11	15.5	6	9.7	17	13
Difficulties in believing in the existence of God			1	1.6	1	0.07
No belief in the existence of God	1	1.4	1	1.6	2	0.1

2.3 *Paternal and maternal groups*

Paternal and maternal groups were distinguished: (a) the paternal group consisted of those subjects who scored higher on the paternal items than on the maternal (sometimes the difference is very small). There were 29 subjects in this group, 18 males and 11 females. (b) The maternal group consisted of those subjects who scored higher on the maternal items than on the paternal. It was composed of 32 subjects, 16 males and 16 females. As regards other variables, the two groups were homogeneous. The total scores for the paternal and maternal item series are:

	Paternal items	Maternal items
Paternal group	99.27	90.39
Maternal group	65.39	105.58

Statistics

The differences of the attribution intensity of the items were tested using multivariate analysis of variance (Cooley and Lohnes 1971). The Spearman-Rho correlation was used to analyze the rank order of the items, comparing the results from the paternal and maternal groups and from the belief groups.

3   RESULTS AND DISCUSSION

3.1   *Intensity Analysis: Paternal and Maternal Groups*

Paternal items   All the items, except who takes the initiative, guiding stimulus towards the future, firmness, and dynamic, differentiate between the paternal and maternal groups (Table 5.9). And, except for dynamic, all were scored more highly by the paternal group. Of the most strongly differentiating items, two types can be distinguished: on the one hand, God as authority and lawgiver (stern, authority, who gives the law, judge) and, on the other hand, God as very actively involved in human life (who gives the directions, who makes the decisions, who maintains order, who has the knowledge, power). It is important to note here that the largest rank differences are found for the items dynamic and who takes the initiative. These two items were given high scores by the maternal group and low scores by the paternal group. Thus, there are no typical paternal items for the paternal group, but there are paternal items for the maternal group. We shall return to these two items in the discussion of the rank orders.

Table 5.9   *Manova of the paternal and maternal items, means of the paternal and maternal groups, pooled SD, univariate F-value, and Eta square*

Paternal items	$\bar{X}V(29)$	$\bar{X}M(30)$	Pooled SD	F^1_{59}	Eta^2
The one who maintains order	5.17	2.56	1.96	27.05	0.3144
Who gives the law	6.17	3.19	1.95	35.54	0.3759
Who takes the initiative	4.48	4.09	2.09	0.53	0.0088
Strength	6.24	4.97	1.90	6.85	0.1040
Guiding stimulus towards the future [1]	5.41	4.69	2.10	1.82	0.0300
Who is the principle, the rule	5.00	3.19	2.10	11.30	0.1608
Firmness	6.00	5.84	1.60	0.15	0.0025
Who makes the decisions	5.86	3.06	1.74	39.23	0.3994
Dynamic	4.59	4.72	2.36	0.05	0.0008
Power	5.72	3.59	1.99	17.45	0.2285
Systematic mind	5.83	3.69	1.97	17.95	0.2333
Judge	6.10	3.56	1.84	28.89	0.3287
Who gives the directions	5.97	3.09	1.69	44.14	0.4280
Authority	6.21	3.25	1.61	51.37	0.4654
The one who acts	4.93	2.56	2.08	19.69	0.2502
Stern	5.31	2.31	1.74	45.04	0.4329
Who has the knowledge	6.21	4.47	1.83	13.78	0.1894
Who examines things	4.07	2.56	1.88	9.81	0.1425

Maternal items	$\bar{X}V(29)$	$\bar{X}M(30)$	Pooled *SD*	F_{59}^{1}	Eta^2
The one who is most patient	6.03	6.53	1.10	3.12	0.0503
Who is always there when needed [1]	5.93	6.34	1.48	1.18	0.0197
Intuition	5.17	5.69	1.68	1.43	0.0236
Who takes loving care of me	6.24	5.69	1.76	1.13	0.0188
Who welcomes me with open arms	5.17	6.03	1.80	3.46	0.0555
Tenderness	4.31	5.75	1.86	9.11	0.1338
Who is always ready with open arms	4.45	6.00	1.93	9.86	0.1432
Who brings out which is delicate	3.62	5.06	2.09	7.21	0.1089
Self-giving love	5.17	6.75	1.57	15.29	0.2058
Who is intimate	4.03	5.56	2.00	8.92	0.1314
Sensitive	5.03	6.34	1.57	10.53	0.1514
Who will sympathize with the child's sorrows	4.62	5.34	1.92	2.15	0.0352
Close to whom one feels at home	5.17	6.44	1.45	11.58	0.1641
Who lets you be a child [1]	4.45	6.03	1.69	13.38	0.1848
Who is always waiting for me	5.14	5.09	1.87	0.01	0.0001
Who gives comfort	4.76	5.59	1.70	3.66	0.0584
Who is all-embracing	5.31	5.75	1.52	1.27	0.0211
A warm-hearted refuge	5.79	5.78	1.56	0.00	0.0000

1. These items do not occur in the English version of the scale.

Maternal items   There is clearly less differentiation here (cf. Table 5.9), the most significant difference being the low scoring of the paternal items by the maternal group. The items that differentiate are, in decreasing order, charming, who lets you be a child, close to whom one feels at home, sensitive, who is always ready with open arms, tenderness, and who is intimate. These items express a kind of contact that is characteristic of the mother–child relationship, a relationship of dependence. Here also the maternal group scored all of the items more highly except for who takes loving care of me, who is always waiting for me, and a warm-hearted refuge. For who takes loving care of me, the difference is rather large though it is not statistically significant.

3.2   *Intensity Analysis: The Three Belief Groups*

Paternal items that differentiate between the three belief groups
The items that differentiate between the three belief groups are: who gives the law, power, judge, who gives the directions, and authority (Table 5.10). These items can be interpreted as applying to a lawgiving and intervening God on whom the human person is dependent and toward whom it is obligated. They stress the lawgiving power of God, which is gradually less emphasized as belief in the existence of God is questioned or doubted. In all likelihood, these elements in the representation of God are felt to come into opposition with human autonomy.

Maternal items that differentiate between the three belief groups
In descending order, the following maternal items differentiate between the groups: who is all-embracing, a warm-hearted refuge, who is always ready with open arms, who takes loving care of me, who gives comfort, who lets you be a child. The scores decrease steadily from the absolute believers, to the believers, to the doubters. Common to these items is that God is described in terms of presence and care for the human individual. A form of dependence on God is stressed. God is near and offers security.

3.3   Rank Order Analysis

Tables 5.11 and 5.12 give the rank order correlations per item series between the various groups. The qualitative interpretation is based particularly on those items for which the rank difference is greater than four. The correlations are somewhat inflated because the subjects of the paternal and maternal groups were drawn from the belief groups. The number of subjects, however, is always roughly proportional, and thus the results can be considered and interpreted as general trends.

Paternal items   The absolute believer group and the believer group correlate very highly with each other and the believers correlate very highly with the doubters (Table 5.11). The absolute believers and the doubters correlate to a lesser, though still significant, degree. The subjects who doubt emphasize more dynamic, who takes the initiative, and guiding stimulus towards the future, while the absolute believers stress more who gives the law. Correlations of the belief groups with the paternal group clearly decrease from the absolute believers, through the believers, to the doubters. On the other hand, the correlations of the belief groups with the maternal group rise in the reverse direction. The absolute believers emphasize very strongly the paternal items that are typical for the paternal group, and the doubters place strong emphasis on the paternal items characteristic of the maternal group, which items, are, in fact, not so characteristic for the paternal group. The believers fall in between with a certain tendency towards similarity with the maternal group. The absolute believers thus place greater stress on the items reflecting the judgment and intervening activity of God.

The particular stress placed by the doubters can be interpreted as follows. These items reflect qualities that one would readily apply to oneself, with which one can identify in a positive manner. It is easier to apply to oneself the items dynamic and who takes the initiative than stern and authority. The items, stern and authority, who gives the directions, and the one who makes the decisions,

Table 5.10 *Manova of the paternal and maternal items, means of the belief groups, pooled SD, univariate F-value, and Eta square*

Paternal items	$\bar{X}5$	$\bar{X}4$	$\bar{X}3$	Pooled SD	F^2_{127}	Eta^2
The one who maintains order	4.00	3.83	3.24	2.19	0.79	0.0123
Who gives the law	5.19	4.19	3.71	2.13	4.59	0.0674
Who takes the initiative	4.28	4.00	4.53	2.13	0.50	0.0078
Strength	5.76	5.17	5.06	2.03	1.56	0.0240
Guiding stimulus towards the future [1]	5.24	4.83	4.82	2.04	0.64	0.0100
Who is the principle, the rule	4.26	3.98	4.12	2.32	0.20	0.0031
Firmness	5.83	5.92	5.53	1.69	0.34	0.0054
Who makes the decisions	4.80	4.17	3.82	2.08	1.99	0.0304
Dynamic	4.61	4.69	4.18	2.24	0.36	0.0056
Power	5.57	4.68	4.18	2.03	4.29	0.0632
Systematic mind	5.37	4.80	3.88	2.03	3.67	0.0546
Judge	5.65	4.85	4.00	2.01	5.00	0.0729
Who gives the directions	5.20	4.42	3.53	2.03	4.98	0.0727
Authority	5.44	4.47	4.29	1.95	4.30	0.0635
The one who acts	4.43	3.81	3.35	2.19	1.97	0.0301
Stern	4.50	3.53	3.71	2.09	3.21	0.0481
Who has the knowledge	5.67	5.03	4.65	1.94	2.43	0.0369
Who examines things	3.85	3.20	3.06	2.03	1.81	0.0277

Maternal items	$\bar{X}5$	$\bar{X}4$	$\bar{X}3$	Pooled SD	F^2_{127}	Eta^2
The one who is most patient	6.35	6.07	6.12	1.27	0.74	0.0116
Who is always there when needed [1]	6.30	5.86	5.47	1.48	2.43	0.0369
Intuition	5.04	5.15	4.94	1.99	0.09	0.0015
Who takes loving care of me	5.93	5.37	4.41	1.67	5.53	0.0802
Who welcomes me with open arms	5.48	5.69	5.47	1.87	0.22	0.0034
Tenderness	5.20	5.12	4.47	1.89	1.01	0.0156
Who is always ready with open arms	5.44	5.25	3.65	1.92	5.94	0.0855
Who brings out which is delicate	4.31	4.37	3.35	2.20	1.52	0.0233
Self-giving love	6.04	5.81	5.18	1.70	1.66	0.0254
Who is intimate	4.94	4.63	4.59	2.11	0.38	0.0059
Sensitive	5.83	5.69	5.06	1.72	1.33	0.0204
Who will sympathize with the child's sorrows	5.54	5.24	4.12	1.91	3.57	0.0533
Close to whom one feels at home	6.04	5.64	5.24	1.53	2.06	0.0314
Who lets you be a child [1]	5.50	5.49	4.12	1.85	4.11	0.0607
Who is always waiting for me	5.15	4.97	4.71	2.00	0.34	0.0053
Who gives comfort	5.70	5.05	4.35	1.67	4.86	0.0711
Who is all-embracing	5.67	5.34	3.94	1.94	15.18	0.1929
A warm-hearted refuge	6.33	5.90	4.53	1.43	10.29	0.1395

1. These items do not occur in the English version of the scale

Table 5.11   *Rank correlations between the groups: Paternal items*

	Paternal group	Maternal group	Absolute believers	Believers
Maternal group	39			
Absolute believers	82	36		
Believers	66	75	91	
Doubters	45	90	53	78

which were strongly stressed by the paternal group and the absolute believers, could constitute a threat to human autonomy, which is emphasized by the doubters through the items particular to them. The believers occupy the intermediate position in this regard in the sense that they place less stress on the specific paternal items and more on the nonspecific paternal items.

Maternal items   It is immediately apparent from the correlation matrix (Table 5.12) that all relations are significant and that there is no clear trend present. For the belief groups, the lowest correlation is that between the absolute believers and the doubters. Our consideration of the rank differences is thus qualitative and interpretative.

Table 5.12   *Rank correlations between the groups: Maternal items*

	Paternal group	Maternal group	Absolute believers	Believers
Maternal group	46			
Absolute believers	75	70		
Believers	72	86	87	
Doubters	53	63	48	61

The items that are ranked higher by the absolute believers are: a warm-hearted refuge, who is always ready with open arms, who is all-embracing, who takes loving care of me, and who gives comfort. These are items that could define the mother–child relationship, involving caring and protection. The items, intuition, who is intimate, and who is always waiting for me, are stressed particularly by the doubters. We can suppose that these subjects stress being accepted and the feeling of contact. We believe that this is affirmed in the items, who is intimate, and who welcomes me with open arms. These items could well reflect the need for personal contact. Doubt and uncertainty are perhaps indicated here by the lower ranking of, who is all-embracing, and sensitive, which could reflect questions and doubts as to whether man has or can have a relationship with God.

Again it is the believers who occupy the intermediate position. They conform somewhat more to the maternal group and emphasize the items sensitive, who lets you be a child, who is all-embracing, intuition, and who takes loving care of me. Stress is laid somewhat more on the deep experience of affection than on the strict aspect of care.

The differentiations of the maternal items are clearly weaker, though it can be said that the absolute believers lay more stress on the caring aspects of the relationship and the doubters more on the affective aspects. The believers span the two groups by stressing the caring aspects somewhat less and the relation as such somewhat more. The doubters also seem to question the possibility of the existence of the relationship.

4 CONCLUSION

By way of summary of the results of this study, we can say that the representation of God of the absolute believers is colored by the concept of a lawgiving and intervening God who displays concern for humanity. For the believers, this lawgiving aspect is still present, but there are also items by which humanity can express its autonomy through the possibility of positive identification. The caring God is still important, but the experienced relationship is more stressed.

The doubters, finally, strongly emphasize their own autonomy with the items reflecting the possibility of identification. Along with this, we note a strong accent by this belief group on the experienced relation as such.

Thus, in function of the belief ratings, item attribution not only differs in intensity, but it also differs as regards rank order. This appears particularly for the paternal item series. The maternal series shows clearly less differentiation, though some stresses are present.

F   PARENTAL IMAGES AND THE REPRESENTATION OF GOD IN SEMINARIANS AND WOMEN RELIGIOUS
by Alfred Vannesse and Therese Neff

1 INTRODUCTION

In the last few years, many studies have shown the existence of a particular psychological bond between clergymen, both Catholic and Protestant, and their mothers. In the USA., a very extensive national study (Potvin and Suziedelis 1969), in which 6420 seminarians and 1130 lay students participated, resulted in the conclusion that a 'special proximity' existed between the seminarian and his mother, as opposed to the nonseminarians. According to the authors, it is this special proximity that accounts for the mother, rather than the father, being the one who fashions the ideals and the desires of the seminarians. In Europe, investigations in several countries have led to very similar conclusions. The most significant are presented by Godin (1975). Although he does not provide any new data, he synthesizes and criticizes with scientific rigor the studies that have dealt with this matter over the last twenty years.

The purpose of the present research is to study the relation of the choice of clerical and religious life to the parental figures and the representation of God.

2 METHOD

2.1 *Instrument*

The French version of the SDPS.

2.2 *Samples*

The sample was composed of 290 subjects of which 170 were religious (110 seminarians and 60 women religious) and 120 were lay people (60 male and 60 female). The average age was 22 years for the seminarians and 27 years for the women religious. Half of the women religious were contemplatives and half belonged to active congregations. All lay people were unmarried university students in philology and applied sciences. They belonged to the Catholic faith and most were practising. The average age was 22 years and 5 months for lay male students and 21 years and 6 months for female students.

For convenience, we shall use 'religious' for the seminarians and the women religious taken together, and 'laity' for the students.

3 RESULTS AND DISCUSSION

The results for the seminarians and women religious presented a remarkable convergence. In both groups, the maternal dimension is very much stressed in the father figure and in the representation of God. Moreover, the parental figures are less saturated with their specific qualities than is the representation of God with these same qualities.

Table 5.13 gives the mean intensity attribution scores of the items to the parental and divine figures. The paternal items are more intensely associated to the father figure by the male students than by the seminarians [$t(168) = 7.33$, $p < 0.001$] and by the female students than by the women religious [$t(118) = 6.10$,

Table 5.13   *Mean intensity scores*

Figures	Items	Male students	Seminarians	Women religious	Female students
Father	Paternal	5.45	4.38	4.39	5.48
	Maternal	4.25	5.03	5.32	4.36
Mother	Paternal	3.58	3.29	3.74	4.09
	Maternal	6.03	5.86	6.21	6.21
God	Paternal	4.89	4.45	4.51	5.32
	Maternal	5.17	5.94	6.38	5.78

$p < 0.001$]. The maternal items, however, are more strongly attributed to the father figure by the seminarians than by the male students [$t(168) = 4.65$, $p < 0.001$] and by the women religious than by the female students [$t(118) = 5.34, p < 0.001$].

There are no significant differences between the groups in the attribution of both series of items to the maternal figure, except that the female students attribute the paternal items more intensely than do the women religious [$t(118) = 2.01, p < 0.05$].

Concerning the representation of God, the paternal items are more intensely associated to it by the male students than by the seminarians [$t(168) = 2.53, p < 0.02$], and by the female students than by the women religious [$t(118) = 3.90$, $p < 0.001$]. The maternal items, on the contrary, are more intensely attributed to the representation of God by the seminarians than by the male students [$t(168) = 3.96$, $p < 0.001$], and by the women religious than by the female students [$t(118) = 3.07, p < 0.001$]. Thus, the religious attribute the maternal dimension more intensely and the paternal dimension less intensely to the representation of God than do the laity. The intensity scores of the two series of items indicate a balanced structuring of the representation of God with regard to the two symbolic dimensions by the laity and that the maternal dimension is distinctly prevalent in the structuring of the religious.

Table 5.14 *Internal structure of the figures – grouped distributions of the mean item scores by item series*

Item series	Male students f	m	Seminarians f	m	Women religious f	m	Female students f	m
Figures Class intervals								
Father 5.5 – 7.0	14	–	3	5	4	8	16	–
4.0 – 5.49	4	3	9	12	8	9	2	3
2.5 – 3.99	–	15	6	1	6	1	–	12
1.0 – 2.49	–	–	–	–	–	–	–	3
Mother 5.5 – 7.0	–	15	1	15	1	16	–	15
4.0 – 5.49	3	3	7	3	6	2	3	3
2.5 – 3.99	12	–	10	–	8	–	12	–
1.0 – 2.49	3	–	1	–	3	–	3	–
God 5.5 – 7.0	2	4	4	16	5	17	2	9
4.0 – 5.49	13	9	6	2	6	1	11	7
2.5 – 3.99	3	5	8	–	6	–	5	2
1.0 – 2.49	–	–	–	–	1	–	–	–

The internal structure of the figures also reveals the resemblances between the seminarians and the women religious, as well as their differences from the groups of the laity. This is what appears when we divide by class the means of the item scores within each series for each figure (see Table 5.14).

For the father: most of the paternal items are located in the top class for the laity, whereas for the religious they are mainly distributed in the second and third class intervals. The maternal items, however, are concentrated mainly in the third class for the laity, whereas for the religious they are nearly all in the first and second classes.

For the mother: The structure is almost the same for all samples.

For God: The paternal items belong primarily to the second class for the laity, while more than a third also belong to the third and fourth classes for the religious. Almost all the maternal items are to be found in the first class for the religious, whereas they are distributed among the first three classes for the laity.

The semantic distance scores yield similar results: the women religious and seminarians resemble each other and also differ in similar ways from the laity.

The distance scores between the figures (Table 5.15) show that (1) the differences between seminarians and women religious are never statistically significant; (2) the differences between the seminarians and the male students are all significant ($p < 0.01$), as well as the differences between the women religious and the female students ($p < 0.01$) with the exception of the paternal semantic distance between the father and God figures; (3) the distances between the figures are always shorter for the religious than for the laity, particularly for the maternal items, which indicates that the religious differentiate the three figures to a lesser degree.

4 CONCLUSIONS

Three conclusions may be draw. (1) The structuring of the figures of the father, of the mother, and of God is very similar for the seminarians and for the women religious. (2) There are distinct differences between the religious and the laity. (3) The points of divergence between the religious and the laity consist mainly in that the former emphasize more the maternal dimension and less the paternal dimension in the father figure and in the representation of God.

How can these differences be interpreted? Generally speaking, sociocultural environment differentiates the religious from the laity. Religious institutions, and, in particular, houses of religious formation, are separated from the sociocultural context in which they are situated. The purpose of this separation seems to be to allow those who live in them to attain to certain values less accessible in the context of ordinary life.

Table 5.15 *Means of distance scores and p-values*

Distance scores	Male students	Seminarians	Women religious	Female students	Male students vs. Seminarians	Seminarians vs. Women religious	Women religious vs. Female students
M_m–F_m	10.31	6.81	7.07	10.71	$p < 0.01$	n.s.	$p < 0.01$
M_m–G_m	9.00	5.76	4.90	7.91	$p < 0.01$	n.s.	$p < 0.01$
F_m–G_m	10.26	7.77	8.15	10.37	$p < 0.01$	n.s.	$p < 0.01$
M_f–F_f	12.48	8.07	7.18	10.09	$p < 0.01$	n.s.	$p < 0.01$
M_f–G_f	11.67	9.27	9.88	11.31	$p < 0.01$	n.s.	$p < 0.01$
F_f–G_f	10.79	8.18	8.84	9.41	$p < 0.01$	n.s.	n.s.

n.s. = not significant

The values reinforced by religious institutions are unconditional welcome of the other, benevolent love, goodness, understanding and the like. These values seem to refer more to the maternal dimension than to the paternal.

If this is so, the differences observed in this research between the results of the religious and those of the laity could be explained on the basis of these sociocultural differences. The maternal items of the SDPS might have a higher subjective value for religious because they are reinforced by the institutions in which they live. If the religious did not strongly attribute these items to the father and to God, they might feel they were depreciating these figures.

Reciprocally, paternal qualities are less stressed by these institutions. Hence the subjects would be less inclined to attribute them to the father and to God because, in their opinion, they have less importance.

Other data complement this interpretation. The results of the personality tests, and in particular the Szondi test (Szondi 1972),[1] administered to the religious at the same time as the SDPS, show that they manifest greater maternal attachment than does the ordinary population (Neff 1973, 1975, 1977; Vannesse 1974, 1977*a*). This attachment to the mother corresponds to an archaic link with the primitive mother (Szondi 1972), and constitutes a kind of clinging to the first object of love or to its substitute (Deri 1949). As such, it can continue to live on, in certain persons, far beyond adolescence. It implies a certain obliteration of the father and of his specific role, as distinct from that of the mother (Erikson 1968).

The presence of this privileged bond with the mother, clearly more present among the religious, both men and women, substantiates the argument that it influences their perception of the

1.   We know of the validation problems associated with the Szondi test. Still, we are convinced that the methodological criticisms of it proceed from a misunderstanding (Legrand 1979). Positive clinical experience with the Szondi test in several therapeutic institutions, in any case, has encouraged us to use it as a supplementary source for the interpretation of our study of specific groups.

parental symbols, and hence their representation of God. More affectively attached to the mother, the religious have a predilection for the items that particularly evoke her. They will thus have a tendency to ascribe them more intensively to the father and to God, because they wish to find them there. Less attached to more specifically paternal values, they do not expect to find them so much in the father and in God, and so they ascribe them with less intensity to these two symbolic figures.

This second interpretation of the results concords with the conclusions of the studies mentioned at the beginning of this section (Potvin and Suziedelis 1969; Godin 1975). The results obtained suggest an exceptional proximity, on the affective level, between the seminarian and his mother. It is necessary to add, however, that there is also a similar proximity between the woman religious and her mother.

Moreover, on the basis of this research certain implications of this structuring of the relationship to the parents of the religious can be clarified. In fact, the religious, while reinforcing the maternal traits of the representation of God, emphasize in it the dimension of unconditional love. This stressing of the maternal items in the representation of God has, of course, many implications. For example, the prophetic dimension of God, the dimension that calls for the concrete building of the future, is diminished along with the corresponding diminuition of the paternal items. This can well lead to a certain passivity with respect to the actual conditions of society.

Finally, this study can contribute to a better understanding of the psychological meaning of the religious and priestly vocation. It is by emphasizing certain values that religious institutions recruit their candidates (Rulla 1971). Probably the attraction felt by the candidates for some of these values corresponds to psychological traits that make them more apt to discover these values and to adopt them as norms in their lives.

The Parental Figures and the Representation of God of Schizophrenics and Delinquents

Because variables such as cultural environment, field of study, age, and religious affiliation influence the perception of the symbolic parental figures and the representation of God, it seems logical to presume that such vital behavioral problems as schizophrenia and delinquency also affect the experience and perception of these figures. As already has been explained, the symbolic parental figures are the result of the interaction between the lived experience of the individual with his own parents and the connotations conveyed by the cultural structures of the milieu of that individual. Modern scientific research has often suggested that schizophrenics and delinquents have deviant or deficient parent–child relationships. These deviant or deficient relationships are often cited in etiological studies of schizophrenia and delinquency. Thus, if the parental figures are in some way the model upon which the representation of God is developed, it seems logical that, for schizophrenics and delinquents, it would be affected by their distorted affective experience with their parents.

The objective of this chapter is to study the characteristics of the figures of the father, the mother, and God of a group of schizophrenics and a group of delinquents. The term 'delinquent' is restricted in this study since the only criterion used in the selection of the subjects was their having been arrested and sentenced to penal institutions for periods from two to twenty-four months.

1 PARENT–CHILD RELATIONSHIPS OF SCHIZOPHRENICS AND DELINQUENTS

Many studies have been done on the parent–child relationships of schizophrenics and delinquents in the attempt to determine their pathogenic significance in the development of schizophrenia and delinquency. There are still enormous methodological problems to be overcome in the study of this topic (Jacob 1975; Riskin and Faunce 1972; Mishler and Waxler 1965; Rosenthal et al. 1975), but the results already obtained allow the formulation of hypotheses on the characteristics of the parental figures of schizophrenic and delinquent subjects.

1.1 *Delinquents*

Many empirical studies have shown that parents of delinquents differ from parents of nondelinquents in their approach to familial discipline and in their manner of supervising their children (Glueck and Glueck 1962; West 1969; Craig and Glick 1965; Sprott et al. 1955). Parental aggressivity (Bandura 1959, 1969) and criminality (West 1973) have also been associated with the development of delinquent behavior in children. In addition, parents of delinquents seem to be incapable of true intimacy so that the parent–child relationship is characterized by the absence of warmth (Cleckley 1964).

Many authors have focused their research on the mother–child relationship. McCord (1964) showed that there is a relation between the tendency to delinquency and attitudes of negligence and passivity of the mother with regard to her child. A previous study (Glueck and Glueck 1964) on the perception delinquents have of their mothers seems to confirm this. They found that only 22 percent of the delinquents as opposed to 71 percent of the nondelinquents perceived their mothers as being preoccupied with their well-being, and 19 percent as opposed to 1 percent respectively, perceived their mothers as having little interest in them, as being egoistical, as harming them, or as rejecting them. They also found that boys who felt that their mothers rejected them or were indifferent to them more often became delinquents or criminals than boys who felt sure of the love and interest of their mothers.

Bowlby (1947) has insisted that privation of maternal care during the first five years of the child's life is one of the most important causes of delinquency. This position, however, has not been confirmed by empirical research (Lewis 1954; Naess 1959; Passingham 1968), and Bowlby himself has altered it somewhat in view of results obtained from the study of children separated from their mothers because of illness (Bowlby et al. 1956). Recently, several studies have been oriented to the significance of paternal rather than maternal deprivation in the etiology of crime and delinquency. Warren and Palmer (1965) found more paternal than maternal deprivation in their sample of 316 delinquents, which has been largely confirmed by several other studies (Little 1965; Oltman and Friedman 1967; Gregory 1965; Newman 1970). In addition, Virkkunen (1976: 383) found significant differences between recidivists and his control group as far as paternal deprivation is concerned but not in maternal deprivation. He concluded that 'the absence of the mother or the mother substitute did not seem to be so important as the absence of the father or the father substitute' in the development of delinquent behavior.

In addition to paternal privation, paternal behavior and personality patterns influence antisocial development. Thus Robins (1966) found that delinquent behavior is strongly linked to the presence of an alcoholic or sociopathic father. Davies and Sinclair (1971) found that the behavior of the delinquent is determined by the need for a firm paternal figure who does not fear emotional attachment and who is backed up by the mother in the discipline he imposes. Some older studies have indicated that paternal rejection correlates with delinquency (Lewis 1954). Recently, Milebamane (1975) observed that delinquents perceive their fathers as having rejecting, punitive, negligent, and overdemanding attitudes. On the other hand, Fodor (1973: 42–43), using the Cornell Parent Behavior Description, found that delinquents perceive their fathers as having expressed less nurturance, as having given less encouragement, as not having helped the child in various learning activities, and as having rejected them. Fodor concludes that 'it is the activity of the father which is most critical for the development of psychopathic characteristics in sons'.

Finally, Lemay (1976) considers that, for delinquents, either the image of the father is undervalued and distant or aggressive and hostile with regard to the child or the mother.

In summary, the literature confirms that disturbances in the parental roles and in the parent–child relationship are associated with the development of delinquent behavior.

1.2 Schizophrenics

Many studies have focused on the psychological characteristics of parents of schizophrenics that differentiate them from parents of other kinds of psychiatric patients and, particularly from parents of subjects without psychiatric troubles.

Tringer (1975) observed that the differences between schizophrenic and normal subjects are less than the differences between their respective parents. Friedman and Friedman (1974), in a pilot study comparing historical factors and current functioning of 'normal' families to families with schizophrenic offspring, found that the mothers of schizophrenics reported more serious medical problems than did the mothers of the control group. In addition, the mothers of schizophrenic daughters had more psychosomatic disorders than did the mothers of the control group or those of schizophrenic sons. Finally, the fathers and mothers of schizophrenic patients obtain poorer results and show more thinking deficiencies in several tasks in comparison to control parents. In addition, the parents of schizophrenic subjects present a deviant transactional style (Jones 1977), high scores in extraversion and psychoticism (Winter 1975), and have contradictory expectations with regard to their children (Lu 1962).

In another study, Friedman and Friedman (1970) showed that parents of schizophrenics have more interpersonal conflicts than parents of nonschizophrenics. They also found in a study of 128 families that the fathers and mothers of schizophrenics manifested more emotional troubles, more psychopathology, and more impoverishment of thought than did the control group parents. These differences were more striking and more substantial for the parents of female schizophrenics than for the parents of male schizophrenics

(Friedman and Friedman 1972, 1973). Finally, many other studies have shown that the mothers of schizophrenic patients are psychically very disturbed (Despert 1951; Rank 1955), anxious (Sullivan 1947, dominant and hostile (Arieti 1955; Waxler and Mishler 1971), incapable of understanding the feelings and needs of their children, and incapable of physical and emotional nearness with them (Alanen 1958).

To what degree do these different characteristics of parents of schizophrenic subjects affect the parent–child relationship? A number of specialists have studied the patterns of the parent–child relationship, and more particularly the mother–child relationship, and many theories on the etiology of schizophrenia have been constructed around this fundamental relationship in the structuring of the individual.

Waxler and Mishler (1971) have reported that, in the process of familial interaction, parents interact differently with a schizophrenic child than with its normal sibling, and that, inversely, the schizophrenic child interacts differently with its parents than does the healthy child.

A number of studies (Wynne and Singer 1963a, 1963b; Singer and Wynne 1965) have shown that parents of schizophrenics have difficulties in establishing, maintaining, and sharing attention in verbal communication. Singer and Wynne classified the thinking style of parents of schizophrenics on a continuum, the poles of which are amorphous attention and fragmented attention. Now if, in the context of the parent–child relationship, the focus of attention is never established (amorphous) or is only fragmentarily established, it is obvious that the child's demands can never be adequately satisfied. In this way, disorders in schizophrenic thought patterns can affect the parent–child relationship. Wild et al. (1975) have shown that fathers and particularly mothers of schizophrenic subjects have amorphous attention scores higher than do control group parents.

The article by Fromm-Reichmann (1948) on the role of the mother in the development of schizophrenia draws attention to the study of the mother–child relationship. Later, Arieti (1955) hypothesized that the mother–child relationship was deficient or disturbed. Many earlier studies on the mothers of schizophrenics seem to confirm this hypothesis (Tietze 1949; Prout and White 1950; Gerard and Siegel 1950; and Lidz and Lidz 1949).

Reichard and Tillman (1950) observed that the mothers of schizophrenic patients can be divided into three quite distinct categories. The most common relational mode is where the mother, who secretly rejects the child, reacts against her hostility by a reaction formation. The second category consists of the overprotective mother whose love is suffocating because of her desire to maintain the child's dependence; her behavior tends to perpetuate the primitive symbiotic relationship that once existed between them. The ego of the child remains fused with that of the mother, and, consequently, the frontiers between the mother and the child are never defined. The third category is defined by the kind of mother who projects her needs of dependence on the child and maintains it in this kind of relationship.

Several investigators (Alanen 1958; Cheek 1964) have found that mothers of schizophrenic subjects are hostilely overprotective. Karon (1963) defined the schizophrenogenic mother as one who, when there is conflict between her needs and those of her child, indirectly satisfies her own needs by manipulating her child so that its behavior satisfies them. This concept has received empirical confirmation in several studies (Meyer and Karon 1967; Mitchell 1968, 1969, 1974), where it was found that the mothers of schizophrenic children differed significantly from mothers of children without psychiatric troubles in the number of stories given in the TAT in which the dominant person either ignored the expressed needs of the dependent person or overrode them when there was conflict. Mitchell (1969, 1974) twice studied the same problem with fathers of schizophrenics but did not find any significant difference between them and the control group.

The Palo Alto group (Bateson et al. 1956) found that one of the causes of schizophrenia is a pattern of contradictory communication in the mother–child relationship that they called the double bind. This has been the object of numerous empirical studies (Watzlawick

1963; Berger 1965; Beavers et al. 1965; Sojit 1969, 1971; Beakel and Mehrabian 1969; Ringuette and Kennedy 1966). Three conditions define the double bind situation:
the individual is involved in an intense relationship;
the individual is caught in a situation in which the other person in the relationship is expressing two orders of message and one of these denies the other;
the individual is unable to comment on the messages being expressed to correct his discrimination of what order of message to respond to, i.e., he cannot make a metacommunicative statement (Bateson et al. 1956: 254).

The double bind thus consists of a contradiction between verbal and nonverbal communication in the context of a relationship that is vital for the child and in which it is completely dependent and physically and/or psychologically incapable of metacommunication. That which the mother expresses on the verbal level generally contradicts that which is done and signified on the action level. The mother thus simultaneously transmits such contradictory messages as acceptance and rejection, as demands for autonomy and dependence. The child is continually and traumatically faced with the fundamental question of being or not being. In this situation, it can never yield to its desires because those desires are never fully recognized and accepted by the mother.

'The most useful way to phrase double bind description is not in terms of a binder and a victim but in terms of people caught up in an ongoing system which produces conflicting definitions of the relationship' (Bateson et al. 1963: 157). It is not a question of a single traumatic experience, but of a specific and constant pattern in the relationship lived with the mother. One of the most significant aspects of the double bind emerges from the fundamental importance and intensity of the relationship in which it occurs (Olson 1972).

This type of mother–child relationship forces family relations into a style that Bowen (1960) describes as follows: 'overadequate mother, helpless patient and peripherally attached father'. The role of the father is fundamentally defined by his failure to neutralize the pathological tendencies of the mother (Clausen and Kohn 1960; Bowen 1960). The father often assumes the function of a maternal substitute, but all his efforts fail (Bowen 1960). This figure of the father in families of schizophrenics agrees with the results of other studies (Lidz 1957; Cheek 1965) in which the father was found to be passive, immature, and reserved.

In summary, research has shown that the parents of schizophrenics have characteristics that distinguish them in many ways from the parents of subjects not afflicted with psychiatric troubles. The mother–child relationship seems to have a significant and specific impact on the genesis of schizophrenia. The mother of the schizophrenic subject appears as someone who, by her behavior and by what she says, prevents the child from emerging from nothingness and from existing as a distinct person. The father–child relationship seems to be affected by the behavior of the mother and has less of a direct effect on the development of schizophrenia.

One of the objectives of the present research is to determine the structures of the parental figures of the schizophrenic. How does he structure, on the basis of his lived relationships with his parents, a father and a mother figure? In the preceding chapters, it has been shown that the mother figure is perceived fundamentally in terms of total availability, welcome, and tenderness. Is it the same for the schizophrenic? On the basis of the literature mentioned above, one would expect to find that the maternal figure for a schizophrenic is poorly defined and profoundly disturbed. Regarding the paternal figure, which is usually characterized by law and authority, one would expect that it be ambiguous for the schizophrenic who apparently had a passive father who, virtually excluded from the paternal role, assumed the role of a maternal substitute.

And is the representation of God of a schizophrenic going to be affected by the deficient parent–child relationship he has experienced? What will be the contribution of each parental figure to this representation of God?

The schizophrenics and the delinquents, though very different from each other, are relevant to our purposes insofar as these individuals seem to have experienced parental relationships fundamentally different – and for the most part negatively so – from those experienced by the subjects not afflicted with psychiatric troubles that have composed the samples of all the studies discussed so far. It would seem reasonable to suppose that the representation of God will be affected by the experience of a disturbed parent–child relationship.

2 METHOD

2.1 *Sample*

The sample was composed of 63 male subjects, 33 of which were schizophrenics and 30 delinquents. The criterion for the choice of the schizophrenics was psychiatric diagnosis; no distinction was made regarding types of schizophrenia. All were involved in institutional treatment for periods of time ranging from two months to eight years and seven months; the number of admissions varied from one to nine. Fourteen subjects had been given psychiatric treatment exclusively, and nineteen a combination of psychiatric treatment and behavioral therapy (token economy). The average age of the schizophrenics was 30.2 years and the average educational level was 10.2 years.

The average age of the delinquents was 25.8 years and the level of education was 10.1 years. They were all serving prison terms varying from two to twenty-four months. Most had been incarcerated more than one time for theft (all categories), drug trafficking, or sexual crimes (rape, incest, exhibitionism).

Ideally, these groups should be compared with control groups from the same milieu, the same social level, and the same educational background. But anyone who has had experience in clinical psychology will realize how unreal the methodological norms of experimental psychology are in this case.

2.2   The Measuring Instrument

The measuring instrument used was the French version of the SDPS. Upon preliminary verification of the instrument with schizophrenic subjects, definitions of the psychological significance of each degree of the scale were added at the head of each column of numbers. This modification was made after it was noticed that the schizophrenics had some difficulty in applying the meaning of the numbers of the scale.

3   RESULTS

3.1   *Relative Importance of the Figures*

The schizophrenics attributed the total item set more intensely to the representation of God than to the mother figure [$t(33) = 2.162$, $p < 0.05$] or the father figure [$t(33) = 5.909, p < 0.001$]. Likewise, the attribution intensity scores of the delinquents were higher for the representation of God than for the mother figure [$t(30) = 4.555$, $p < 0.001$] or for the father figure [$t(30) = 10.522$, $p < 0.001$]. In addition, the attribution intensity scores were higher for the mother figure than for the father figure for both the schizophrenics [$t(33) = 3.425$, $p < 0.01$] and the delinquents [$t(30) = 4.890$, $p < 0.001$]. Thus the sequence of attribution is $G > M > F$.

Regarding the attribution of the nonspecific items to the parental figures, the attribution of maternal items to the father figure was not significantly higher than the attribution of paternal items to the mother figure in either of the two groups:

M_f is equivalent to F_m.

There was more intense attribution of maternal items to the representation of God than to the father figure for both the schizophrenics [$t(33) = 5.497, p < 0.001$] and the delinquents [$t(30) =$

9.419, $p < 0.001$]. Similarly, there was more intense attribution of the paternal items to the representation of God than to the mother figure for both the schizophrenics [$t(33) = 2.941, p < 0.01$] and the delinquents [$t(30) = 4.434, p < 0.001$]. Thus,

$$G_m > F_m$$
$$G_f > M_f.$$

For the delinquents, the maternal items were more intensely attributed to the representation of God than were the paternal items [$t(30) = 2.942, p < 0.01$]. Thus,

$$G_m > G_f \quad \text{for the delinquents}$$
$$G_m \cong G_f \quad \text{for the schizophrenics.}$$

In summary, (1) the representation of God seems to be more complex than the two parental figures for both groups: the total item set is attributed to the representation of God with more intensity than to either the father or the mother figure. (2) For both groups, the representation of God is more paternal than the mother figure and more maternal than the father figure. This confirms what was reported in the preceding chapters. (3) For the group of delinquents the representation of God is more intensely maternal than paternal, while for the schizophrenics it is equally paternal as maternal. (4) Regarding the parental figures, the two groups of subjects attribute the nonspecific items with equivalent degrees of intensity. Nevertheless, from the perspective of the total item set, the mother figure seems to be more complex than the father figure. As has been pointed out already, the degree of complexity of the parental figures could be dependent on the cultural milieu.

3.2   Similarity of the Figures

The distance scores have been calculated for the maternal item set, the paternal item set, and the total item set. Three analyses of variance (split-plot factorial design, unweighted means solution, 2 X 3; Kirk 1968) have been calculated to test the differences between the maternal, paternal, and total item mean distance scores.

Table 6.1   *Mean distance scores between the figures using the maternal items, the paternal items, and the total item set, and the p-values* between the differences*

	Schizophrenics			Delinquents		
	Maternal	Paternal	All items	Maternal	Paternal	All items
MF	7.2127	7.4966	10.5475	6.3590	6.7787	9.5277
MG	6.0957	8.0242	10.3181	5.6519	7.6393	9.6258
FG	8.2300	8.2460	11.8600	7.4019	8.3570	11.3767
MF > MG	0.01	n.s.	n.s.	n.s.	n.s.	n.s.
MF < FG	0.05	n.s.	0.05	0.05	n.s.	0.01
MG < FG	0.01	n.s.	0.05	0.01	n.s.	0.01

MF = mother–father distance
MG = mother–God distance
FG = father–God distance
n.s. = not significant
*   determined by the Tukey q-test (Kirk 1968).

Using the maternal item distance scores, analyses of variance shows that the semantic relations had a significant effect $[F(2) = 14.07, p < 0.01]$. The Tukey q-test (Table 6.1) indicates that the mother-father distance is greater than the mother–God distance for the schizophrenics $[q(124, 3) = 4.29, p < 0.01]$, and less than the father–God distance for both the schizophrenics $[q(124, 3) = 3.91, p < 0.05]$ and the delinquents $[q(124, 3) = 4.01, p < 0.05]$. Finally, the mother–God distance is less than the father–God distance for the schizophrenics $[q(124, 3) = 8.21, p < 0.01]$ and for the delinquents $[q(124, 3) = 6.73, p < 0.01]$.

Using the paternal item distance scores, analysis of variance reveals no significant effect. Using the total item distance scores, however, analysis of variance showed a significant effect of the semantic relations $[F(2) = 6.2088, p < 0.01]$. The Tukey q-test (Table 6.1) indicates that the mother–God distance is less than the father–God distance for both the schizophrenics $[q(124, 3) = 4.13, p < 0.05]$ and the delinquents $[q(124, 3) = 4.69, p < 0.01]$. In addition, the mother–father distance is less than the father–God distance for both the schizophrenics $[q(124, 3) = 3.52, p < 0.05]$ and the delinquents $[q(124, 3) = 4.96, p < 0.01]$.

It follows from these analyses that there is very little difference between the schizophrenics and the delinquents as far as the relations of the semantic distances between the three figures are concerned. For both groups, the representation of God manifests a more pronounced similarity with the mother figure than with the father figure and this from the perspectives of the total item set and of the maternal item set. This result seems to be more definitive for the delinquents than for the schizophrenics since the levels of significance are higher for them ($p < 0.01$ vs. $p < 0.05$). Also serving to confirm this is the fact that, for the delinquents, the intensity of attribution of the maternal items to the representation of God is higher than that of the paternal items. Semantically, the differences between the two groups are minimal.

3.3 Factorial Structure of the Figures

Six factor analyses were calculated, three for each subject group, in order to arrive at the factorial structure of each of the three figures. The factors, extracted by the principal factor solution, were subjected to orthogonal rotation using the Varimax method. Only the factors having eigenvalues greater than two were retained in this study. The degrees of congruence between the factors derived from the six factor analyses were determined by the calculation of Phi-coefficients (Tucker 1951; Harman 1960).

Results of factor analysis   Table 6.2 gives the factors obtained for the three figures for the schizophrenic group. The mother figure is composed of five factors, which account for 74.4 percent of the variance. Four of these factors have no item that is significantly loaded, i.e., having a loading coefficient equal to or greater than 0.60 so that it was impossible to determine their nature or content. These are factors M_1, M_2, M_3, and M_4. These four factors account for 65.9 percent of the total variance. The fifth factor is designated by the term 'judge', and is composed of only one significantly loaded item. It accounts for 8 percent of the variance.

The figure of the father is made up of three factors: availability-decision (F_1), norm–presence (F_2), and tenderness (F_3). The first two are composed of both maternal and paternal items and the last of maternal items exclusively. These three factors account for 72 percent of the variance.

The factors obtained for the representation of God are: receptivity–order (G_1), sternness (G_2), decision–sensitivity (G_3), and action–giving (G_4). Together they account for 83.2 percent of the total variance. The sternness factor is composed exclusively of paternal items while the others have a combination of maternal and paternal items.

Table 6.3 gives the loading coefficients and the percentages of variance for the factors of the three figures for the group of delinquents.

The mother figure is composed of four factors, which account for 71 percent of the variance. These are initiative (M_1), delicacy (M_2), giving (M_3), and law (M_4). Initiative and law are composed of paternal items and the other two of maternal items.

The factors obtained for the father figure are systematic mind (F_1), organization (F_2), and presence (F_3). The first two are composed of paternal items and the last of maternal items. These three factors account for 69 percent of the variance.

The representation of God is composed of three factors: familiarity–dynamism (G_1), protection (G_2), and norm (G_3), which account for 78.5 percent of the total variance. The first is composed

Table 6.2   *Loading coefficients and percentages of variance for each factor of the mother, father, and God figures: Schizophrenics*

Items	Mother					Father			God			
	M_1	M_2	M_3	M_4	M_5	F_1	F_2	F_3	G_1	G_2	G_3	G_4
Who is always ready with open arms						0.85			0.79			
Close to whom one feels at home						0.82						
Self-giving love						0.78			0.84			0.68
Who welcomes me with open arms						0.72						
Who is always there when needed [1]						0.65						
Intuition							0.60					
Tenderness								0.75				
Who is all-embracing								0.72				
Who takes loving care of me									0.78			
Who brings out which is delicate									0.76			
The one who is most patient									0.61			
Sensitive											0.79	
Who gives comfort					0.70						0.61	
Judge						0.79					0.73	
Who makes the decisions						0.73					0.80	
Power						0.70						0.87
The one who acts						0.70						
Who takes the initiative						0.63						
Firmness						0.60						
The one who maintains order							0.83		0.76			
Who is the principle, the rule									0.76			
Who gives the law									0.66			
Stern										0.73		
Authority										0.70		
Who examines things											0.73	
The one who has the knowledge											0.65	
Protection											0.63	
Percentage of variance	27.3	15.6	12.7	10.5	8.3	48.1	15.0	8.9	47.5	13.5	12.8	9.4

1. This item does not occur in the English version of the scale.

Table 6.3 *Loading coefficients and percentages of variance for each factor of the mother, father, and God figures: Delinquents*

Items	Mother				Father			God		
	M_1	M_2	M_3	M_4	F_1	F_2	F_3	G_1	G_2	G_3
Who brings out which is delicate		0.85						0.85		
Close to whom one feels at home		0.73						0.75		
Who takes loving care of me		0.79								
Sensitive		0.68							0.65	
Who is always waiting for me		0.63								
Self-giving love							0.63		0.68	
Who is always ready with open arms			0.82				0.73			
Who is always there when needed [1]			0.80				0.80			
Who welcomes me with open arms								0.76		
Who is all-embracing								0.72		
Who will sympathize with the child's sorrows									0.77	
The one who is most patient									0.74	
Who gives comfort									0.62	
Who takes the initiative	0.83									
The one who acts	0.72							0.64		
Power	0.69									
Who makes the decisions	0.64							0.64		
The one who maintains order	0.66			0.85						0.81
Judge				0.69	0.81			0.75		0.80
Who gives the law					0.77			0.73		
Who examines things						0.78				
Dynamic						0.70			0.79	
Who gives the directions						0.68				
Protection										0.69
Strength								0.68		
Firmness										0.84
Who is the principle, the rule										
Percentage of variance	40.2	13.8	9.1	8.0	47.3	12.3	9.0	56.4	12.0	10.1

1. This item does not occur in the English version of the scale.

of both maternal and paternal items, the second of maternal items, and the third of paternal items.

Factor congruence   All possible combinations of the factors were involved in the calculation of congruence. No congruent factor pairs emerged, i.e., none had a Phi-coefficient equal to or higher than 0.9398. There are seven pairs of semicongruent factors (Table 6.4) and four exclusive factors, i.e., factors having coefficients of congruence with all other factors less than 0.4597 (Table 6.5).

Table 6.4   *Highest coefficients of congruence between the factors of the mother, father, and God figures*

Factors	Coefficients
M_1d vs F_2d	0.77047
M_2d vs G_1d	0.72149
M_3d vs F_3d	0.76422
F_1d vs G_1d	0.78634
F_1s vs F_3d	0.83222
F_1s vs G_1d	0.72415
F_2s vs G_1s	0.75749

$M_{1,2,3}d$: factors 1,2, and 3 of the mother figure of the delinquents
$F_{1,2,3}d$: factors 1,2, and 3 of the father figure of the delinquents
G_1d : factor 1 of the representation of God of the delinquents
$F_{1,2}s$: factors 1 and 2 of the father figure of the schizophrenics
G_1s : factor 1 of the representation of God of the schizophrenics

Figure 6.1 illustrates the relations between the figures within and between the two groups on the basis of congruence. The uniqueness of the mother figure of the schizophrenics is remarkable: it is the only figure with no semicongruent relations with any of the other figures. In addition, four of its factors are exclusive, i.e., they have nothing in common with any of the other factors obtained by the six factor analyses.

For the schizophrenics, there is semicongruence between the father figure and the representation of God. This involves the norm-

Table 6.5   *Coefficients of congruence of the four exclusive factors*
(M_1, M_2, M_4, M_5) *of the mother figure with all the other factors*

	M_1	M_2	M_4	M_5
$F_1 s$	0.223	0.355	0.249	0.222
$F_2 s$	0.308	0.196	0.379	0.126
$F_3 s$	0.410	0.218	0.171	0.073
$G_1 s$	0.251	0.347	0.359	0.195
$G_2 s$	0.184	−0.022	0.441	0.029
$G_3 s$	0.379	0.262	0.208	0.319
$G_4 s$	−0.113	0.052	0.073	0.200
$M_1 d$	0.105	0.169	0.348	0.311
$M_2 d$	0.299	0.448	0.260	−0.113
$M_3 d$	0.210	0.215	0.316	0.024
$M_4 d$	0.150	−0.082	0.429	0.445
$F_1 d$	0.285	0.256	0.295	0.127
$F_2 d$	0.089	0.190	0.385	0.224
$F_3 d$	0.403	0.188	0.259	0.195
$G_1 d$	0.256	0.213	0.349	0.127
$G_2 d$	0.417	0.232	0.211	0.045
$G_3 d$	0.252	0.052	0.436	0.155

$F_{1,2,3} s$: factors 1,2, and 3 of the father figure of the schizophrenics
$G_{1,2,3,4} s$: factors 1,2,3, and 4 of the representation of God of the schizophrenics
$M_{1,2,3,4} d$: factors 1,2,3, and 4 of the mother figure of the delinquents
$F_{1,2,3} d$: factors 1,2, and 3 of the father figure of the delinquents
$G_{1,2,3} d$: factors 1,2, and 3 of the representation of God of the delinquents

presence factor (F_2) of the paternal figure and the receptivity–order
factor (G_1) of the representation of God.

For the delinquents, the relations of semicongruence between
the figures are quite complex. There are two pairs of semicongruent
factors for the mother and father figures: initiative (M_1) and organization (F_2) on the one hand, and giving (M_3) and presence (F_3) on
the other.

Between the representation of God and the parental figures there
are two sets of semicongruent factors: familiarity–dynamism (G_1)

	Schizophrenics		Delinquents	
Mother	*M_1	(27.3)	┌---Initiative	(40.2)
	*M_2	(15.6)	│ Delicacy	(13.8)---┐
	M_3	(12.7)	│ ┌-Giving	(9.1) │
	*M_4	(10.5)	│ │ Law	(8.0) │
	*Judge	(8.3)	│ │	│
			│ │	│
Father	Availability-Decision	(48.1)	│ │ Systematic mind	(47.3)-┐ │
	┌-Norm-Presence	(15.0)	└-┼-Organization	(12.3) │ │
	│ Tenderness	(8.9)	└-Presence	(9.0) │ │
	│			│ │
God	└-Receptivity-Order	(47.5)	Familiarity-Dynamism	(56.4)---┘
	Sternness	(13.5)	Protection	(12.0)
	Decision-Sensitivity	(12.8)	Norm	(10.1)
	Action-Giving	(9.4)		

* Exclusive factors (Phi $<$ 0.4597)
Factors connected by dashes (--------) are semicongruent
(0.7000 $\leqslant$ Phi $\leqslant$ 0.9398)
The figures between parentheses indicate the percentage of variance accounted for by the factor.

Figure 6.1   *Factor structure of the three figures and the percentage of variance accounted for by each factor*

is semicongruent with systematic mind (F_1) of the father figure and delicacy (M_2) of the mother figure.

Intergroup comparison reveals that the availability-decision factor (F_1) of the father figure of the schizophrenics is semicongruent with both the presence factor (F_3) of the father figure and the familiarity-dynamism factor (G_1) of the representation of God of the delinquents.

4 DISCUSSION

Regarding the mother figure, the most striking result is that, for the schizophrenics, it is composed for the most part of factors of which the content is impossible to define. The only factor with definable content, judge, not only accounts for the smallest percentage (8.3 percent) of variance, but also is composed of only one item. In addition, four of the factors of the maternal figure, including the judge factor, are exclusive to this figure, i.e., they are not congruent with any of the seventeen other factors obtained. These data do not agree with any of the results obtained elsewhere with the SDPS; they are specific to the schizophrenic subjects.

Such data could raise the question of invalidity of the SDPS for schizophrenic subjects. However, the SDPS functions in another way with these same subjects for the descriptions of the father figure and the representation of God. Comparison of the semantic distance scores and especially of the mean intensity scores of the items within and between the groups indicates that the mother figure of the schizophrenics was treated in the same way as the other figures.

This clear difference in the factor structure seems therefore to be directly linked to the very nature of the mother figure of the schizophrenic. Even though the sample was too small to allow reliable factor analysis, the results obtained can be considered as valid indications of the mother figure of the schizophrenics.

This phenomenon seems to be adequately explained by the typical mother–child relational pattern of schizophrenics. The constant contradiction between the mother's actions and speech in the relationship with her child invalidates that relationship and deprives the child of the effective presence of one of the fundamental poles in its personality structure. When appealing to the other, the child encounters absence or a presence that invalidates the appeal. In such a situation, the connotations of the maternal figure that originate in lived experience profoundly contradict those borne by the culture. The result is a symbolic maternal figure that is impoverished, elusive, and defined by factors without definite content and by a factor having a rather negative significance – especially in the context of so fundamental a relationship.

The maternal figure of the schizophrenics thus contrasts with the well-structured maternal figure of the delinquents. This figure is composed of the factor initiative, which seems to be the most fundamental as it alone accounts for 40 percent of the variance, and of three less important factors: delicacy, giving, and law. This clear difference between the schizophrenics and the delinquents in their perception of the maternal figure is quite adequately accounted for by the different ways they lived the mother–child relationship.

In all the studies discussed in the preceding chapters, the mother figure was fundamentally characterized by total availability, tenderness, or receptivity. This contrasts with the results obtained with the schizophrenics and the delinquents and can be explained by the disturbed mother–child relationship.

The father figure of the schizophrenics seems also to be specific to them. It is characterized by a richness of content that contrasts with the poverty of the maternal figure. Two of the three factors that compose it consist of maternal and paternal items, which is very rare in studies with the SDPS, and the third factor, tenderness, is clearly maternal. The fundamental factor of the father figure is availability–decision (48.1 percent of the variance). In the other studies, availability is the characteristic factor for the mother figure. Thus it is significant to find here the availability dimension in the fundamental factor of the father figure. This dimension is defined by such items as who is always ready with open arms, close to whom one feels at home, self-giving love, who is always waiting for me, who welcomes me, and intuition. Nevertheless, availability does not exhaust the significance of this factor. There is a second aspect, apparently incompatible with the first, that is expressed by decision, firmness, order, power, initiative, action — all paternal items. Availability is thus partially denied by a disciplinary function. The second factor also has two aspects: norm and presence.

The factors of law and authority, which appear in the father figure in all the preceding studies, are absent in the paternal figure of the schizophrenics. Thus, this is an ambiguous figure having contradictory elements in which the specific maternal aspect is overdeveloped at the expense of the paternal aspect. This ambiguity could be explained by the fact that the schizophrenic seems to have experienced a disturbed father–child relationship in which the father projected a contradictory image of the paternal role, since he was more concerned with assuming the role of substitute mother than affirming his paternal role (Fleck et al. 1963; Bowen 1960; Clausen and Kohn 1960).

For the delinquents, the father figure also deviates from the results reported in the preceding chapters. It is constituted by three factors expressing secondary dimensions in the factor structure of the paternal figure: systematic mind, organization, and presence. The law (or authority) factor, which is fundamental to the father figure (cf. Chapters 4 and 5), is absent here. The fact that the delinquent does not perceive his father as law seems to be of particular interest, since deficient acquisition of social norms and lack of introjection of law are essentially characteristic of the delinquent personality (Hare 1968; Cassiers 1968; Cleckley 1964).

Regarding the parental figures, it is further significant that they have no elements in common. The father figure is quite distinct from that of the mother. This phenomenon is more pronounced for the schizophrenics who manifest a maximum degree of polarity between the parental figures, there not even being any semicongruence between them. The delinquents have two pairs of semicongruent factors.

This polarity of parental figures of the two psychiatric groups is opposed to the results obtained in the preceding studies where the factor structures of the parental figures were always roughly equivalent, the factors defining the father figure being identical with those defining the mother figure (see Chapters 4 and 5). It is therefore clear that there is a more pronounced polarity between the parental figures of the two psychiatric groups than between those of subjects not afflicted with psychiatric troubles.

Regarding the representation of God three main points are apparent. First the representation of God is more complex than the two parental figures. It seems to be a synthesis of maternal and paternal values. This result agrees perfectly with the results obtained for the subjects without psychiatric difficulties.

Second, the representation of God is semantically more maternal than paternal for both the schizophrenics and the delinquents. As reported in Chapters 4 and 5, similar results were obtained by Tamayo and Dugas with a group of Canadian university students, and by Tamayo with a group of Belgian females. Thus, this is not a characteristic peculiar to the groups of psychiatric subjects. Nevertheless, it does seem surprising that, for the schizophrenics, the mother figure is more involved than the father figure in the symbolization of God because the mother figure has so little structure for them.

The preference of the delinquents for using maternal values to describe God also seems problematic. Maternal values are actually values of intimacy and affectivity, but the delinquent is characterized by, among other things, a lack of affectivity and an incapacity for profound intimacy (Cassiers 1968; Cleckley 1964). Why should he then favor, for his representation of God, values that seem to have so little existential resonance in his life?

Finally, in spite of this favored semantic similarity with the mother figure, the representation of God seems to differ between the two groups when it is considered from the perspective of its factor structure. For the delinquents, the representation of God is composed of the factors of familiarity–dynamism, protection, and norm. For the schizophrenics, the representation of God contains contradictory elements as does the father figure. Three of the four factors are composed of items having some degree of incongruence. The fundamental factor seems to be receptivity–order (48 percent of the variance) that is composed of two series of items, the first of which stresses unconditional receptivity and the second the function of imposing order and law. Two other factors, decision-sensitivity and action–giving, also contain incongruent elements. This tendency to contradiction has also been observed by Gruba and Johnson (1974) who found that the self-concept of schizophrenics contains more contradictory elements than that of the control group. They explained this phenomenon by the fact that the schizophrenic subjects experienced patterns of contradictory communication, such as the double bind, in the context of the parent–child relationship (Bateson et al. 1956). In our opinion, this explanation also applies to the contradictions observed in the father figure and the representation of God.

The results obtained in the exploratory research discussed in this chapter give rise to many questions. These questions could open the way for further research that would refine and, perhaps, establish the interpretations advanced here.

The Representation of God and Parental Figures Among North American Students

The main purposes of the present research were, first, to reexamine thoroughly the content of the SDPS in order to determine if the items contain the fundamental characteristics of the parental figures as they are conceived in the culture of the United States, and second, to study, with the revised form of the SDPS, the representation of God and the parental figures of American students.

1 METHOD

1.1 *The SDPS II*

For the reformulation of the SDPS, a new list of items was drawn up, consisting of the old SDPS items plus new ones selected from United States literature, mainly sociological and psychological studies on the family (Bossard and Boll 1956; Brenton 1967; Christensen 1964; Farber 1964; Fluegel 1939; Friedan 1964; Ginott 1965; Gray 1967; Handel 1967; Harding 1965; Henry 1955; Kephart 1961; Kirkpatrick 1963; Mead 1955, 1965; Sirjamaki 1953; Williamson 1966; Winch 1962).

The new list of 500 items was finally reduced to a validated instrument of 72 items, of which 39 were paternal and 33 maternal. The 500 items were tested on three groups of high school and college students (100, 250, and 120 subjects, referred to as administrations I, II, and III, respectively). The results of administrations II and III were factorized into 20 factors (factorial method: principal components and Varimax solution). The criteria used in determining the final form of the questionnaire were:

Saturation: Items were retained in the questionnaire if they showed a sufficient degree of saturation in all three figures. The attribution means of the items to the figures in the final application (i.e., administration III) verified the saturation.

Discriminability: Items were selected that produced significant differences when applied to each parental figure.

Linearity: Items were retained if they offered purity of loading. Items that had high loadings in different scales as well as the same direction were probably not linear; assuming that the factors were independent (the rotation of the factors was orthogonal), these items lacked independence and, consequently, were eliminated from the sample of items.

The following are the items of the SDPS II.

Paternal items

1. Systematic mind
2. Who studies issues
3. Strong-minded
4. Who takes the initiative
5. Strength
6. Protection against danger
7. Is leader
8. The authority
9. Is the principle, the rule
10. The judge
11. Lays down the law
12. Has guts
13. Who gives the law
14. Stern
15. Decisiveness
16. Self-sufficiency
17. The one who acts
18. Guardian and protector
19. Disciplinarian
20. Power
21. Strong-willed
22. Intelligent when it comes to organization
23. Inspires a sort of fear, reverence
24. Who has the knowledge
25. Methodical mind
26. Realistic

27. Firmness
28. Maintains order
29. Provider
30. Demanding
31. Who makes the decisions
32. Supervisor
33. Hard thinker
34. Dynamic
35. Ability to solve problems
36. Gives the directions
37. Independent-minded
38. Independent responsibility
39. Who takes action

Maternal items

40. Most patient
41. Close to whom one feels at home
42. Warmth
43. Is intimate
44. Tenderness
45. Strong emotional involvement
46. Emotional support
47. Most compassionate
48. All-solicitous about the well-being and happiness of others
49. Takes loving care of me
50. Welcomes me with open arms
51. Sensitive
52. Surrounds one with comfort
53. Most concerned with what is related to human beings
54. Feels things very deeply
55. Nourishing
56. Is all-embracing
57. A warm-hearted refuge
58. Intuition
59. Sympathetic understanding
60. Loving companionship
61. Self-giving love
62. Who gives comfort
63. Nurturing
64. Will sympathize with the child's sorrows
65. Mildness

66. Heart-felt closeness
67. Tender attachment
68. Endearing
69. Mercy
70. Is touched deeply by events
71. Gentle
72. Demonstration of affection

All the items were randomly arranged. The scales were set up for simultaneous application to the father and mother figures instead of successively, as was the case for the original SDPS.

1.2   *The Sample*

What follows is based on data gathered from a sample of 120 individuals (administration III), which consisted of two subsamples of 60 high-school (mean age 17.3) and 60 college science students (mean age 19.5). Each subsample had 30 male and 30 female subjects. The students resided in the Rochester, New York metropolitan area. All were Roman Catholic, students in Catholic institutions, unmarried, and from stable family units of the middle and upper social strata.

2   RESULTS AND DISCUSSION

2.1   *The Factors*

Table 7.1 shows that at least 45 percent of the total variance of the original matrix of intercorrelations is accounted for by the first five factors in each figure. Table 7.2 presents the Phi-coefficients (Tucker 1951). These coefficients indicate that the first factor is identical in all three figures. Factors II, III and IV present semi-congruence in all three figures.[1]

1. For the definition of semicongruence see Chapter 4, p. 74.

Table 7.1 *Percentages of the total variance of each of the three figures accounted for by the five factors*

Factor	Father	Mother	God
I	16.26	17.22	21.03
II	9.53	10.36	9.60
III	8.96	9.24	9.51
IV	6.34	3.93	6.79
V	3.22	3.17	4.92
	44.31	44.62	51.85

Table 7.2 *Coefficients of congruence between factors in the parental figures and in the representation of God*

Factors	Father–Mother	Father–God	Mother–God
I	F_1M_1 0.9471584	F_1G_1 0.9439165	M_1G_1 0.9325381
II	F_2M_3 0.8183173	F_2G_2 0.8210036	M_3G_2 0.8310633
III	F_3M_2 0.8975135	F_3G_3 0.8177395	M_2G_3 0.8019256
IV		F_2G_4 0.6224496	M_3G_4 0.7436913

Factor I is constituted in all three figures by the maternal items taken as a whole (item 40 to 72). The basic items of factor I may be outlined as follows:

Security: a warm-hearted refuge, gives comfort, welcomes me with open arms, surrounds one with comfort, close to whom one feels at home, emotional support, protector, provider, a safe place of refuge.

Intimacy: closeness, all-embracing, friendly companionship, tender attachment, intimate, warmth, gentleness, affectionate, gentle, mildness, compassionate, sympathetic understanding, endearing, mercy.

Tender loving care: takes loving care of me, solicitude, concern, nurturing, nourishing.

Sensitive: is touched deeply by events, feels things very deeply, strong emotional involvement, tenderness, sensitive.

The general characteristics of factors II and IV are:

Disciplinarian: lays down the law, stern, strong-willed, strong-minded, maintains order, firmness, supervisor, inspires a sort of fear and reverence, demanding, takes action.

Norm: gives the law, authority, the principle and rule, the judge, makes the decisions, is leader.

Protection: guardian and protector, protection against danger, provider, strength, power, has guts.

The items highly loaded in factor II lend to an interpretation of this factor in terms of law and order, while those highly loaded in factor IV suggest the idea of authority and law.

Factor III is characterized by:

Autonomy: independent-minded, independent responsibility; self-sufficiency, (provider, protector); leadership, gives the directions, is leader, takes the initiative, makes the decisions.

Dynamism: he who takes action, dynamic, decisiveness, the one who acts.

Mental ability: hard thinker, ability to solve problems, organizing brain, methodical, systematic mind, studies issues, has the knowledge.

Factor V is characterized by items expressing the idea of realism, initiative, and decisiveness. The five factors are:

Factor I $(F_1=M_1=G_1)$ = Intimacy and security
Factor II (F_2,M_3,G_2) = Law and order, disciplinarian
Factor III (F_3,M_2,G_3) = Autonomy and action
Factor IV (F_2,M_3,G_4) = Authority and law
Factor V (F_4) = Realism, systematic, and decisiveness

2.2 Factorial Structure of the Figures

When the means of the attribution of each factor to each figure are considered, certain characteristics become immediately apparent. On the basis of Table 7.3, the figures may be expressed in the following specific and structured factorial components:

Mother = I + II, III, (IV), (V)
Father = (IV), III, V, II + I
God   = IV + III + (V), II + I

Factors in parentheses represent dimensions that are not structured into factors in the particular figure although the items contained in these dimensions are also applied to that figure.

Table 7.3 *Attribution means of the factors for the father, mother, and God figures*

	Father	Mother	God
Factor I	3.37	5.05	4.10
Factor II	5.05	3.40	4.43
Factor III	5.22	3.68	4.88
Factor IV	5.32	3.58	5.32
Factor V	5.10	3.74	4.64

The mother figure is composed and structured first in terms of factor I (17.22 percent of the variance). It represents the characteristics of intimacy and security. In addition, the mother figure assumes all the paternal factors (i.e., factors whose content is composed of paternal items) to an important degree. However, the mother figure integrates only two of these factors as structured dimensions (factors II and III); Factors IV and V are not integrated as factors in the mother figure, although their components, i.e., the items, are also highly attributed to the mother. All paternal factors are attributed to the mother figure with a lower degree of intensity than factor I ($p < 0.01$). Thus, the mother figure is defined primarily in terms of intimacy and security. It is also characterized by law and order (factor II), and by autonomy and action (factor III).

The father figure is much more complex than the mother figure. Its basic content is comprised of three structured factors that characterize the father as the representation of law and order, as autonomous and active, and as approaching the world systematically and realistically. The father figure also contains values that specifically characterize the mother (viz., intimacy and security), though to a lesser degree.

From the point of view of intensity of attribution, the representation of God is primarily characterized by factor IV (authority an law), then by factor III (realism and systematic attitude) and factor II (law and order), and finally by factor I (intimacy and security). Factor IV is the most intensely attributed to the representation of God, and factor I is the most fundamental since its percentage of variance is the highest (cf. Table 7.1) In addition, factor I (security and intimacy) is attributed to God to a significantly higher degree than it is to the father ($p < 0.01$). Factor IV is attributed to God with the highest degree of intensity of all the factors ($p < 0.01$), and factor III ranks higher than factor II ($p < 0.05$). Consequently, the representation of God may be conceived as the discriminated synthesis of parental characteristics. The representation of God is a synthesis because it assumes all the parental factors to a high degree. In fact, it integrates the paternal factors much better than the mother figure and also the maternal factors better than the father figure; it is a synthesis of contrasts superior to the composition of both the maternal and the paternal figures. In addition, it is a discriminated composition of contrasts because the four paternal factors are integrated into it in clearly different degrees of intensity whereas they are integrated into the parental figures with equivalent degrees of intensity.

Briefly, in the father figure, the factors reveal the very important feature of possessor of authority, the symbol of law and discipline, to a much greater degree than to the items considered only in terms of individual intensity scores. Furthermore, the father figure is the symbol of freedom, autonomy, action, realism, decision and a systematic approach to things and to the world. It also incudes, to a lesser extent, the characteristics of intimacy and security. On the other hand, the mother figure is primarily a symbol of safety, security, and trust, and of one who gives the feeling of together-ness and heart-felt closeness. It also includes strong components of the autonomy and action – the independent woman oriented towards achievement.

As far as the figure of God is concerned, it must be said that it integrates well all the parental characteristics. However, it is also imperative to recognize that the maternal items are less relevant to the divine figure than the paternal items. A further distinction must be made with respect to the latter: the paternal items most attributed to the representation of God are not those which best describe the father. The most typical paternal items of the rep-resentation of God are those which compose factor IV. The items most intensely attributed to the father figure are those highly loaded in factor II.

2.3   Relational Structure of the Figures

The paternal items are attributed most to the father, then to God, and finally to the mother; and the maternal items are attributed most to the mother, then to God, and finally to the father. The distribution of items seems to be specific because the profile of any one figure does not coincide with the profile of any other figure. Nevertheless, this specificity is relative, the coefficients of correlation between the mean intensity scores of attribution of each item to each figure (Table 7.4) support this.

Table 7.4   *Correlation coefficients between intensity score means*

	rF_fM_f	rF_fG_f	rM_fG_f	rF_mM_m	rF_mG_m	rM_mG_m
Males	0.093	0.396*	0.125	−0.004	0.263	0.158
Females	0.470**	0.400**	0.234	0.581**	0.528**	0.463**
Total	0.328*	0.383*	0.181	0.352*	0.462*	0.343*

* $= p < 0.05$
** $= p < 0.01$

The general tendency among males is to consider the three profiles as being independent (i.e., not related to each other), but there is a similarity in the distributions of the same items when they are applied to God and to the father, especially in the case of the paternal items ($r = 0.40$, $p < 0.05$). Females manifest the opposite tendency in correlating the profiles, with one exception: the paternal profiles of the mother (M_f) and of God (G_f) are not related to each other.

The following important points can be derived from the above: (a) Both males and females express a relation (similarity of structure) between the father figure and the representation of God in the paternal items. (b) Correspondence of structure between the profiles of the mother figure and the representation of God is only manifested by the female students when they express those figures in terms of maternal items. (c) Unlike males, females conceive a very high correspondence between the paternal and maternal profiles in both sets of items. And (d), the paternal items evoke more differentiated reactions than do the maternal items. In fact, males show three independent figure profiles whereas females show the tendency to express all three figures with a similar maternal item profile. In the paternal items, however, both males and females give two different configurations for the figure profiles. For the males, there is a configuration of paternal items that is identical for the figures of God and the father, and another configuration specifically determined by the mother figure. For the females, there is one configuration for the father and God, and another for the father and the mother. When applied to God, therefore, the paternal items are strikingly different from their distribution in the mother figure.

2.4 *Semantic Differences on the Basis of the Items*

Two types of distance scores are available. One was derived from the analysis of the figures using only the items and the second using only the factors. We treat first the item semantic distances.

(a) The representation of God is closer to the figure of the father than to that of the mother. This is true on several accounts: (1) the total figures, $FG < MG$, $[t(119) = 5.62, p < 0.01]$, (2) the figures considered from the perspective of the paternal items, $FG_f < MG_f$, $[t(119) = 6.96, p < 0.01]$ and (3) the figures considered from the perspective of the nonspecific items, $FG_m < MG_f$, $[t(119) = 7.70, p < 0.01]$.

(b) The father figure is an adequate symbol for God not only in its specific dimension but also in its nonspecific dimension. It is, in fact, close to God in its specific as well as its nonspecific items. We find that

$FG_f < FG_m$ $[t(119) = 2.05, p < 0.05]$
$FG_f < MG_f$ $[t(119) = 6.96, p < 0.01]$
$MG_m < MG_f$ $[t(119) = 5.86, p < 0.01]$
$FG_m < MG_f$ $[t(119) = 7.70, p < 0.01]$

and can state that:

paternal God is closest to paternal father
maternal God is closest to maternal mother
maternal God is very close to maternal father
paternal God is close to paternal mother

and in general terms:

the representation of God is very close to the father figure
the representation of God is close to the mother figure.

As a total figure, the father figure seems to be a better symbol for God, but in the specific items both parental figures seem equally to be adequate symbols for God. The father, however, prevails in this symbolic function because the integration of the maternal items within the father figure more closely resembles the maternal dimension in God than the paternal dimension in the mother resembles the paternal dimension in God.

(c) The main differences observed in the distance scores in relation to the sex of the subjects are that the distances between the figures tend to be generally smaller for the female students than they are for the males. However, this tendency is significant only for the father–mother distance, in both the paternal [$t(59) = 3.93$, $p < 0.01$] and maternal items [$t(59) = 2.68$, $p < 0.01$], and the mother–God distance in the total figures [$t(59) = 2.23$, $p < 0.05$] and in the figures described from the perspective of the paternal items [$t(59) = 2.09$, $p < 0.05$].

2.5 *Semantic Distances on the Basis of the Factors*

Factor I (intimacy and security)   The factor I semantic distances between the figures in the total sample are equivalent. However, the females present a greater similarity between the figures of the mother and God than between the figures of the father and God [$t(59) = 2.52$, $p < 0.05$]. Thus, it seems that factor I represents a set of existential characteristics that are closer to the females' experience of the similarity between the mother and God figures than to their experience of the similarity between the father and God figures.

The distance between the mother and God figures in factor I is smaller than the same distance in factors II [$t(119) = 4.13$,

$p < 0.01$], III [$t(119) = 3.42, p < 0.01$], IV [$t(119) = 5.33, p < 0.01$] and V [$t(119) = 3.29$, $p < 0.01$]. This shows that the paternal items significantly loaded in factors II, III, IV, and V do not fit in the mother–God relation as well as the maternal characteristics of intimacy and security.

Factor II (law and order) and factor IV (authority and law)   These two factors will be considered simultaneously since they have much in common. Factor II generates very definite differences between the three figures, particularly by stressing a mother–God distance larger than the father–God [$t(119) = 3.94$, $p < 0.01$] and the father–mother distances [$t(119) = 2.64$, $p < 0.01$]. The paternal component of law and order seems to contain a dimension that is distinctly less intensively applied to the mother than it is to the father and to God. Factor IV produces also a mother–God distance larger than the father–God [$t(119) = 10.81$, $p < 0.01$] and the mother–father distances [$t(119) = 5.52$, $p < 0.01$]. Factors II and IV seem to lead to a remarkable likeness between the paternal and the divine figures, particularly when compared to the similarity of the figures of the mother and of God.

Factor IV contains items which are just as relevant to the father and to the mother as the items contained in Factor II. However, it includes items that are definitely more pertinent to God than the items contained in factor II ($p < 0.01$). The items most relevant to God (factor IV) are also those that establish the most marked dissimilarity between the mother and God when compared to the other factors, and also that establish the greatest similarity between the paternal and divine figures. The items contained in factor II, although less relevant to God than those of factor IV, produce the same results as factor IV in terms of similarity of figures, though to a lesser degree.

Therefore, it is clear that paternity includes two aspects of a very different nature. The first, expressed by factor II, is not specific to the father figure: one finds it in a similar way in the mother figure. The second of these aspects, expressed by factor IV, is, on the contrary, specific of the father figure and places it closer to the representation of God. This set of items is, in fact, attributed with a greater intensity to the father than to the mother, and is at the origin of the greatest father–mother distance and of the smallest father–God distance. Factor IV, then, indicates a-more-than-human paternity or, at least, a paternity that the father shares with God.

The relationship between the figures is not the same when given in terms of distances as when given in terms of intensity of attribution of the items. Factor I is significantly more intensely attributed to the mother than to God [$t(119) = 7.45, p < 0.01$] or to the father [$t(119) = 16.26, p < 0.01$]. However, factor I represents an equivalent semantic dimension for all three figures. Its structure does not vary when applied to the three figures though the intensity of application does vary. Factors II and IV are both applied to the father with equivalent degrees of intensity. They are applied also to the mother with equivalent, though inferior, degrees of intensity. In the representation of God, however, factor IV produces highly significant differences because it is applied more intensely than factor II, factor V ($p < 0.01$), or factor III ($p < 0.05$). In addition, factor III is more intensely applied to the representation of God than factor II ($p < 0.05$).

The intensity scores of the paternal items, in addition to being significantly more intensely attributed to the father and to God than to the mother, introduce additional differences in the representation of God. The influence on the representation of God is even more apparent in the relation between the figures when the semantic distances are taken into consideration.

This seems to suggest two conclusions. (1) The representation of God is decidedly closer to the paternal figure than to the maternal one, since it is more similar to the father figure than to the maternal figure. In fact, it consistently assumes the items significantly loaded in the paternal factors to a higher degree than the items composing the maternal factor, and is always similar to the father figure in all factors. The similarity of the representation of God to the mother, however, is significant only in factor I. (2) The representation of God is more complex than the father figure, because it assumes factor I to a significantly higher degree than does the father figure, and introduces differences within the paternal factors in terms of intensity (factor IV over factor II, factor III, and factor V, and also factor III over factor II) and semantic distance. The God figure is, therefore, a paternal figure that is richer than the figure of the human father, even a father figure that has incorporated the maternal characteristics contained in factor I.

The distance between the father and mother figures may be considered as a standard measure of the similarity between the figures. This distance is virtually identical in all factors and in all samples. Therefore, the relation of the parental figures in terms of distance is the same, irrespective of the dimension involved (i.e., maternal or paternal). On the basis of the distance and intensity scores it may be said that the parents are different figures, but are not estranged from one another; they are not interchangeable, but they are highly similar; they are independent in meaning, but are also complementary; they present a semantic polarity; they are both simultaneous components of the experience of all subjects, but they are also discriminable. All paternal factors, if conceived in a slightly different fashion can, as shown by the distance scores, also be used to describe the mother. Support for this assertion is found in the constant distance between the father and the mother figures in all factors. The introduction into the comparison of the representation of God introduces the greatest differences in the semantic scores. There are items attributed in a similar way to the representation of God and to the father figure (for instance, factor IV) that do not apply to the mother figure in the same way. These items express strictly paternal characteristics and are applied to the representation of God with the opposite degree of intensity than they are applied to the mother figure. This phenomenon is not observed when the maternal items are attributed to the three figures. In fact, the maternal items consistently fit all figures and exhibit small and equal distances between all three figures. They represent characteristics of a fundamental and primitive importance, characteristics typical of the mother–infant relationship. For the individual, the characteristics expressed by the paternal items are of more recent psychogenetic origin, and, when compared to the maternal items, they assume a very specific content, so as to appear, at times, opposed to the latter.

Consequently, the mother figure may also be an adequate symbol for God. However, there are aspects of the representation of God that do not correspond to characteristics found in the mother because they arise from a specific paternal base. This leads to the conclusion that the figure of the father is a more adequate symbol for God because it is more complex than the figure of the mother. Not only does the father figure involve a greater number of dimensions (four factors for the father, and three for the mother), it also assumes these dimensions with greater intensity. The representation of God has a superior assimilation of parental contrasts and is therefore more similar to the father figure than to the mother figure. In fact, it most often appears closer to the father figure than to the mother figure.

Overview and Theoretical Perspective

1 THE PARENTAL FIGURES

1.1 *The Components of the Parental Figures*

The studies presented above establish three things that are of major importance and virtually constant. First, the preliminary tests of the discriminative attribution of the items show that the subjects of both sexes, from whatever cultural milieu, clearly differentiate the paternal and maternal items. Second, the application of these items to the symbolic figures of the father and the mother shows that each parental figure also possesses, to varying degrees and on different levels, the characteristics of the other parental figure. And finally, the differentiated attribution of the parental items to both parents seems to imply that both parents fulfill complementary functions with respect to the child. The mother is characterized primarily by availability and tenderness, and secondarily by authority. The father is characterized primarily by law and authority, and secondarily by availability or receptivity. The applications of the SDPS, therefore, confirm and augment the results of the choices required by the preliminary test of the differential capacity of the items.

Postadolescents, adults, and elderly persons give these same results. Moreover, an exploratory study with children (see Appendix I) suggests that the essential components of the parental symbolic figures are formed very early, at about seven years old. The parental symbolic figures remain stable and are not significantly modified by the life situation or the psychological transformation of the individual.

1.2   The Maternal Symbolic Figure

The mother is primarily and essentially, the one who is available. Thus, the fundamental factor of the mother figure is called availability, receptivity, or tenderness. The reader is reminded that, in most of the factor analyses, the factors were named after the most loaded items in the composition of the factors. In reality, the components of the fundamental maternal factor are almost equivalent. Therefore, it can be designated here as affective availability. Her capacity to welcome, to take loving care of the child, to give security, to be a warm-hearted refuge is not limited to the actual care that the mother provides during early infancy, even if this care is indelibly impressed on the psyche. The stability of the symbolic figure of the mother through the years for both sexes and in various cultural milieux shows that it represents unconditional love (Fromm 1962).

This fundamental characteristic can be understood if it is associated with maternity as the gift of life. She who bears the new life and places it in the world is also she who surrounds it with her care and her warmth, who nourishes it, and who always remains, on the level of symbolic representation, the figure of unconditional acceptance. From the total acceptance by the mother, the child derives affective security. The experience and the memory of maternal availability normally confirm the child in its personal value and develop in him a fundamental confidence in life and in humanity, which is a necessary condition for the acquisition and maintenance of the sense of personal identity (Erikson 1968).

Recent studies (Bowlby 1951, 1969, 1973; Spitz 1968; Zazzo 1974) have insisted on the importance of the attachment to the mother. In making this point, they recapitulate and elaborate a theme that has been previously illustrated (Hermann 1936; Szondi 1952). In our opinion, the availability factor, as it is constructed, perfectly describes the object of the attachment to the mother. This attachment, in fact, is not to be taken only in a physical sense, it must also be understood in the sense of an affective bond with the person who, in being entirely attentive, is capable of receiving the attachment of the child. Certainly, the vital need for care, protection, consolation, and warmth stimulates and sustains this attachment. But these needs also respond to the desire of the mother, which the child perceives. In this way, the mother also awakens in the child the desire to be wanted. In the satisfaction of its needs, which the child expects from and demands of the mother, it always demands more: it demands to be loved. Thus a psychic process is established in which demands and desires are formed on the basis of needs (Lacan 1966, 1973). This is also what Freud (1957) meant when he wrote that love is formed partially on the anaclitic mode, that is, it is supported by needs (Laplanche 1970). In this attachment, therefore, the capacity to bind oneself with confidence emerges. Maternal availability represents the objective pole and the condition for the development of such an attachment.

The results obtained from schizophrenics and delinquents (Chapter 6) lend particular weight to the significance of the maternal figure. Though these subjects are capable of differentiating the maternal and paternal items, they are the only ones for whom the mother is not characterized by availability. No well-defined factorial structure is found for the schizophrenics.

It may be presumed that the schizophrenics are able to verbally distinguish the maternal characteristics, but that these characteristics do not form a configuration in their psychic relations. Behind the words there is no affective gestalt that these words would normally sustain. This radical lack may not be entirely imputed to the mother, but that her attitude is partially responsible for this grave lacuna is supported by the studies cited in Chapter 6. The observations regarding the double bind phenomenon and the incapacity of the mother to focus her attention on the child can be summarized in these terms: she lacks fundamental availability. Consequently, the symbolic figure of the mother as availability is not formed. The capacity to form bonds with confidence is also not developed, nor is the sense of personal identity.

The results obtained from the delinquents do not give evidence of an absence in structure in the maternal figure, but well of a lack of her affective significance. The factors delicacy and giving are much less important than the dominant factor, initiative.

It seems that, for the delinquents, the capacity to put oneself empathetically in the place of others is lacking. Probably they also feel themselves to be emotionally frustrated, and a feeling of revindication probably dominates their relations with others and to society. One may suppose that, characterized by active initiative the mother was indeed the one who gave them the necessary things but that, not being emotionally available, she left them emotionally bereft.

The term 'symbolic figure' now takes on its full meaning. By being-for-the-child, the mother or the maternal substitute represents, well beyond the real dependence of the child, the figure that remains the sign of confident love formed in response to unconditional availability for the other. The necessities of new life condition the formation of this figure. The bioaffective bond that unites the mother and the child naturally predestine the mother for her function. But there is more. The language that the various cultures have developed around the mother consecrates her function. The term 'mother' is charged with affective connotations that render present the symbolic figure of the mother. The presence of this cultural symbol causes the experience of a physical presence that does not support the desired availability to be all the more bitter, for the physical presence is experienced as absence and contradiction.

Authority, the specific characteristic of the father according to the results reported in the preceding chapters, is almost always included in the maternal figure but always secondarily and rather far behind the dominant factor. From the semantic analysis presented in Chapter 4 it appears that the authority factor, when it is attributed to the mother, retains its paternal sense. In assuming authority, the mother refers to the father, who retains it as father. The perception that maternal authority is referential agrees with the relatively minor importance attributed to the authority and strength items. The most important paternal items in the maternal figure refer to concrete behavior; the mother is the one who maintains order, and who examines things.

It is possible to see here just a simple reflection of old established family customs, which may or may not be supported by laws that still discriminate between the sexes. But this would be to misunderstand the symbolic meaning of the parental figures. Considering only the mother figure, it has to be stressed that unconditional availability harmonizes with the function of authority only with difficulty. Thus the reference to the father can be understood as a safeguard both of maternal specificity and of the alliance with the father. For the child, from whose point of view the interpretation must be made, the mother can only be conceived in terms of two essential elements: first, what she is by virtue of her direct bond with the child, and second, what she is as a parent along with the father. The family, in fact, is not the sum of autonomous entities, but a field of relations structured around three poles. The results obtained with the SDPS show that the subjects perceive this structure. Indeed, to the direct relationship that is in the foreground is added that which the mother has with the child because of the third party with whom she shares parenthood. In the family structure, this second type of relationship consists of precisely the factor that specifies the father.

It is striking that judge is the only factor that characterizes the mother figure of the schizophrenics. This concurs with the clinical data cited above according to which the father of the schizophrenic does not assume his paternity. We do not think that the paternal absence is simply due to the father's vague personality. Clinical experience supports the opinion that the absence of the father results just as much from the desire of the mother to eliminate him from the family triangle. Doing this, she imposes herself on the child with an authority that contradicts her availability. She becomes the judge. Grouping together the set of characteristics stressed in the attitude of the mothers of schizophrenics, their disturbing effects are better understood. In arrogating the authority to herself, it is no longer positive. It reinforces that which is already indicated in the elimination of the father: the mother keeps the child for herself, absorbing the life that she should engender for its own autonomous existence.

These results and interpretations will not fail to encounter the serious questions raised by the modern movements fighting discrimination against women. Is not the maternal figure, as we have defined it, a contingent stereotype produced by centuries of masculine dominance that new social relations should and will overturn?

This study is not predictive but rather positive and interpretative. That which we have observed indicates that the family structure is not something born from an accident of history, but that it is founded on reasons more essential than an abuse of power. The sexual difference cannot be denied. It determines in every way the different positions in the family constellation. To hold this reality to be completely secondary would be to separate the body from rational behavior — by a rather rationalist and dualist preconception. We have insisted here that the affective relationship of the mother with the child, as both of them perceive it, takes up and prolongs the corporal and vital bond in which new life is created. Social changes that would deny the inherency of the affective bonds formed in the birth event shatter the spontaneity of the emotions. We recall the warning that Margaret Mead (1955) drew from her studies in cultural anthropology:

> The mother's nurturing tie to her child is apparently so deeply rooted in the actual biological conditions of conception and gestation, birth and suckling, that only fairly complicated social arrangements can break it down entirely. Society must distort their sense of themselves, pervert their inherent growth-patterns, perpetrate a series of learning-outrages upon them, before they will cease to want to provide, at least for a few years, for the child they have already nourished for nine months within the safe circle of their own bodies.

The psychology of the formation of personal identity, though more hypothetical, provides a second indication. The sense of being accepted unconditionally by the available mother seems indeed to be a condition necessary for the development of fundamental security and confidence. In any event, the results obtained with the schizophrenic subjects constitute a serious warning against arbitrary manipulation of the symbolic relations, the foundations of which are rooted in the difference between the sexes, the meanings of which have been developed by the culture.

It first must be made clear that the results of our study as well as the interpretations we present can be understood as antiegalitarian only in a certain sense. If, on the basis of equal social and political rights for men and women and of the necessity for equal task distribution in the home, one concludes that the parental images must be simply identical, then, of course, our study will appear to be antiegalitarian. But some critical questions arise: why transpose to the family the conceptions that apply in the working world? Is this not to fail to recognize that the family is structured in function of the human being in becoming and not, as other types of society, in function of adults? There is nothing that proves that the difference in parental functions would necessarily produce similar differences in societies that have other foundations and other purposes. One may wonder also what affective and cultural impoverishment would result from an egalitarianism that would abolish the differences in the extremely personal relationships in the constellation of the family.

1.3 *The Paternal Symbolic Figure*

Among the items that the groups first distinguished as specifically paternal, one set clearly emerges as the law and authority factor. It constitutes the most important component in the paternal symbolic figure. There are three groups for which this does not apply: the schizophrenics, the delinquents, and the Hindus. We turn first to the results that are the most uniform.

For our subjects, who come from diverse milieux and who, for the most part, belong to the younger generation, the father still possesses the law and authority function that has been traditionally specific to him. The semantic analysis given in Chapter 4 furnishes the elements necessary to understand the primacy of this factor. The father, as father, takes on this function of himself, while the mother in the exercise of this function refers to the father. Our subjects cannot conceive of paternity without this function.

To arrive at the significance of the father as representative and custodian of the law, we shall first consider the various terms that are assembled in this factor and then we shall situate this semantic set within the family structure.

The item who gives the law is often the most important in this factor, and thus the factor is named after it. The authority item is very close to it and designates in the most comprehensive manner the one who gives the law, who is the principle, and who judges. The item rule has a more concrete flavor, evoking rules of conduct. The item stern designates the manner of exercising that authority. In fact, this last item presents a low degree of saturation in the paternal symbolic figure. Our subjects, in attributing authority to the father, did not therefore intend to characterize the father as authoritarian. From this one can conclude that the term law, insofar as it identifies the paternal function does not connote a petty and oppressive legalism.

The term law consists of two elements that go together: it designates an imperative rule for behavior and it signifies that that rule comes from the exterior. Even if one gives interior consent to the law and makes it one's own, it remains a rule that, surpassing one's particular desires, has a universal character. And it is because of this universality that scientific language has adopted the term law to express the constant relations between phenomena of nature. The imperative nature of law is consistent with the fact that it addresses the human person as a being responsible for his own future.

This brief analysis of the term law allows us to situate the meaning of the paternal function as it occurs in the family constellation within the parental polarity. The mother actually represents the origin and the object of the affective bond and of the relation of desire. But a human being in becoming is not just a being of immediate desires to be satisfied. He must become himself and must form himself for an autonomous and responsible position in the social world. In the microsociety that is the family this vector of the personality finds its response and its support in the father. In this manner, the presence of the father rouses and sustains another type of desire than that which seeks security in unconditional acceptance. If the child desires that his father occupy the place that justifies the name 'father', it is because he wants to have a pole for the orientation of his future and for his relations with the social world. As found in exploratory interviews with children (see Appendix I) this requirement of a father is present at a very early age; in their language they witness to it, saying that the father must be stern. In responding to the SDPS, the adolescents and the adults recognized this function of the father by attributing it to the symbolic figure.

It is noteworthy that both males and females present the same paternal figure. This observation contradicts the simplified representation of psychoanalytic theory concerning the Oedipus complex. In this conception, the oedipal conflict represents for the girls the same scheme as for boys but simply inverted. Desiring the father, the daughter comes into conflict with her mother as rival. The mother would represent from then on the prohibitive law in the oedipal relationship. We do not deny the reality and the effect of this problematic, but we are convinced that it takes on its true significance in reference to the symbolic parental functions, which are the same for both sexes. With regard to the theory of the Oedipus complex, we would say that in face of a daughter's oedipal desire, the father represents in the first place prohibitive law by signifying that it is the mother for whom he has sexual desire. In the case where the father does not assume his authority in the affective relations with the daughter, the rivalry with the mother has its full disturbing effect.

It is in the group of delinquents that the function of authority is the most lacking in the paternal figure. Based on this alone, it is obviously not possible to say to what degree this is an absence that developed afterwards or if it is primal and determinative. Those who have studied the psychological laws of becoming and the psychology of delinquency would no doubt agree with the idea that delinquency does not arise, in a formed personality, as a simple effect of privations and conflicts imposed by society. The human being does not learn to resolve his contradictory desires and to treat others as brothers and sisters in a common humanity unless he has succeeded in interiorizing law as a universal rule of conduct. It is therefore necessary in the first society, the family, that the parents assume this function. And the texture of the family requires that it be primarily the father who does this. We may correctly presume that in some way the fathers of the delinquents were deficient. According to the SDPS, his figure is essentially characterized by the rational trait of systematic mind, a trait which, in the absence of law, doubtless takes on the sense of efficacious calculation. Direction, the second and less important paternal factor with the delinquents connotes a more concrete exercise of authority in practical affairs. It does not have the universality of a norm commanding ethical respect.

The law-authority set is also absent in the paternal figure of the schizophrenics. The primary factor is composed of two opposing dimensions, one expressing the idea of decision, a more concrete term than law-authority, and the other containing the idea of availability. The father here is therefore not really the symbolic father that was found with the other subjects. In addition, with the more concrete quality of exercise of authority, he assumes at the same time the maternal function absent in the mother. If the structuring effectiveness of the parental polarity is taken into account, the grave disturbing effect of such a father is obvious. He applies a double bind different from that explained by clinicians. By simultaneously neglecting his function and substituting for the mother, he constantly contradicts the position that is his according to the nature of the family constellation. It is this double bind imposed by the father that is expressed in the first of the two paternal factors.

The responses of the Hindus have to be understood within their cultural context, determined as it is by their religion. One can not understand their paternal figure, characterized first by receptivity and then by principle, without taking into account their particular representation of God. God is overwhelmingly described in terms of law and only very minimally in terms of availability. It can be presumed that the father retreats behind the reference to God who, omnipresent in the culture, alone provides the law for becoming and acting.

The item who gives the law, takes on its full meaning when it is placed in its context. The law is presented as a gift offered in answer to a child's felt need, even if no demand has been expressly formulated. As clinical experience attests, if the father does not give the child the law, the child will be insecure, exposed as he is to contradictory desires and not having support to order his impulses and to construct for himself a competent human personality. Neither will the child separate himself from the maternal bond that, becoming the exclusive pole, encloses the child in a proximity that destroys its autonomy. The physical presence of a nourishing and protecting father cannot sufficiently compensate for that which he ought to be symbolically. And if the physical absence of the father renders more uncertain the efficacy of his symbolic significance, it can still be exercised if the mother refers to the absent father, thus rendering him symbolically present in the familial triangle.

The maternal factor of availability is secondary in the father figure, giving the law factor its properly paternal significance. The items that the subjects identify as paternal do not connote a specifically paternal relationship. Taken in themselves, one can interpret them as characterizing different relations between man and society. This peculiarity of the paternal characteristics reflects the position of the father; intervening as a third party in the family constellation, he comes, in a certain sense, from the outside. While a direct bond unites the child to the mother, the father becomes father by assuming his paternity. His active recognition creates a bond of tenderness so strong that, for many groups, the items of the maternal availability factor are among the most saturated even though factor analysis places it second in the composition of the paternal figure. Semantic analysis, however, does not show that the father's availability has reference to the mother's as is the case for the law factor in the mother figure. Availability, of itself, seems to imply a direct personal relationship without the presence of a mediating third party. Because it is precisely a very personalized affective bond, availability must be situated in the father himself. In our opinion, the second place of this factor can be explained by the fact that the father intervenes by intentionally recognizing the child and by affectively and effectively adopting him. The availability of the father is not as primal as that of the mother in the sense it was described in the analysis of the maternal figure and its sources in the primal bioaffective bond.

The two factors of the father figure mutually support each other and intermingle in the perception of the child. Being the one who gives the law, the father, unlike the mother, loves conditionally. If he does not assume his proper function, he absents himself as father and the child does not realize that he is interested in him. Paternal love is therefore not conditional in the sense that it can be withdrawn. It is conditional as love; it expects a response to the giving of the law, and it reserves a surplus of recognition for what the child wants to become. The father must be receptive, giving himself in active concern and self-giving love. But, while the maternal items are attributed to the father figure in largely the same way as in the maternal figure, tenderness, which is highly saturated in the mother figure (Chapter 3), is virtually absent in the father figure. Does this difference not indicate that the function of law gives paternal availability a special vigor that diminishes the quality of maternal tenderness?

Our study affirms the importance of a warm, affective relationship of the father with the child. This has also been indicated by various other studies (MacKinnon 1938; Mussen and Distler 1960). Contrary to much misunderstanding, however, our study shows that this paternal relational form is intrinsically bound to law and authority, as psychoanalysis has emphasized. In any case, the socializing influence of the father does not consist primarily of the instrumental function that Parsons (1954, 1955) stresses.

And the crisis of paternity? According to the results presented above, the modifications in the intrafamily relationships do not seem to essentially affect the significant relationships that make up the family as such. In the same way, the contemporary instability of marriages also does not seem to affect them. Perhaps what is called the crisis of paternity is rather a crisis of fathers who have to exercise their paternity. For many reasons, it is apparently more difficult these days for the father to correspond to his symbolic function. A certain number of men doubtless feel that their paternal position has been supplanted by the social and juridical equality of women. The position given to children in contemporary civilization requires a mode of exercising paternity that is less authoritarian; the new forms of familial relations require considerably more personal qualities than did the authority officially consecrated by all the social norms. Then, too, in a society where customs and values are unstable, contradictory, and contested, there is no longer a culturally diffused paternity that would provide secure support for the father. This situation renders his position particularly fragile. For, while representing the law within the famial relations as the child perceives them and wants them, the father does not draw his authority from himself lest he render it arbitrary and consequently destroy his function. Consider the group of Hindus: like the mother and like the entire society, the father defers here to the divine law so that he almost nullifies his own function of giving the law. In our opinion, this situation is analogous to that of primitive societies where the maternal uncle assumes the paternal function of representing, and being the guarantee of, the law of the ancestors. These are civilizations where the permanence of the symbolic references strongly dominates the discontinuities. But in contemporary Western society, the historical ruptures and the contradictions in values that are invoked place the father in a delicate position: he is more directly the one who gives the law, but, in this function, he is less supported and authenticated by universally recognized values.

One wonders also if the expression 'crisis of paternity' does not betray a certain intolerance for the conflict that is part of paternity. It is obvious that the law, even when required by the child, represents a pole of conflict. The mother is situated more directly in the desire vector. In our data, this is reflected in the greater saturation of the maternal items, and this even in the father figure. Still, the mother also arouses profound conflicts insofar as she never can respond adequately to the child's desire because this desire is limitless and because the child projects an idealized mother figure. These demands, however, do not challenge the mother as mother, but only the imagined insufficiency of her responses. But the father by his very function cannot avoid the aggresivity that law inherently provokes.

The theme of a crisis of paternity reflects, moreover, theories and ideologies relative to the changes in the various societies so that, by the influence of the society on the family, the term 'paternity' has come to connote all that is involved in any authority function whatsoever. Now with regard to the great centralizing and anonymous powers, the political ideal of democratic equality is being pursued in the search for self-managing societies of more human dimensions, and this on the social, economic, and political levels. From these critical movements tending to 'a fraternal society', one can then infer the idea that contemporary society is moving towards the elimination of 'paternal' kinds of authority. But is this not to be deceived by a confusion between the family and the society? Is it not an illegitimate extension or projection first to transpose the model of the family to the society, and then to reapply the objections against a certain kind of society to the family? The paternal function in the family does not rest on the nature of social authority, even if the practical exercising of paternity is subject to the influences of social models and ideals. To speak of a crisis of paternity because there is a crisis in adult society is to foster ideological confusion between the family and the society.

1.4   *The Variations between the Groups*

Only the differences between the sexes and the differences between the cultural groups will be discussed here. The Hindu subjects and the psychiatric groups have already been discussed. The results of the group of religious will be discussed in the section on the representation of God.

The influence of sex   The equivalence that uniformly appears in the results from the two sexual groups provides striking evidence that the parental figures do not derive from the particular affective relations that the males or females have with their two parents individually, but well from their position in the family structure as it is established by the bond of birth and by the paternal mediation of a cultural law that transcends the family unit.

Some minor differences, nevertheless, regularly distinguish the results from the two sexes. Females generally score slightly higher than the males. To explain this differential phenomenon, the element of social desirability that supposedly is more stressed by the females is often cited. Suggested too is that the more affective female disposition would differentiate the items less than would the more critical reason of the males. In Chapter 5, Neff (1977) and Vannesse (1977*b*) have reported that the high scorers, males or females, have a different Szondi test profile. In Szondi's terminology, subjects having high scores show a tendency to conform to what is desired of them and to have a form of hypochondriac existences, i.e., they have a tendency to eliminate their representations of desire (in Szondi's terminology, 'hypochondriac existence' does not have pathological implications). Subjects with low scores, on the other hand, manifest a form of existence characterized by guilt and by a marked tendency to sublimate sexuality; critical judgment and control are characteristic of this form of existence. If verified by further research, this observation could probably furnish an element for the interpretation of differential scoring tendencies.

The sexual differences in the results obtained with the SDPS apparently pertain to differential psychology. The males have a tendency to accentuate more the paternal characteristics of the father and to differentiate the two figures according to the items that are specific to them. Among the paternal items, the males stress more the items of giving the law and judge. The females have the tendency to accentuate more certain paternal items in the mother figure: strength, maintains order, initiative. These slight differences can be understood as the differential effects of identification with the parent of the same sex. The males stress the specific aspect of the father who, among others, is their identification model. Because of their idenfication with the mother, the females present the mother somewhat more than do the males as a complex being, endowed with more embracing characteristics. In the context of the psychoanalytic theory of oedipal conflict, one can also consider that the mother is slightly more of an authority for the females than for the males, while for the males, the mother is situated more clearly in the desire vector. Finally, that the males score the items of law and judge slightly higher is not surprising, since from the age of eight years on, males show more sense of law and guilt (Jaspard and Dumoulin 1973).

Intercultural differences: The mother figure   The maternal items are less differentiated semantically than the paternal items. Virtually all of them are variations on the theme of affective availability, the fundamental maternal factor. This structural simplicity of the maternal dimension is also manifest in the fact that, in the parental figures and the representation of God, the maternal structure remains essentially the same. Availability, with its qualities of receptivity, presence, patience, and tenderness is inherent in the mother figure as such. This simple unity of the maternal figure explains why there are few intercultural variations in the maternal dimension. In Chapter 4, only three characteristics composing the maternal factors were noted that could be distinguished from the central factor. The Zairian and Filipino groups attribute the factor protection to the mother figure. The Belgian group attributed the peripheral factor of feminity to the mother, the Indonesian group that of intuition. It therefore seems that the maternal qualities that are capable of differentiating the mother figure are either her active concern that provides security or the feminine charm and finesse of her personal relationships. The first characteristic reflects a type of mothering that is present in some family traditions. The other characteristic reflects a more developed feminine culture. This shows that the differential characteristics that psychology would sometimes consider as belonging to the nature of woman are, in fact, largely possibilities that the various cultures develop and evaluate differently.

According to the intercultural study presented in Chapter 4, only one group that attributes a peripheral maternal factor to the mother figure, also attributed to it a peripheral paternal factor. This is the Filipino group for which the mother figure also includes the factor power. We have insufficient information to interpret this fact. That the same group would also be the only one to attribute the same factor power to God, however, leads one to think that, in virtue of the religious context, the mother and God are joined in representing the origin of life as emanating from a divine-maternal generative power. In favor of this hypothesis, we recall that similar representations are quite common in many religions (Eliade 1958; Bergounioux and Goetz 1958) and that it is found among children and preadolescents in Western Christian cultures (Deconchy 1967). On the other hand, it seems significant that the two other groups that attributed a secondary paternal factor to the mother figure, are the same ones for which the mother figure does not have a second maternal factor. The Colombian group characterized the mother figure with the factor order, the American group with that of authority. Order belongs to paternal authority, designating its concrete exercise.

With one exception, the differences in the maternal figure are therefore reduced either to the development of a specific maternal trait (protection, feminity) or to the characteristic assumption of a paternal function.

Intercultural differences: The father figure   By subjective factorization of the paternal items, classification into three dimensions seems to be indicated: authority, dynamic power, and knowledge. The factor analyses presented in Chapters 4 and 5 did derive these three dimensions and significantly nuanced our semantic hypothesis. In fact, law appears as the central factor and is universally present. We have already stated that this semantic element marks the structural position of the father in the family sphere at the open frontier between the family and the world. Factor analysis did not demonstrate power to be an identified paternal factor with the exception of the Filipino group as mentioned above. Dynamism, on the other hand, occurs in four groups and knowledge in two. Because of the introduction of a new item series, the study done by Pasquali (Chapter 7) is not exactly comparable with the others. The large number of items led to the derivation of four paternal factors for his American group. The results of this study however, do concur with the other studies on the same cultural population. Law, authority, and dynamism reoccur. And, as regards the significance of the fourth factor, realism and systematic mind, is it not included among the aspects of dynamic action?

Two cultural groups, the Belgian and the Filipino, attribute to the father figure the factor dynamism associated with the maternal factor protection. This could be the effect of family traditions in which the father is very much actively present in the family, occupying himself for a long period with the welfare of his children and remaining a support for their psychological and social security.

The Colombian and American groups also attribute dynamism to the father figure, but associate it with factors that, by their semantic content, are connected to that of law: order and authority. He who maintains order exercises authority by his concrete initiatives in the family. Authority, on the other hand, evokes the person who is the representative of the law. Moreover it has been noted that these two factors can equally characterize the primary quality of the father figure, as has been presented in Chapter 5. One can infer from this that the father figure of the American group represents both the embodiment of ethical authority and the model of the socially enterprising man. Another American group (See Chapter 3) emphasizes in an exceptional way the paternal dimension of the father to the point that, for this group, in contrast with the others, the difference between the father figure in its paternal dimension (F_f) and the mother figure in its maternal dimension (M_m) is almost nil. In the American group presented in Chapter 7, the factors authority–law and autonomy–action also present the highest attribution scores.

As the American group presents the most striking results for both parental figures, these results will be considered at greater length and an interpretation will be proposed that, of course, will have to be verified by more extensive research and clarified by sociological and historical studies. The results obtained with the American groups converge to distinguish a clear American type of father, characterized by two traits: authority and enterprising spirit. If to authority is given the ethical sense that the word evokes in the context of the paternal function, and if dynamism is taken as the spirit of enterprise in the business world, we essentially have the two elements that, according to Max Weber (1930), comprise the 'ideal type' of a certain society, namely, that which results from the interaction between the 'Protestant ethic and the spirit of capitalism'. In any case, it is striking that the American group (cf. Chapter 4) was also the only one to attribute to the mother figure the peripheral factor of authority, previously distinguished as specifically paternal. This seems to be a convincing argument for the predominance, in the American family, of paternity as ethical authority. The absence of a secondary maternal factor in the father figure, the absence of a secondary maternal factor in the mother figure, the bond between dynamism and authority in the father figure, and finally the exceptional emphasis on paternal items in the father figure — these are the converging cultural characteristics. Even if the father and the mother figures present central factors that identify their particular relationships with the child, one has the feeling that the cultural milieu holds maternal and feminine values to be less important.

The Indonesian and Zairian groups attribute the peripheral factor of knowledge to the father figure. Knowledge means something other than managerial intelligence, which is obviously bound to initiative and action. Without sufficient data to support our interpretation, but taking into account the absence of this factor in the other groups as well as the circumstances in the 'developing countries', we suppose that knowledge has to do with initiation of the father into the secrets of the 'knowledgeable' world. In these countries, the prestige of knowledge is in fact still largely reserved to men. In any event, it is interesting to note that this factor is not attributed to the father in any of the countries where knowledge is shared to a larger degree by both sexes.

The set of cultural variations are centered around a stable core where both symbolic differentiation and union in parenthood are present. The factor analyses revealed a polar structure at the center of the parental figures, and showed that different units of meaning characterize the various dimensions of these figures. This diversity could depend both on the family customs and on the ideals of the various cultural milieux. The factor protection, which was attributed twice to the mother and twice to the father, suggests family traditions that emphasize security. The factors feminity and intuition express a cultural ideal of the woman that gives maternity its particular form. Dynamism, which appeared four times as a peripheral factor of the father figure, indicates that the father brings to the family relationships a cultural appreciation of the enterprising man. Authority, which is the only secondary factor in the American group and this in the mother as well as in the father figures, suggests the cultural specificity discussed above.

2 THE REPRESENTATION OF GOD

The language of Christianity allows the presumption that the father figure symbolizes God. The following hypothesis was formulated: the father, as a symbolic figure in the family structure, supports the metaphor of divine paternity. Nevertheless, the research was not confined to this hypothesis. On the one hand, the same idea of the parental symbolic figures leads to the supposition that the differentiation between these figures ought to consist of a significant variation around a common axis, which gives rise to the hypothesis that the mother also mediates the representation of God. On the other hand, the desire of union with a God who is present leads to the supposition that the maternal element adds a dimension proper to the representation of God (Vergote 1969).

To go directly from a parental figure to the representation of God, moreover, would seem to be a biased procedure. The representation of God apparently results from a complex interaction between the individual and his milieu, and it cannot be assumed that the idea of God merely reproduces, by some well-determined psychological mechanism, the content of a parental figure. The concept of symbolization itself constitutes a problem that perhaps the studies reported here can clarify to a degree.

The hypotheses, questions, and instrument set limits. It was not intended to explain the faith of the subjects, nor even to define exhaustively their representation of God. The purpose was exclusively to study the degree to which the parental figures mediated that representation. However, something essential of religion can be grasped by this method. As the parental figures are initiators and supports of very personal relationships that are constitutive of the personality, it is likely that some fundamental vectors of religion as it is lived can be isolated. As the objective pole of a subjective relationship, the manner in which God is represented ought to disclose something of this relationship.

First the similarities and differences between the representation of God and the parental figures will be considered, and then the differences between some of the groups. This will allow the determination of which figure symbolizes God the more adequately. After that, the process of symbolization will be taken up and, in this regard, the results will be considered with reference to the Christian conception of God, which most of the subjects accept or at least refer to.

2.1 *The Fundamental Structure of the Representation of God and Its Meaning*

Setting aside the exceptional groups (the pathological, religious, and Hindu groups), there is a remarkable universality in the representation of God.

The representation of God integrates to a high degree the two parental dimensions, and is therefore more complex than the father figure. In a certain way, the representation of God is more maternal than paternal because it stresses more the maternal qualities than the paternal, the only exception being made by the American group presented in Chapter 3. Nevertheless, the representation of God is less maternal than the mother figure, but it is more maternal than the father figure; just as it is less paternal than the father figure, but more paternal than the mother figure.

Semantic analysis (Chapter 4) shows that, when applied to God, the maternal items combine the direct sense of their maternal significance and the transposed sense of the significance they take on when attributed to the father. Thus the divine presence is perceived, as an affective relation, as immediate as the attachment of the child to the mother. But at the same time, like the father, God is present as model thus again giving to presence the meaning that it receives by its insertion into the linguistic domain of law. On the other hand, the paternal items in the representation of God maintain the immediate signification that they have in the paternal figure, whereas the mother figure assumes them only in reference to the father.

Factor analysis (cf. Chapters 4 and 6) shows that the representation of God is composed of two factors, the one maternal, availability, and the other paternal, law and authority. Availability accounts for a very high percentage of variance in all the groups, while law and authority accounts for a very low percentage. Factorially, therefore, the representation of God presents more affinity with the mother figure than with the father figure because it is composed essentially of the fundamental factor of the mother figure.

The distance scores show that the semantic relations between the representation of God and each of the parental figures are not uniform for all the groups. In most of the cases, the distances between the representation of God and the parental figures are equivalent, but sometimes it is semantically closer to the father figure than the mother figure and sometimes it is semantically closer to the mother figure than the father figure.

The evidence shows first of all that God is represented as a complex unity holding the two parental dimensions in tension. Although, in Christian language, God is addressed as father, God is, just as well, a maternal figure in virtue of his immediate, available, and welcoming presence.

Not only is the representation of God more saturated in maternal qualities than the father, but these qualities also maintain their direct meanings. This peculiarity acquires its full meaning if it is considered in terms of human paternity. The father, in fact, is not truly father until he makes himself present by actually taking up the paternal role. God, on the contrary, is always present and unconditionally available. For the subjects studied, the biblical and Christian idea of paternal adoption by God is obliterated by the effect that it produces in religious awareness: the idea of a quasi-natural bond, resembling the vital and intimate bond with the mother. The contrast is considerable with the Hindu group (Chapter 5) as will be discussed further on.

The paternal dimension is no less pronounced in the representation of God, even if the paternal items are there less saturated than those of the maternal dimension. The factor law predominates in the paternal component of the representation of God. Logically, this is a contradiction and for this reason the logical term of 'synthesis' of opposites is avoided. What occurs is that the symbolic functions, which are differentiated in the familial structure, coincide in the same relational pole. At one and the same time, God is unconditionally available and the relation to him is conditioned by his paternal demands. This internal tension is present up to the point of a certain dissociation in the signification of the maternal items, which are there charged with references to the paternal function. In the commentary on the paternal functions, the signification that the parental bipolarity has for becoming was pointed out. The question now is if the internal tension in the representation of God and, as a consequence, in the religious relationship, is only the effect of an intellectual effort to gather into God all the qualities of humanness, or if this tension has its impact on religious becoming. Perhaps, it is not just a matter of intellectual desire to conceive of a divine absolute beyond human limits, but what is involved is that the internal tension in the representation of God is operative within lived religion. The items are, in fact, not metaphorical but rather are expressions of relational modalities. This question will be returned to later.

The less intense attribution to God of the more concrete items indicates that God is not conceived of as intervening contingently in the events of daily life, neither by his security giving presence, nor by his function of law and authority, nor by his dynamism and power. It is not to be concluded from this that the representation is reducible to an abstract philosophical concept. Certainly, the separation of God from the idea of punctual intervention could lead to the religious idea of a *Deus otiosus* (Eliade 1958). But it can just as well express a fundamental relationship that invests life and even affects it in its circumstantial aspects, without thereby interfering by particular initiatives. In other words, the relationship can be experienced as personal and singular without being particular.

The results of another study made in the Center for Religious Psychology (Vercruysse 1972) concur with these observations. Among the four factors derived by this study as constituant of the meaning of God for adults, that of presence is the most important. This factor is composed of three subfactors. First, the personal relationship to God implies that the human being is responsible before God for his/her activity in the world and that he/she has confidence that God will perfect what is done. There is a similarity here with the law factor. The second subfactor is that of presence as such, which is comparable to the unconditional availability of the maternal figure. The third and much less affirmed subfactor consists of the idea of a divine providence that intervenes helpfully in the vicissitudes of daily life. The three other factors of this study are not comparable to the results of the SDPS because they were derived from different scales (God as ultimate and inclusive truth and finality; the divine as a diffuse sacredness in the cosmos).

2.2 *Differences between the Groups*

Intercultural differences Distance analysis in Chapter 3 already shows certain differences that seem to be culturally based, even if the lack of perfect homogeneity of the groups imposes a degree of caution in their interpretation. Thus, in the Belgian-French groups, the mother figure is as close to the representation of God as is the father figure; in the maternal dimension, the maternal figure is even closer to the God figure than is the father figure in the paternal dimension. According to the factorial comparison of Chapter 4, another Belgian-French group is, moreover, the only one to attribute to God the peripheral factor feminity, which factor it also attributes, exceptionally, to the mother. Obviously, there is a transfer in the religious relationship of an affective relational quality that the culture has developed by esteeming a feminine ideal and that characterizes, from the beginning, maternal presence.

The Belgian-Dutch groups differ from their national partners in that their representation of God is mediated more by the maternal qualities of the father figure than by the paternal qualities of the father figure or the maternal qualities of the mother figure. Lacking factorial analysis for this study, we can only propose hypothetically that these groups accentuate in God that which is of the order of active protection.

The American group of Chapter 3 is clearly distinct from the others by its greater stress on the paternal dimension in God; this is also the only group for which the God figure is closer to the paternal figure in the paternal dimension than to the mother figure in the maternal dimension. This does not prevent this group from integrating maternal qualities into the God figure: the distance between the God figure and the two parental figures is the same for the entire item set. Furthermore, another American group (Chapter 4) is also exceptional as regards the parental figures as has been seen. This group attributes to God the peripheral factor of dynamism. The representation of God is thus specified there by the transfer to God of dominant values in the culture. In Chapter 7 an equivalent process is observed in another American group. The

Colombian group, which manifests a cultural resemblance to the American group as regards the parental figures, also shows this resemblance in its representation of God; it is the only group to attribute to God the peripheral factor of order, and also the only one to attribute it to both the father and mother figures.

The Zairians associate with the representation of God a secondary maternal factor that they attribute to the mother, and the Filipinos associate a paternal factor that is also peripheral in their maternal figure. An hypothesis of the maternal–divine signification that power takes on in the Filipino context has already been presented. In any case, for both of these groups, a cultural peculiarity of the maternal figure is characteristic also of the representation of God. In the Indonesian group, on the other hand, in contrast with a mother figure with distinct feminine qualities, it is the paternal peripheral factor of knowledge that is related to God. It is to be noted that intuition and knowledge differentiate the father and mother figures in the same order of knowing.

A general rule appears from these comparisons. The representation of God contains only one peripheral factor, which is always a factor that characterizes either the father or the mother. It must be concluded that, in its cultural specificity, the representation of God comes under the influence of the religious tradition and does not derive from individual psychology. That a parental factor mediated the differentiated representation of God arises from psychology. But it is the culture as bearer of a religious tradition that determines which components of the parental figures are attributed to God.

The belief groups and the religious group   The religious group is treated as a group apart because, in addition to their vocational option, these subjects give, in general, unique results on the SDPS. Particular attention will be given to the comparison between the belief and the religious groups since their contrasting results are puzzling.

Those who affirmed absolute belief placed significantly higher stress on the paternal items in the representation of God, and particularly on the function of law. In the maternal dimension, this group emphasized particularly a warm-hearted refuge, who is always ready with open arms, who is all-embracing, who takes a loving care of me, who gives comfort — thus secure and protective presence. Those who doubt showed preference for dynamism, intiative, and orientation toward the future, among the paternal items. These items are, moreover, preferred by the group that favors the maternal dimension in the representation of God. In the maternal series, on the other hand, the doubters stress the items intuition, who is intimate, who is always waiting for me. The degree of believing conviction thus modifies the rank order of the items. Those who believe absolutely relate to God according to his most specific paternal function and his active maternal presence. Those who doubt showed preference for dynamism, father and as patiently and intimately available like a mother.

The author of this study, Dirk Hutsebaut, suggests that the doubters experience the divine law as a menace to their autonomy with which they are shown to be quite preoccupied. This hypothesis is certainly supported by the greater stress these subjects place on practically all maternal items, reflecting a pronounced concern for security.

But what is the intrinsic bond between these choices in the parental dimensions and the faith conviction? Is it that doubt causes withdrawal in the face of the paternal exigency of God, or is it that religious affirmation of the divine law causes doubt? Or is there another element, not uncovered in this study, that is responsible for the correlation of these two elements? The fact that one's autonomy is experienced as menaced by divine law does not provide an answer, for this concern for autonomy is a psychological tendency that could derive from a multitude of factors. Considering the great complexity of the psychological elements involved and the long personal history from which doubt and the conflict between law and autonomy are always the result, it would be naive to attempt to specify a causative chain for the observed correlations. Nevertheless, it can be stated that those who affirm absolute belief do not perceive adhesion to the paternal God as being in opposition with their autonomy. They also insist on a protective maternal presence in God rather than on a maternal presence that is characterized by patience and affective intimacy. This perception of God recalls the results of a different study (Vercruysse 1972) according to which the most important factor in the idea of God is composed of two elements: the God before whom one is responsible and the God who is a personal presence. We would propose that convinced faith involves taking a personal position with respect to God, a position where confidence and acceptance of his law mutually support each other. In other words, as a personal relationship with a God recognized as personal, convinced faith harmonizes the paternal and maternal dimensions that remain unresolved for the doubting group. To account completely for these data, it would be necessary to analyze thoroughly the relations between law, guilt, and personal relationships (Vergote 1978).

One would expect that the religious group would react to the SDPS in the same way as the absolute believers. But instead, there are surprising differences between the results of these two groups. The religious, young and old, men and women, emphasize very strongly the maternal dimension in the representation of God and in the father figure, and more in the former than in the latter.

It is difficult to put the religious into the same category as the doubters though their SDPS results are similar. As Neff and Vannesse, the authors of this study, propose, it is my opinion that the life milieu of this group, stressing as it does the qualities of benevolent reception, partially explains these results. Certainly the spiritual climate of contemporary Catholicism also exercises particular influence over the religious. In fact, after having overstressed divine law and judgement, Catholicism is today emphasizing more the less dramatic elements of its doctrine in somewhat of a reaction against its recent past. Neff and Vannesse also rightly refer to depth psychology in their explanation. On the basis of the psychological profiles of the religious, which manifest a 'maternal attachment' more intense than is usual, the authors interpret their results on the SDPS as being essentially explainable by this psychological factor. As they say, this factor does not imply a particular bond with the mother on the biographical level of affectionate attachment. What is certainly involved, according to the Szondi psychological profiles, is archaic impregnation of the object of attachment that the mother represented at the origins of psychic life. Besides, among the religious of another study (Van Cottem 1977) only a small group idealized the mother and manifested a lack of affection or contempt for the father. These data seem to confirm the necessity of distinguishing, on the one hand, the affective bond with the mother and, on the other hand, the attachment with the object of desire of which the mother obviously constitutes the foundation and the archaic paradigm. How then to conceive of the transfer to God of the intense attachment to the primordial object? We are confronted here with a key question in psychology of religion. Only the cumulative experience of in-depth individual analyses will be able to provide some clarification.

Comparing the absolute believer group with the religious group, it is clear that, among subjects equally convinced of their faith, very personal factors can determine and differentiate the religious relationship and orient the representation of God in various directions.

Two different religions: Christianity and Hinduism   In the commentary on the father figure, it was noted that, for the Hindu group, the father clearly leaves the function of law to God. The very feeble presence of availability in the God of the Hindus is another radical difference from the God of the Christians.

These differences, taken together, lead to an explanation based on the difference between the two religions. To understand this difference, it is sufficient to recall that Jesus of Nazareth gave new content to the divine name of father (Marchel 1960; Jeremias 1966). Saint Paul (Rom. 8) bears witness to the transformation of religious consciousness that, following Jesus, addresses itself personally to God in saying 'Father'. In the Christian groups, the respectful intimacy that takes on and expresses the name of father given to God is shown in the stress on the maternal items, which have so little importance for the Hindu group.

The results from the Hindu group also provide an important indication of the influence of the religious tradition on the culture as it takes form in the family structure. The contrary hypothesis, which would have that the family and the culture alone can explain religion, seems improbable.

In the Hindu group the absence of semicongruence between the factors of the representation of God and those of the parental figures indicates that the parental figures apparently do not mediate the representation of God here. The divine law that arches over the society does not allow here for mediation by a father who himself is almost completely deprived of his function. Moreover, the absence of an affective bond with God obviously manifests much less dependence on maternal mediation.

The elderly   The group studied in Chapter 5 presents unique results, with the factor presence being by far the most important. With only this one study available, one can only hypothesize on the influence of advanced age. It could be that the absence of law as well as the substitution of presence for availability indicate a confident intimacy that is both beyond a confrontation with divine law and the need for a maternal bond. Probably a long life of religious faith forms in a tranquil conscience a personal presence that has a certain mystical tenor. This needs to be verified.

The pathological groups   The most important factor with the schizophrenics (receptivity–order) is a double factor, that is both paternal and maternal. Differing from the father figure, the representation of God thus includes here the law element, but in the modality of the one who exercises authority. The duality of this factor corresponds to the duality of the two primary factors attributed to the father. Thus, the double bind is reproduced in religion. One can recognize here the same fundamental uncertainty of the schizophrenics who experience themselves totally vulnerable to meanings that their internal contradiction renders unresolvable.

For the delinquents, the most important divine factor is familiarity–dynamism. In the comparison of this factor with the two
primary factors attributed to the mother (initiative and delicacy,
the latter being much less important), the impression is given that
the delinquents expect from God the affectionate maternal presence
that was frustrated in the relationship with the mother. Second, the
dynamism of the representation of God reproduces the initiative
attributed to the mother and lacking in the father. What is absent
in the representation of God as well as in the father figure is law.
Religion, therefore, does not compensate for the paternal deficiency
that determined their destiny.

2.3 *The Father Figure: The Most Adequate Symbol of God?*

Setting aside for the moment the important question of the specific
meaning that the divine name of father has acquired in the religion
founded by Jesus Christ, the discussion will be directed to the consideration of if and in what degree the representation of God as
mediated by the parental figures rests preferentially on the paternal
symbol. In addressing God, the subjects spontaneously employ the
name of father, which they inherited from the Christian tradition.
But is this name consonant with their representation of God? This
question is posed here within the limits defined by the present
problematic and by the instrument used to deal with it.

The scientific strategy of these studies requires us to answer the
question posed by distinguishing the different approaches.

The analyses of Chapter 3 indicate that, for the groups studied
there, the father figure better symbolizes God than does the mother
figure. In general, the father figure integrates the two parental
dimensions more completely than does the mother figure. This is
not because the representation of God contains more paternal
qualities than maternal, nor even because it is assigned the set of
items just as intensely as the father figure, it is because of the greater
simplicity of the maternal figure as opposed to the greater complexity of the father figure. This difference is equally apparent in

the high paternal distance scores between the mother figure and the representation of God. Nevertheless, the paternal dimension is structured differently in the representation of God than in the father figure. Law, authority, and knowledge are more intensely attributed to God than to the father, with the inverse being the case for dynamism, initiative, and systematic mind. Regarding the maternal dimension, it is structured in the same way in the representation of God as in the father figure, but differently in the mother figure. Tenderness, for example, is attributed to a high degree to the mother figure but is hardly present in the father figure and in the God figure.

Factorial analysis (Chapters 4 and 5) did not show a greater complexity of the paternal figure. On the contrary, it showed that the mother figure and the representation of God are composed of the same central factors present in the same order, availability and law, while the order is inverted in the father figure. It is to be noted that factor analysis also does not permit a decisive answer to the question under discussion here. The intensity of item attribution must still be taken into account.

Though factor analysis demonstrates a greater similarity between the representation of God and the mother figure concerning the nuclear factors, this phenomenon is nuanced, at least for the six groups of the intercultural study (Chapter 4), by the fact that four groups attribute only one peripheral factor to God, which is paternal. In addition, the factorial analysis done by Pasquali (Chapter 7) after adding a new item series, brought out a greater resemblance between the representation of God and the father figure.

The semantic analyses in Chapter 4 attest to a greater similarity between the representation of God and the signification of the paternal figure. While the paternal items, and particularly those that are related to law, imply a reference to the father in the maternal figure, when applied to God they maintain the same immediate signification that they have for the father figure. The paternal function is applied to God in the same direct and specific manner as to the father. In other words, one cannot attribute a paternal dimension to the mother without situating her in the parental couple while paternity is inherent in the representation of God as in the father figure.

The semantic distance scores between the representation of God and each of the parental figures are not uniform for the groups. Sometimes the representation of God is closer to the mother figure, sometimes closer to the father figure, and sometimes the distance is equal for both figures.

Even in the religious group, the exceptional saturation of God in maternal qualities and the exceptionally weak attribution of paternal items to the father and to God do not prevent this group from bringing God nearer to the father figure than to the mother figure in the paternal dimension.

The different technical approaches, therefore, do not give the same results. If one considers exclusively the factor analysis one would have to say that for all the Christian groups, the mother mediates the representation of God better than the father since the most important factor there is maternal. However, this does not permit the conclusion that the mother figure is the privileged symbol in the representation of God. The attribution scores reported in Chapter 3 place the representation of God nearer to the paternal figure. Semantic analysis reveals shifts of signification that factor analysis cannot measure. Even within the limits of this study there is thus no simple answer to the question of a privileged capacity for symbolization by one or the other parental figure. Disregarding the attribution scores, one must say that in some respects, the representation of God is more maternal than paternal and, in other respects, it is more paternal than maternal. And this precisely because, on the one hand, it is primarily characterized by availability and, on the other hand, law and authority pertain to it directly as they do to the father figure. But more refined methods are necessary to explain adequately the complex signification of the representation of God as it is constituted by the transposition of the parental qualities.

The presence of the respective parental items in the representation of God is, furthermore, not the same for all of the groups.

If it is considered that, in general, the paternal figure better symbolizes the representation of God, there is reason to say that some groups — the French-speaking Canadians (Chapter 5), the French-speaking Belgian females (Chapter 4), and both psychiatric groups (Chapter 6) — clearly prefer the maternal symbol. How to interpret this phenomenon? In any case, there is no question of a decisive option between two names for God. These subjects were not asked if they preferred to address God as father or as mother, leaving them the liberty to place God into one or the other sexual category. They composed their representation of God with parental qualities that they had first discriminated. Certainly, it could be that these groups were reluctant to sanction an apparent paternal privilege and that, in consequence, their responses express a more positive appreciation of the maternal dimension than is encountered elsewhere. Another explanation, which could be linked to the preceding, is also possible. What is known of the revolution that has occurred in religious orientation seems to imply that the references that risk evoking a guilt-causing law are avoided, and that, in reaction to a moral and religious style characterized by paternal demands, maternal values of sensible contact and affectionate benevolence are sought.

From the elements making up the SDPS, one must conclude that the religious relationship is not the same if the maternal symbol or the paternal symbol dominates. There is no doubt that the lived religious content is different in the two cases. In addition, the study comparing the more fervent believers and the doubters (Chapter 5) indicates that the difference in semantic content correlates with the difference in the degree of faith assent. Obviously, it is necessary to verify further what was observed in this study. The following are the essential points. There is a correlation between faith conviction and the proportional stress on items in the representation of God that are considered, by this group, as the most specifically paternal: law, direction, decision. The less one is assured of one's faith, the more one emphasizes the other paternal qualities: dynamism, initiative, orientation towards the future. For the doubters, these latter items express a kind of divine power, diffuse and immanent, that favors the initiative, rendering the individual more involved in the future. In other words, these subjects perceive these items more from their own point of view than from the point of view of a God who takes real and active initiative. Those who believe more strongly are also those for whom God is more maternal in a relationship of protective presence that reflects concern for the other. In contrast, the others stress more the maternal items of intimacy and who is always there.

The preference accorded to the paternal symbol is therefore not a matter of a greater love for the father than for the mother or of a sociological or sexist prejudice, at least not in this group. Certainly, the fact that those who believe more strongly give clearer preference to the paternal symbol could lead one to think that they accept more docilely the religious tradition and also maintain the traditional attitudes about the power of the father. But with regard to the meaning of the items, both paternal and maternal, that are stressed by the believer group, such an interpretation is not justified. The firmest believers see the relationship with God as being clearly more personal in both the maternal and the paternal dimensions. For this group, God is simultaneously law and active maternal presence. The results from the less convinced believers show a God who is rather an impersonal dynamism and a being with whom one has a distant affective contact, an object towards which is directed a vague nostalgia for intimacy. The study on the meaning of God cited above (Vercruysse 1972) showed that the factor of personal presence is composed essentially of the sense of responsibility before God, of the confidence that he will bring human enterprises to a good end, and of the sense of dialogical presence. From this it is seen that the sense of responsibility, which corresponds to paternal law, is a constitutive element of the faith in a God who is personal because he is qualified by his paternal function. And it is significant that, in this personal relationship, confidence is also placed on the protective maternal concern of God.

The preference of the paternal symbol for the symbolization of God seems therefore to have a properly religious sense. It structures the religious relationship in a specific manner. For religious becoming, the reference to divine paternity has a capacity for structuration analogous to that which the paternal function accomplishes in the family constellation. The child is situated in the presence of two different and conjoint poles that correspond to two essential elements of his becoming: the desire to be unconditionally loved and accepted and the paternal law and promise that calls him to assume his responsibility, to orient himself toward his personal future in extrafamilial society. In an analogous manner, the divine law introduces the exigency of accepting responsibility along with the religious desire for confident intimacy. If the father symbolizes God better than does the mother, it is thus because of that which the paternal law effects in the family triangle. To call God mother would be to eliminate from religion one of its fundamental components.

Some would hold that the paternal metaphor for God derives from sexist prejudice (Daly 1973; Russell 1974) and perceive it as a prolongation and comfirmation by religion of the privileged power role that men have in contemporary society. The reports on masculine domination, however, forget the affective power that pertains to the mother and, in particular, underestimate the extent to which the paternal metaphor is derived from the function of the father who, for the child, is the transitional figure between the family cell and the society of responsible adults. The terms father and mother have symbolic meanings that, while being supported by the consequences of the sexual difference, depend on a different order.

The limits of these studies on the religious sense of the paternal symbol must be noted. Linguistics and the philosophy of language have given us a keen awareness of them. A word takes on its meaning in the entirety of its context. Now, it should be evident for those familiar with Christianity that the essential element of the Christian message about divine paternity is not present in the SDPS. That which Christianity proposes about divine paternity is too complex to be contained in a few simple and nonambiguous statements. Nor do we see how this fundamental element can be incorporated into a semantic scale. According to the foundational texts of Christianity, which have been taken up, amplified, and elaborated into highly varied conceptual systems, God accomplished his paternity by means of an historical initiative. In giving his own divine glory to Jesus of Nazareth, who was predestined to this divinization, God claims him as his son. At the same time, he fully fulfills and manifests his paternity. Via Jesus, to whom God conferred divine filiation in its plenitude, believing Christians also participate in this divine filiation and can address themselves to God saying, in an unprecedented way, Father.

In a psychological study, it is essential to recognize the religious context within which the subjects are situated. This does not imply that they completely take up the faith proposed to them and to which they try more or less to adhere. The degree to which the subjects have personally appropriated this faith is not known. To learn this, it would not have been sufficient to pose a few simple questions on the content of their faith, as is too often done in investigations on this subject. Simple responses to questions on the content of beliefs do not permit appraisal of the degree of interior assimilation of that content. The distance can be more or less great between the verbal acceptance of the Christian message and the real and personal transformation in the sense of the paternal metaphor. On the other hand, cultural anthropology (Evans-Pritchard 1962; Needham 1972; Douglas 1973) has shown that religion is a symbolic, cultural, and linguistic practice in which the words are charged with connotations of which the subject is not totally conscious in a reflexive way.

The SDPS, therefore, cannot register the personal faith in regard to that which is the most essential to the Christian idea of divine paternity: the paternal act by which God accomplishes his paternity. The paternity of the Christian God resembles in this way human paternity. This must be insisted upon: the father must accept his paternity. This signification of human paternity has also not been directly measured, but it has been referred to because it permits a better interpretation of the semantic content that designates the paternal function. And also for the representation of God, the SDPS only measures the representational content, which does not express the paternal act of the Christian God. It can be presumed that, to varying degrees that are not measurable here, the subjects of these studies relate to God as he is proposed to them by the message of their Christian religion. The divine name of Father, then, derives from the Christian message a surplus of signification that goes beyond the symbolization studied here. It is our opinion, nevertheless, that the concrete form of this symbolization contributes an essential part to the Christian meaning of Father. It is difficult to separate completely the representational content from the faith reference. The correlations observed between the believing groups and the representation of God furnish an indication of this bond.

2.4 *Symbolization, That which Animates the Paternal Metaphor*

We return to the complex, variable, and multiple determination of the paternal metaphor by which the Christian subjects orient themselves to God. Whatever may be the content attributed to the divine name given to them by the Christian tradition, the process of the symbolization of God by the parental figures must be examined. And to do this, the 'paternal metaphor' will be discussed, it being understood that symbolization by the maternal figure is included in this term.

The SDPS studies lead, first of all, to the conclusion that, when attributed to God, the word 'father' keeps its proper sense and that it does not designate God by derived predication as Kant held (1960). It is not the image of the father that permits an imaginary representation of God. 'Father' signifies a function in a structured intersubjective relationship; the person is so named insofar as his position in the relational order designates him rightfully as clothed with the paternal function. In the religious relationship, God assumes this function in the strict sense. To speak of a paternal metaphor with respect to God, therefore, implies that, based on the recognition of the symbolic paternal function in the human order, the name of father is applied to God to designate him as being father in this strict sense. It is assumed, obviously, that the one who gives God this name also gives the term its precise signification.

In one sense, the name of father is addressed even more properly to God than to the paternal figure. It has been shown that the characteristics that appear as the most specifically paternal — those of law, authority, judge — are generally more attributed to God than to the father. In another sense, nevertheless, the divine name of father is a metaphor because of a surplus of content in the representation of God, namely, the maternal dimension. Still, as this dimension is also constitutive of the paternal figure, be it to a very minor degree and metaphorically, the divine name of father is not a derived predication.

Our semantic data contain evidence for the psychological interpretation of the representation of God and of the religion related to it. It may be assumed that psychological processes sustain and motivate the relationship to a God who is called Father in the sense delineated here, otherwise religion would remain excluded from the affective life. The whole tenor of our results makes this highly improbable however.

There seems to be no psychological theory that could account for our observations regarding the representation of God. The Freudian theories are the most famous and, in our opinion, they are the only ones that have made a real attempt to explain paternal religion by psychological processes. Nevertheless, as far as our observations are concerned, they seem to be full of gaps. The explanation proposed by Freud in *The Future of an Illusion* (1943) collects, structures, and tries to justify the vague and wandering explanations that run through the idea of a 'projection' based on needs. But the theme of nostalgia for the father that Freud develops in this book does not take into account two essential elements that we have isolated. On the one hand, the father as described by Freud is only the one who responds to the demands for help caused by the distresses and frustrations of life. According to the studies we have reported, it is by his very presence that God responds to desire, like the mother who is the prototype of personalized desire. On the other hand, the father figure proposed by Freud lacks the specifically paternal function, i.e., that which does not correspond to illusory desires, but which obliges the acceptance of responsibility. Freud himself recognized that his popularized psychological work did not do justice to the signification of paternity that his psychological theories powerfully illustrated. Therefore, his last work on religion took another direction. In *Moses and Monotheism* (1939), Freud intended to restore fully the paternal function. It even appeared to Freud to be so contrary to the illusory image created by disappointed needs, that he considered that humanity needed a long history of spiritual renunciation for divine paternity to be truly recognized. Thus, the psychology of the individual no longer explains paternal religion. Freud brings up the subconscious guilt for the murder — hypothetical — of the primitive father. But how can this barbarian monster without faith or law be the origin of paternal law? Moreover, in the description given by Freud, paternal law is always simply the expression of the struggle waged by the father to safeguard his unique position. It is not a function that structures a symbolic relationship. Freud also considers Christianity as the elimination of the father by substitution of the son. The father of *Moses and Monotheism* (1939) is a father without the bond of paternity, a father who does not become father in recognizing his children, a unidimensional father who renders impossible the cohabitation in God of the differentiated paternal and maternal poles.

No psychological hypothesis will be constructed here to account for the origin of paternal religion. We are convinced that any hypothesis explaining this origin either presupposes what it would explain or rests on the reduction, a priori, of the phenomenon studied to a ridiculous artifact. We have tried to understand how the representation of God is formed by the subjects of our studies. From all evidence, there is an encounter between a religious message and psychological structures. The representation of God is not invented, it is received. But one encounters the religious message with one's own psychology and one's own cultural symbols. The pathological groups prove that, in the absence of the parental references constituted in their symbolic signification, the name of father given to God does not have the meaning that the received religion proposes. The results from the religious groups and the differences between the cultural groups also show that the believers appropriate in a particular way the content of the name of father derived from the same religious tradition.

The psychological formation of the personality within the familial constellation occurs under the aegis of parents who correspond to their respective symbolic positions. By this formation, the names of father and mother take on the signification that continues to structure the personality. In the cases where the parental figures are not formed as symbolic references, their absence is responsible for an essential lack that destructures the personality. Entrance into the religious relationship as it is specified in Christianity by the divine name of father presupposes the psychological formation of the parental symbolic figures, for the modes of relationship offered by this religion are the same. From the psychological point of view, the divine name of father is thus indeed a metaphor: its effective recognition is motivated by a complex mode of relations already psychologically constituted. Nevertheless, the transfer to God of the name of father responds to the invocation of religious language. Its signifying power and the psychological motivation of the individual conjoin.

APPENDIX I: SOME DEVELOPMENTAL CHARACTERISTICS OF THE PARENTAL FIGURES AND THE REPRESENTATION OF GOD *by Hervé Coster*

1 INTRODUCTION

The genesis and early development of the parental figures and the representation of God has yet to be the object of rigorous empirical research. An exploratory study in this area has been conducted and what follows is a synthesis of the results. Because this is merely an exploratory study, these results must be approached with a maximum degree of caution and all the more so because the method used does not guarantee sufficient control of the variables considered.

2 METHOD

2.1 *Sample*

The sample was composed of 300 boys and girls ranging from 6 to 11 years old. They were all French-speaking Belgians from stable homes of the middle socioeconomic level.

2.2 *Procedure*

The small group interview technique was used. The 300 children were separated into 60 groups of five children each according to age, scholastic year, and sex. All the interviews were taped and later transcribed. The objective of the interviews was to clarify, in turn, the children's perception of the father, mother, and God figures. The instructions were standardized and adapted to the different age levels of the children (6–7, 8–9, and 10–11). After the presentation of the stimulus figure, the children were allowed to speak spontaneously without substantive interference, intervention being limited to coordinating the reactions. In the second session, a series of qualities was introduced into the discussion and it was asked if these qualities occupied an important place in the description of the figure under consideration. This series of qualities was derived from preliminary interviews based on items from the SDPS with 52 children from six to eleven years old.

The reactions of the children to each stimulus figure were placed in four categories:

(1)   the qualities that received spontaneous approval by all the children of the group without any intervention on the part of the interviewer;

(2)   the qualities that emerged later in the course of the interviews, either spontaneously or indirectly, following the remarks or questions of the interviewer;

(3)   the qualities that were specifically presented for the judgement of the children and that met with obvious approval;

(4)   the qualities introduced by the interviewer and that received only a weak response.

3 RESULTS

3.1 *The Parental Figures*

The perception of the parental figures seems to develop in two phases:

— During the first phase (from six to eight years old), the parents are perceived essentially as persons revolving around the child and being attentive to his immediate needs and desires.

— During the second (from nine to eleven years old), the parents are perceived fundamentally as models and guides for the future.

The six to eight year olds   The child of from six to eight years old sees the father and mother as fundamentally attached to himself: they care for him, encompass him, protect him, and are near him as he plays and does other things. In short, the child perceives them as those who guarantee basic security. They are, therefore, indispensable.

There is one important sexual difference in the perception of the father that must be stressed: the father is perceived as being more distant, more of a 'stranger' than the mother. The boys perceive this characteristic of the paternal figure differently than do the girls. For the boys, this paternal 'distance' is seen exclusively on the level of the principal activity of the father: his work removes him from the daily life of the child and involves him in a relatively unknown and alien universe. The girls perceive this paternal characteristic more fundamentally: the father is seen to be distant not only on the level of the separation caused by his work, but also on the level of his sexual otherness.

The nine to eleven year olds   The children from nine to eleven years old perceive the father fundamentally as a model to be imitated and as the one who orients towards the future. The mother is seen principally in terms of relational qualities, though the girls also stress here the dimension of model to be imitated.

3.2   *The Representation of God*

In the development of the representation of God, two phases can be identified that correspond rather well to the phases observed for the parental figures.

The six to eight year olds   For the child from six to eight years old, God is a being preoccupied with him: God gives him things by placing everything at the child's disposal and by giving to each one what is asked for; God is tolerant, kind, and protective. These are, of course, the dimensions that the child would particularly like to find in his parents and that define God as a being who is fundamentally near.

God is described repeatedly as 'master of the world', as 'creator and master of the whole earth'. This transcendence, this going beyond the small universe of the child, is perceived by the boys primarily on the level of action, of 'power', of 'the ability to do'. And the authority of God over the world originates in this 'ability to do'. The boys are impressed by God's extraordinary power of intervention in the world. This intervening power of God (principally in the act of creation) seems to have the same importance in the representation of God as work has in the father figure. Indeed, this analogy was offered by the boys themselves, who spontaneously compared divine action with the work of the father.

The girls, on the other hand, perceive this 'transcendence' more on the level of the person of God. God is master of the world because of his grandeur, his majesty. And this grandeur implies a relational aspect: God protects us, God loves us because he created the world. As mentioned above, the girls also perceived this relational dimension in the father's work: 'he goes to work to earn money because he loves us very much'.

The nine to eleven year olds   Around the age of nine, the child insists strikingly on the educative aspect of the representation of God, as he does for the parental figures. And the two poles, which distinguished the parental figures, are reunited in a structuring tension.

On the one hand, God is perceived as someone who 'shows the child what he must do', as someone who 'punishes or approves his behavior' and who 'tells him what to do'. It seems to be significant that the majority of the comparisons made between God and the father bear precisely on these points. These comparisons clearly state that, while these qualities are shared by the father and God, God realizes them in a superior manner: 'the intentions of God are more spiritual', 'his words are heard from within', 'he does not limit himself to the appearances, he knows the intentions', 'his criticisms are calmer and always right', 'his punishment is just and not direct'.

On the other hand, God is also described as being open to the child, available, comforting, trusting, considerate: in short, all the relational qualities that were found in the mother figure of the children of this age group.

Therefore, there seems to be an analogy of structure between the parental world and the representation of God. This analogy is not confined to the level of the structures themselves, but appears also in the evolution of the structures as the child grows older and in the different perceptions that the boys and girls have of them.

APPENDIX II: THE MATERNAL AND PATERNAL ITEMS IN ENGLISH, FRENCH, DUTCH, SPANISH, AND ITALIAN

Maternal items

The one who is most patient	patience	geduldig	paciencia	pazienza
A warm-hearted refuge	refuge	toevlucht	abrigo donde se encuentra la quietud	rifugio
Who takes loving care of me	qui prend soin de	zorgend	quien cuida	che ha cura costante
Who will sympathize with the child's sorrows	partage les peines de l'enfant	deelt de zorgen van het kind	comparte las penas del hijo	condivide le pene del figlio
Tenderness	tendresse	teder	ternura	tenerezza
Who is intimate	intimité	intimiteit	intimidad	intimità
Who gives comfort	qui apaise	helend	quien apacigua	che rasserena
Who is always ready with open arms	toujours disponible	dienend	siempre disponible	sempre disponibile
Who brings out which is delicate and refined	fait apparaître ce qui est délicat	ontdekt het tere	hace aparecer las cosas delicadas	delicatezza
Close to whom one feels at home	auprès de qui l'on se sent chez soi	geborgenheid	a cuyo lado uno se siente bien	vicino al quale ti senti a proprio agio
Self-giving love	don	mild	don de si	che dona e si dona
Sensitive	qui ressent profondément les choses	diep aanvoelend	siente profundamente las cosas	profondamente sensibile
Who welcomes me with open arms	qui accueille	ontvangend	quien acoge	accogliente
Who is always waiting for me	qui est attente	wachtend .	siempre a la espera	che ti attende sempre
Intuition	intériorité	innerlijkheid	interioridad	interiorità
Who is all-embracing	qui m'entoure	omringt mij	quien me rodea con su amor	che mi circonda di affetto
Charming	qui est toujours là	altijd daar	siempre presente	sempre vigilante
Warmth	vous laisse être 'enfant'	laat u 'kind' zijn	intuicion	ti ama quale sei

Paternal items

Strength	force	kracht	fuerza	forza
Power	puissance	macht	el poder	potenza
Who gives the directions	qui dirige	bestuurt	quien dirige	che dirige
Systematic mind	intelligence qui ordonne les choses	ordenend verstand	inteligencia organizadora	intelligenza organizzatrice
Who is the principle, the rule	norme	norm	norma	principio e norma
Who takes the initiative	initiative	initiatief	quien toma la iniciativa	che prende l'iniziativa
The one who has the knowledge	le savoir	kennis	el saber	il sapere
Authority	autorité	gezag	la autoridad	autorità
The one who acts	qui agit	presteert	quien actúa	che agisce
Who makes the decisions	qui décide	die beslist	quien decide	che prende le decisioni
Firmness	fermeté	onwankelbaar	firmeza	fermezza
The judge	juge	rechter	juez	giudice
Dynamic	dynamisme	dynamisch	dinamismo	dinamismo
The one who maintains order	qui maintient l'ordre	handhaaft de orde	mantiene el orden	che stabilisce l'ordine
Who gives the law	qui donne la loi	wetgever	cuya palabra es ley	che detta legge
Stern	sévère	streng	severo	severità
Who examines things	qui examine	onderzoekt	quien investiga	che prende in esame le cose
Protection against danger	qui oriente vers l'avenir	richt op de toekomst	orienta hacia el futuro	che orienta verso l'avvenire

APPENDIX III: SOURCES OF THE ATTRIBUTES USED IN
CONSTRUCTING THE SDPS

Bachelard, G. (1958). *La psychanalyse du feu*. Paris: Gallimard.
– (1959). *L'air et les songes. Essai sur l'imagination du mouvement*. Paris: Corti.
– (1960). *L'eau et les rêves. Essai sur l'imagination de la matière*. Paris: Corti.
Bachofen, J.J. (1897). *Das Mutterrecht. Eine Untersuchung über die Gynaikokratie des alten Welt nach ihrer religiösen und rechtlichen Natur*. Basel: Denno Schwabe.
Baur, F. (ed.). (1943). *Guido Gezelle's dichtwerken*. Antwerpen: Standaard.
Bitter, W. (1954) Eröffnungsansprache. In *Vorträge über das Vaterproblem in Psychotherapie, Religion und Gesellschaft, W. Bitter (ed.)*, Stuttgart: Hippokrates.
– (1954b). Die Vaterübertragung in der Psychotherapie. In *Vorträge über das Vaterproblem in psychotherapie, Religion und Gesellschaft, W. Bitter (ed.)*, Stuttgart: Hippokrates.
Bopp, L. (1962). *Zeige uns den Vater. Christliches Vatertum und seine Leitbilder*. Freiburg: Herder.
Bovet, P. (1951). *Le sentiment religieux et la psychologie de l'enfant*. Neuchâtel: Delachaux et Niestlé.
Buytendijk, F.J.J. (1962). *De vrouw. Haar natuur, verschijning en bestaan, een existentieel-psychologische studie*. Utrecht: Spectrum.
De Beauvoir, S. (1949). *Le deuxième sexe*. Paris: Gallimard.
Debesse, M. (1960–1961). Le rôle du père dans l'éducation. *Bulletin Psychologique* 14, 408–414; 770–774.
De Meester, P. (1947). *De vader*. Brussels: Desclée.
Deutsch, H. (1948). *Psychologie der Frau*. Bern: Huber.
Eliade, M. (1944). *Traité d'histoire des religions*. Paris: Payot.
Fluegel, J.C. (1950). *The Psycho-Analytic Study of the Family*. London: The Hogarth Press.

Freud, S. (1921). *Massenpsychologie und Ich-Analyse.* Gesammelte Werke, vol. 13, 71--161.

— (1923). *Das Ich und das Es.* Gesammelte Werke, vol. 13, 235–289.

— (1939). *Der Mann Moses und die Monotheistische Religion.* Gesammelte Werke, vol. 16, 101–246.

Geist, W. (1954). Das Vaterproblem in der psychotherapeutischen Praxis. In *Vorträge über das Vaterproblem in Psychotherapie, Religion und Gesellschaft,* W. Bitter (ed.), 26–43. Stuttgart, Hippokrates.

Gelber, L. and Romaeus, P. (eds.) (1964). *Werken van Edith Stein,* vol. 2. Utrecht: Desclée.

Gijsen, M. (1948). *Het huis.* The Hague: Stols.

Godin, A. (1963a). *Le Dieu des parents et le Dieu des enfants.* Tournai: Casterman.

— (1963b). *La relation humaine dans le dialogue pastoral.* Bruges: Desclée De Brouwer.

Groeger, G.N. (1958). Das Liebesbedürfnis der Heranwachsenden. *Unsere Jugend* 10, 275–281.

Haendler, O. (1954). Unbewusste Projektionen auf das christliche Gottvaterbild und ihre seelsorgerliche Behandlung. In *Vorträge über das Vaterproblem in Psychotherapie, Religion und Gesellschaft,* W. Bitter (ed.), 187–212. Stuttgart: Hippokrates.

Hart de Ruyter, Th. (1959). *De vader van het kind.* Nijkerk: Callenbach.

Hesse, H. (1962). *Narziss und Goldmund.* Frankfurt: Fischer.

Hollenbach, J.M. (1958-1959). Die Rechtsgrundlagen der Vaterautorität. *Stimmen der Zeit* 164, 453–461.

— (1959). Entwurzelte Vaterschaft. *Geist und Leben* 32, 34–38.

Jung, C.G. (1928). *Die Beziehungen zwischen dem Ich und dem Unbewussten.* Darmstadt: Reichl.

— (1944). *Psychologie und Alchemie.* Zürich: Rascher.

— (1950). *Seelenprobleme der Gegenwart.* Zürich: Rascher.

— (1952). *Symbole der Wandlung. Analyse des Vorspiels zu einer Schizophrenie.* Zürich: Rascher.

— (1954). *Von den Wurzeln des Bewusstseins. Studien über den Archtypus.* Zürich: Rascher.

Kafka, F. (1962). *Brief an den Vater.* Munich: Piper.

Kardiner, A. (1947). *The Individual and his Society. The Psychodynamics of Primitive Social Organization.* New York: Columbia University Press.

Kittel, G. (1954). *Theologisches Wörterbuch zum neuen Testament* vol. 5. Stuttgart: Kohlhammer.

Koeberle, D.A. (1954). Vatergott, Väterlichkeit und Vaterkomplex im christlichen Glauben. In *Vorträge über das Vaterproblem in Psychotherapie, Religion und Gesellschaft,* W. Bitter (ed.), 14–26. Stuttgart: Hippokrates.

Kriekemans, A. (1958). *Gezinspaedagogiek.* Antwerp: Nederlandse Boekhandel.

Malinowski, B. (1927). *The Father in Primitive Psychology.* London: Kegan-Trench-Trubner.

Marcel, G. (1944). Le voeu créateur comme essence de la paternité. In *Homo Viator,* G. Marcel (ed.), 135–170. Paris: Aubier.

Maurois, A. (1934). *L'institut du bonheur. Oeuvres complètes,* vol. 2. Paris: Fayard.

Mead, M. (1949). *Male and Female.* New York: Morrow.

Michel, E. (1954). Das Vaterproblem heute in soziologischer Sicht. In *Vorträge über das Vaterproblem in Psychotherapie, Religion und Gesellschaft,* W. Bitter (ed.), 44–74. Stuttgart: Hippokrates.

Murdock, G.P. (1949). *Social Structure.* New York: Macmillan.

Murray, H.A. and Morgan, C.D. (1945). A clinical study of sentiments: II. *Genetic Psychology Monographs* 32, 153–311.

Neumann, E. (1949). *Ursprungsgeschichte des Bewusstseins.* Zürich: Rascher.

Oraison, M. (1957). *Amour ou contrainte. Quelques aspects psychologiques de l'éducation religieuse.* Paris: Spes.

Perrin, A. (1956). *Le Père.* Paris: René Julliard.

Porot, M. (1963). *L'enfant et les relations familiales.* Paris, P.U.F.

Ranke, B. (ed.) (1960). *Mijn moeder was een heilige vrouw. Vlaamse moederlyriek.* Hasselt: Heideland.

Rogers, C.R. and Kinget, M. (1960). *Psychotherapie en menselijke verhoudingen. Theorie en praktijk van de non-direktieve therapie.* Antwerp: Standard.

Rosenberg, A. (1954). Die Gestalt und Entstaltung des Vaters. In *Vorträge über das Vaterproblem in Psychotherapie, Religion und Gesellschaft*, W. Bitter (ed.), 138–171. Stuttgart: Hippokrates.

Rouzic, L. (1927). *Le Père*. Paris: P. Tèqui.

Rustoew, A. (1954). Autorität und Freiheit. In *Vorträge über das Vaterproblem in Psychotherapie, Religion und Gesellschaft*, W. Bitter (ed.), 172–183. Stuttgart: Hippokrates.

Speck, O. (1958). Kinder brauchen auch den Vater. *Unsere Jugend* 10, 269–275.

Trier, J. (1947). Vater. Versuch einer Etymologie. *Zeitschrift der Savigny-Stiftung für Rechtsgeschichte. Germanische Abteilung* 65, 232–260.

Trilles, H. (1933). *Les Pygmées de la forêt équatoriale*. Paris: P.U.F.

Van Benthem Jutting, W. (1959). *Onderzoek naar het vaderschap. Het vaderschap als ethisch en godsdienstig vraagstuk*. Arnhem: Van Loghum Slaterus.

Van den Berg, J.H. (1958). *Dubieuze liefde in de omgang met het kind*. Nijkerk: Callenbach.

Van der Kerken, L. (1962). *Menselijke liefde en vriendschap*. Antwerp: Patmos.

Van der Leeuw, G. (1948). *La religion dans son essence et ses manifestations. Phénoménologie de la religion*. Paris: Payot.

Van de Woestijne, K. (1903). *Het Vader-huis*. Amsterdam: L.V. Veen.

Vergote, A. (1962–1963). Grondige studie van vraagstukken uit de godsdienstpsychologie. Unpublished course, Faculty of Psychology, Louvain.

Von le Fort, G. (1934). *Die ewige Frau. Rede über die Bestimmung des Weiblichen*. Munich: Kösel and Pustet.

Westermarck, E. (1891). *The History of Human Marriage*. London: Macmillan.

Wiechert, E. (1934). *Der Todeskandidat. La femme morte. Der Vater. Drei Erzählungen*. Munich: A. Langen and G. Müller.

References

Alanen, Y.O. (1958). The mothers of schizophrenic patients. *Acta Psychiatrica Neurologica Scandinava* 33, suppl. 124, 1-361.

Allport, G. (1953). *The Individual and his Religion. A Psychological Interpretation*. New York: Macmillan.

Anzieu, D. (1973). *Les méthodes projectives*. Paris: P.U.F.

Ariès, Ph. (1960). *L'enfant et la vie familiale sous l'Ancien Régime*. Paris: Plon.

Arieti, S. (1955). *Interpretation of Schizophrenia*. New York: Robert Bruner.

Balestrieri, I. (1974). Couples et images symboliques du père, de la mère et de Dieu. Unpublished manuscript, University of Louvain.

Bandura, A. (1969). Social-learning theory of identificatory processes. In *Handbook of Socialization Theory and Research*, D.A. Goslin (ed.). New York: Rand McNally.

Bandura, A. and Walters, R.H. (1959). *Adolescent Aggression*. New York: Ronald Press.

Barton, K. and Cattell, H. (1972). Personality characteristics of female psychology, science and arts majors. *Psychological Reports* 31, 807-813.

Bateson, G., Jackson, D.D., Haley, J. and Weakland, J. (1956). Towards a theory of schizophrenia. *Behavioral Science* 1, 251-264.

-- (1963). A note on the double bind – 1962. *Family Process* 2, 154-161.

Beakel, N.G. and Mehrabian, A. (1969). Inconsistent communications and psychopathology. *Journal of Abnormal Psychology* 74, 126-130.

Beavers, W.R., Blumberg, S., Timken, K.R. and Weiner, M.F. (1965). Communication patterns of mothers of schizophrenics. *Family Process* 4, 95-104.

Benedict, R. (1953). *Patterns of Culture*. New York: Mentor.

Berger, A. (1965). A test of the double bind hypothesis of schizophrenia. *Family Process* 4, 198-205.

Bergounioux, F.M. and Goetz, J. (1958). *Les religions des préhistoriques et des primitifs*. Paris: Fayard.

Bernardi, G. (1972). Les images symboliques du père, de la mère et l'image de Dieu: Une étude différentielle sur une population italienne. Unpublished manuscript, University of Louvain.

Bettelheim, B. (1969). *The Children of the Dream*. New York: Macmillan.

Bonami, M. (1966). Le symbole du père et de la mère dans l'image de Dieu. Unpublished manuscript, University of Louvain.

Bossard, J.H.S. and Boll, E.S. (1956). *The Large Family System: An Original Study in the Sociology of Family Behavior*. Philadelphia: University of Pennsylvania Press.

Bovet, P. (1951). *Le sentiment religieux et la psychologie de l'enfant*. Neuchâtel: Delachaux et Niestlé.

Bowen, M.A. (1960). A family concept of schizophrenia. In *The Etiology of Schizophrenia*, D.D. Jackson (ed.). 295-320. New York: Basic Books.

Bowlby, J. (1947). *Forty-four Juvenile Thieves. Their Characters and Home-Life*. London: Bailliere, Tindall and Cox.
– (1951). *Maternal Care and Mental Health*. New York: Columbia University Press.
– (1969, 1973). *Attachment and Loss*. 2 vols. London: Hogarth.
Bowlby, J., Ainsworth, M.D., Boston, H. and Rosenbuth, M.D. (1956). The effects of mother–child separation: A follow-up study. *British Journal of Medical Psychology* 29, 211–215.
Brenton, M. (1967). *The American Male*. New York: Fawcett World Library.
Cassiers, L. (1968). *Le psychopathe délinquant*. Brussels: Dessart.
Cheek, F.E. (1964). The 'Schizophrenogenic Mother' in word and deed. *Family Process*, 3, 155–177.
Cheek, F.E. (1965). The father of the schizophrenic, the function of a peripheral role. *Archives of General Psychiatry* 13, 336–345.
Christensen, H.T. (ed.) (1964). *Handbook of Marriage and the Family*. Chicago: Rand McNally.
Clausen, J.A. and Kohn, M.L. (1960). Social relations and schizophrenia: A research report and a perspective. In *The Etiology of Schizophrenia*, 295–320. New York: Basic Books.
Cleckley, H. (1964). *The Mask of Sanity*. St. Louis: Mosby.
Cooley, W.W. and Lohnes, P.R. (1971). *Multivariate Data Analysis*. New York: Wiley.
Corin, E. (1972). Repères oedipiens et structure familiale. Problème de psychanalyse. *Recherches et Débats* 78, 99–114.
Coster, H. (1972). Images parentales chez les enfants de 6 à 12 ans. Unpublished manuscript, University of Louvain.
– (1973). Structure génétique de l'image divine dans son rapport aux images parentales. Unpublished manuscript, University of Louvain.
Craig, M.M. and Glick, S.J. (1965). *A Manual of Procedures for Applications of the Glueck Prediction Table*. London: University of London Press.
Daly, M. (1973). *Beyond God the Father*. Boston: Beacon Press.
Davies, M. and Sinclair, I. (1971). Families, hostels and deliquents: An attempt to assess cause and effect. *British Journal of Criminology* 11, 213–229.
Deconchy, J.P. (1967). *Structure génétique de l'idée de Dieu chez des catholiques français*. Brussels: Lumen Vitae.
Deri, S. (1949). *Introduction to the Szondi-Test*. New York: Grune and Stratton.
De Saussure, F. (1955). *Cours de linguistique générale*. Paris: P.U.F.
Desjardins, L. and Tamayo, A. (1976). Imagenes del padre, de la madre y de la Divinidad en los Cristianos y en los Hindues. Paper read at the XVI Inter-American Congress of Psychology, Miami Beach, Florida.

Despert, J.L. (1951). Some considerations relating to the genesis of autistic behavior in children. *American Journal of Orthopsychiatry* 21, 335–350.
Dolto, F. (1939). *Psychanalyse et pédiatrie*. Paris: Amedée Legrand.
– (1971). *Le cas Dominique*. Paris: Seuil.
Douglas, M. (1973). *Natural Symbols*. London: Barrie and Jenkins.
Eliade, M. (1958). *Patterns in Comparative Religion*. London: Sheed and Ward.
– (1966–1967) Australian religions. *History of Religions*, 6, 108–134; 208–235.
– (1967–1968) Australian religions. *History of Religions* 7, 61–90; 159–183; 244–268.
– (1976). *Histoire des croyances et des idées religieuses*. Paris: Payot.
Erikson, E.H. (1963). *Childhood and Society*. New York: Norton.
– (1968). *Identity, Youth and Crisis*. New York: Norton.
Evans-Pritchard, E.E. (1962). *Essays in Social Anthropology*. London: Faber and Faber.
– (1967). *Theories of Primitive Religion*. Oxford: Clarendon.
Farber, B. (1964). *Family: Organization and Interaction*. San Francisco: Chandler.
Fleck, S., Lidz, T. and Cornelison, A. (1963). Comparison of parent–child relationships of male and female schizophrenic patients. *Archives of General Psychiatry* 8, 1–7.
Florence, J. (1978). *L'identification dans la théorie freudienne*. Brussels: Publications des Facultés Universitaires Saint-Louis.
Fluegel, J.C. (1939). *The Psychoanalytic Study of the Family*. London: Hogarth.
Fodor, E.M. (1973). Moral development and parent behavior antecedents in adolescent psychopaths. *The Journal of Genetic Psychology* 122, 37–43.
Freud, S. (1927). *Totem and Taboo*. New York: New Republic.
– (1939a). *Civilisation and its Discontents*. London: Hogarth.
– (1939b). *Moses and Monotheism*. New York: Knopf.
– (1943). *The Future of an Illusion*. London: International Psychoanalytical Library.
– (1957). *On Narcissism: An Introduction*. London: Hogarth.
Friedan, B. (1964). *The Feminine Mystique*. New York: Dell Publishing Company.
Friedman, C. and Friedman, A.S. (1970). Characteristics of psychogenic families during a joint family story-telling task. *Family Process* 9, 333–354.
– (1972). Sex concordance in psychogenic disorders: Psychosomatic disorders in mothers and schizophrenia in daughters. *Archives of General Psychiatry* 27, 611–617.

– (1973). Parental factors in schizophrenia. *Archives of General Psychiatry* 28, 318.
– (1974). *Mental Factors and Schizophrenia*. (MH 11547) Philadelphia: Philadelphia Psychiatry Center.
Fromm, E. (1952). *Psychoanalysis and Religion*. New Haven: Yale University Press.
– (1962). *The Art of Loving*. London: Unwin Books.
Fromm-Reichmann, F. (1948). Notes on the development of treatment of schizophrenics by psychoanalytic psychotherapy. *Psychiatry* 11, 263–273.
Geertz, C. (1975). *The Interpretation of Cultures. Selected Essays*. London: Hutchinson.
George, R.L., Marshall, J.C., Hoemann, V.H. and Minkevich, G. (1972). Personality differences among community college students. *College Student Journal* 6, 30–36.
Gerard, D.L. and Siegel, J. (1950). The family background of schizophrenia. *Psychiatry Quarterly* 24, 47–73.
Ginott, H.G. (1965). *Between Parent and Child: New Solutions to Old Problems*. New York: Macmillan.
Girgensohn, K. (1930). *Der seelischen Aufbau des religiösen Erlebnis*. Gütersloh: Bertelsman.
Glueck, S. and Glueck, E.T. (1962). *Family Environment and Delinquency*. London: Kegan Paul.
– (1964). *Unraveling Juvenile Delinquency*. Cambridge, Mass.: Harvard University Press.
Godin, A. (1975). *Psychologie de la vocation. Un bilan*. Paris: Cerf.
Godin, A. and Hallez, M. (1964). Parental Images and Divine Paternity. In *From Religious Experience to a Religious Attitude*, A. Godin (ed.), 79–110. Brussels: Lumen Vitae.
Goldman, R.D., Kaplan, R.M. and Platt, B.B. (1973). Sex differences in the relationship of attitudes toward technology to choice of field of study. *Journal of Counseling Psychology* 20, 412–418.
Goldman, R.D., Platt, B.B. and Kaplan, R.M. (1973). Dimensions of attitudes toward technology. *Journal of Applied Psychology* 57, 184–187.
Gray, M. (1967). *The Normal Woman*. New York: Scribner.
Gregory, I. (1965). Anterospective data following childhood loss of a parent. *Archives of General Psychiatry* 13, 99–109.
Gruba, F.P. and Johnson, J.E. (1974). Contradictions within the self-concept of schizophrenics. *Journal of Clinical Psychology* 30, 253–254.
Hameline, D. (1972). La créativité. Fortune d'un concept ou concept de fortune? *La Maison-Dieu* 111, 84–109.

Handel, G. (ed.) (1967). *The Psychosocial Interior of the Family: A Source Book for the Study of Whole Families.* Chicago: Aldine.

Harding, M.E. (1965). *The Parental Image: Its Injury and Reconstruction. A Study in Analytical Psychology.* New York: Putman.

Hare, R.O. (1968). *Psychopathy: Theory and Research.* New York: Wiley.

Harman, H.H. (1960). *Modern Factor Analysis.* Chicago: University of Chicago Press.

Harvey, O.J. (1963). Authoritarianism and conceptual function in varied conditions. *Journal of Personality* 31, 462–470.

– (1964). Some cognitive determinants of influenceability. *Sociometry* 27, 208–221.

– (1966). System structure, flexibility and creativity. In *Experience, Structure and Adaptability*, O.J. Harvey (ed.), 39–65. New York: Springer.

– (1967). Conceptual systems and attitude change. In *Attitude, Ego-Involvement, and Change*, C.W. Sherif and M. Sherif (eds.) New York: Wiley.

– (1970). Belief systems and education: Some implications for change. In *The Affective Domain*, J. Crawford (ed.). Washington, D.C.: Communic Service Corps.

Harvey, O.J. and Beverly, G.D. (1961). Some personality correlates of concept change through role playing. *Journal of Abnormal and Social Psychology* 63, 125–130.

Harvey, O.J., Hunt, D.E. and Schroder, H.M. (1961). *Conceptual Systems and Personality Organisation.* New York: Wiley.

Harvey, O.J., White, B.J., Prather, M.S., Alter, R.D. and Hoffmeister, J.K. (1966). Teachers' beliefs and preschool atmospheres. *Journal of Educational Psychology* 57, 373–381.

Hauser, R. (1963). *The Fraternal Society.* New York: Random House.

Henry, G.W. (1955). *All the Sexes: A Study of Masculinity and Feminity.* New York: Rinehart.

Hermann, I. (1936). Sich-Anklammern-Auf-Suche-Gehen. *Internationaler Zeitschrift für Psycho-Analyse* 22, 349–370.

Hoffmeister, J.K. (1965). Conceptual determinants of strength and certainty of beliefs. Unpublished manuscript, University of Colorado.

Hudson, H. (1966). *Contrary Imagination.* London: Methuen.

Hutsebaut D. (1976). Geloven als geleefde relatie. Psychologisch onderzoek naar haar componenten en structuur. Unpublished manuscript, University of Louvain.

Jacob, T. (1975). Family Interaction in disturbed and normal families: A methodological and substantive review. *Psychological Bulletin* 82, 33–65.

Jaspard, J.-M. and Dumoulin, A. (1973). *Les médiations religieuses dans l'univers de l'enfant.* Louvain: University Press.

Jeremias, J. (1966). *Abba. Studien zur neutestamentlichen Theologie und Zeitgeschichte.* Göttingen: Vandenhoeck and Ruprecht.

Jones, E. (1923). The psychology of religion. In *Essays in Applied Psychoanalysis*, E. Jones (ed.). London, Vienna: International Psychoanalytic Press.

Jones, J.E. (1977). Patterns of transactional style deviance in the TAT's of parents of schizophrenics. *Family Process* 16, 327–337.

Jung, C.G. (1947). *Psychology of the Unconscious. A Study of the Transformations and Symbolisms of the Libido.* New York: Dodd and Mead.

– (1961). *The Significance of the Father in the Destiny of the Individual.* The Collected Works of C.G. Jung, vol. 4, 301–323. London: Routledge and Kegan.

Kant, I. (1960). *Religion within the Limits of Reason Alone.* New York: Harper and Row.

– (1964). *Critique of Pure Reason.* New York: Dutton.

Kardiner, A. and Linton, R. (1939). *The Individual and His Society.* New York: Columbia University Press.

Karon, B.P. (1963). The resolution of acute schizophrenic reactions: A contribution to the development of non-classical psychotherapeutic techniques. *Psychotherapy* 1, 27–43.

Kephart, W.M. (1961). *The Family, Society, and the Individual.* Boston: Houghton Mifflin.

Kirk, R.E. (1968). *Experimental Design: Procedures for the Behavioral Sciences.* Belmont, California: Brooks and Cole.

Kirkland, J. (1974). Divergent thinking and academic course orientation. *Psychological Reports* 35, 518.

– (1976). Epistemic curiosity and cartoon preference. *Psychological Reports* 38, 354.

Kirkpatrick, C. (1963). *The Family as Process and Institution.* New York: Ronald Press.

Klein, M. (1965). *Contributions to Psychoanalysis.* London: Hogarth.

Kline, P. (1971). Obsessional traits and academic performance in the sixth form. *Educational Research* 13, 230–232.

Krech, D. and Crutchfield, R.S. (1948). *Theory and Problems of Social Psychology.* New York: McGraw-Hill.

Lacan, J. (1966). *Ecrits.* Paris: Seuil.

– (1973). *Le sommaire, livre XI. Les quatre concepts fondamentaux de la psychanalyse.* Paris: Seuil.

Lamb, M.E. (1975). Fathers: Forgotten contributors to child development. *Human Development* 18, 245–266.

– (1976). *The Role of the Father in Child Development.* New York: Wiley.

Lang, A. (1937). *Encyclopedia of Religion and Ethics.* Edinburgh: James Hastings.

Laplanche, J. (1970). *Vie et mort en psychanalyse.* Paris: Flammarion.

Leach, E. (1961). Asymetric marriage rules. Status difference and direct reciprocity. *South-Western Journal of Anthropology* 17, 343–351.

Legrand, M. (1979). *Leopold Szondi. Son test, sa doctrine.* Brussels: Mardaga.

Lemay, M. (1976). *Psychopathologie juvénile.* Paris: Editions Fleurus.

Lévi-Strauss, Cl. (1949). *Les structures élémentaires de la parenté.* Paris: P.U.F.

– (1969). *Structural Anthropology.* London: Allen Lane.

Lewis, H. (1954). *Deprived Children (The Marshall Experiment). A Social and Clinical Study.* London: Oxford University Press.

Lidz, R.W. and Lidz, T. (1949). The family environment of schizophrenic patients. *American Journal of Psychiatry* 106, 332–345.

Lidz, T. (1957). The intrafamilial environment of the schizophrenic patient: I. The father. *Psychiatry* 20, 329–342.

Little, A. (1965). Parental deprivation, separation and crime: A test on adolescent recidivists. *British Journal of Criminology* 5, 419–430.

Lord, F.M. and Novick, M.R. (1968). *Statistical Theories of Mental Test Scores.* New York: Addison-Wesley.

Lu, Y.C. (1962). Contradictory parental expectations in schizophrenia. *Archives of General Psychiatry* 6, 219–234.

MacKinnon, D.W. (1938). Violations of prohibitions. In *Explorations in Personality*, H.A. Murray (ed.). New York: Oxford University Press.

Malinowski, B. (1924). *Mutterrechtliche Familie und Oedipus Complex.* Vienna: Internationale Psychoanalytischer Verlag.

Marchel, W. (1960). *Abba, Père! La prière du Christ et des chrétiens.* Rome: Pontifico Istituto Biblico.

Masserman, J. (1959). *Individual and Familial Dynamics.* New York: Grune and Stratton.

McCord, W. and McCord, J. (1964). *The Psychopath: An Essay on the Criminal Mind.* New York: Van Nostrand.

Mead, M. (1955). *Male and Female. A Study of the Sexes in a Changing World.* New York: The New American Library.

Mead, M. and Ken, H. (1965). *Family.* New York: Macmillan.

Meyer, R.C., and Karon, B.P. (1967). A study of the schizophrenogenic mother concept by means of the TAT. *Psychiatry* 30, 173–179.

Michel, E. (1954). Das Vaterproblem heute in soziologischer Sicht. In *Vorträge über das Vaterproblem in Psychotherapie, Religion und Gesellschaft*, W. Bitter (ed.), 44–74. Stuttgart: Hippokrates.

Milebamane, B.M.M. (1975). Perception des attitudes et pratiques éducatives du père par les délinquants et les normaux. *Canadian Psychiatric Association Journal* 20, 229–303.

Mishler, E.G. and Waxler, N.E. (1965). Family interaction processes and schizophrenia: A review of current theories. *Merrill-Palmer Quarterly of Behavior and Development* 2, 269-315.

Mitchell, K.M. (1968). An analysis of the schizophrenogenic mother concept by means of the Thematic Apperception Test. *Journal of Abnormal Psychology* 73, 571-574.

— (1969). Concept of 'pathogenesis' in parents of schizophrenic and normal children. *Journal of Abnormal Psychology* 74, 423-424.

— (1974). Relationship between differential levels of parental 'pathogenesis' and male children diagnoses. *Journal of Clinical Psychology* 30, 49-50.

Mitscherlich, A. (1969). *Vers la société sans pères. Essai de psychologie sociale*. Paris: Gallimard.

Mussen, P.H. and Distler, L. (1960). Child rearing antecedents of masculine identification in kindergarten boys. *Child Development* 31, 89-100.

Maess, S. (1959). Mother-child separation and delinquency. *British Journal of Delinquency* 10, 22-35.

Nagel, E. (1968). *The Structure of Science*. London: Routledge and Kegan.

Needham, R. (1972). *Belief, Language and Experience*. Oxford: Basil Blackwell.

Neff, T. (1973). Etudes des résultats du test Szondi appliqué à 120 religieuses francophones. Unpublished manuscript, University of Louvain.

— (1975). La représentation de Dieu à la lumière du test de Szondi. Paper read at The International Congress of Fate Psychology, Paris.

— (1976). Représentation de Dieu et structure de la personnalité. Unpublished manuscript, University of Louvain.

— (1977). Image of God and psychic structure. *Lumen Vitae* 32, 399-422.

Nelson, M.O. (1971). The concept of God and feeling towards parents. *Journal of Individual Psychology* 27, 46-49.

Nelson, M.O. and Jones, E.M. (1957). An application of the q-technique to the study of religious concepts. *Psychological Reports* 3, 293-297.

Newman, G. and Denman, S.B. (1970-1971). Felony and paternal deprivation: A socio-psychiatric view. *International Journal of Social Psychiatry*, 17, 65-71.

Nunnally, J.C. (1967). *Psychometric Theory*. New York: McGraw-Hill.

Olaerts, R. (1971). Symbool-en herinneringsbeelden van de ouders in hun relatie tot het godsbeeld. Unpublished manuscript, University of Louvain.

Olson, D.H. (1972). Empirically unbinding the double bind: Review of research and conceptual formulations. *Family Process* 11, 69-94.

Oltman, J. and Friedman, S. (1967). Parental deprivation in psychiatric conditions. *Diseases of the Nervous System* 28, 298-303.

Osgood, C.E., Suci, G.J. and Tannenbaum, P.H. (1971). *The Measurement of Meaning*. Urbana: University of Illinois Press.

Parsons, T. (1954). The father symbol: An appraisal in the light of psycho-analytic and sociological theory. In *Symbols and Values*, L. Bryson, L. Kinkelstein, R.M. MacIver, and R. McKeon (eds.), 34–55. New York: Harper and Row.

Parsons, T. and Bales, R.F. (1955). *Family, Socialization, and Interaction Process*. Glencoe, Ill.: Free Press.

Pasquali, L. (1970). The parental images and the concept of God. Unpublished manuscript, University of Louvain.

Passingham, R.E. (1968). A study of delinquents with children's-home background. *British Journal of Criminology* 8, 32–45.

Pattyn, M.R. and Custers, A. (1964). Het vadersymbool en het moedersymbool in de godsvoorstelling. Unpublished manuscript, University of Louvain.

Pohier, J. (1969). La primauté du Père comme attribut du Fils dans la foi chrétienne. *Interprétation* 3, 49–90.

Potvin, R. and Suziedelis, A. (1969). *Seminarians of the Sixties*. Washington, D.C.: Center for Applied Research in the Apostolate.

Prout, C.T. and White, M.A. (1950). A controlled study of personality relationships in mothers of schizophrenic male patients. *American Journal of Psychiatry* 107, 251–256.

Radcliffe-Brown, A.R. (1969). *Structure and Function in Primitive Society: Essays and Addresses*. London: Cohen and West.

Rank, B. (1955). Intensive study of preschool children who show marked personality deviations or atypical development and their parents. In *Emotional Problems of Early Childhood*, G. Caplan (ed.), 491–502. New York: Basic Books.

Reichard, S. and Tillman, C. (1950). Patterns of parent–child relationships in schizophrenia. *Psychiatry* 13, 247–257.

Ricoeur, P. (1969). La paternité. *Interprétation* 3, 173–214.

Ringuette, E.L. and Kennedy, T. (1966). An experimental study of the double-bind hypothesis. *Journal of Abnormal Psychology* 71, 136–141.

Riskin, J. and Faunce, E. (1972). An evaluative review of family interaction research. *Family Process* 11, 365–456.

Rizzuto, A.M. (1974). Object relations and the formation of the image of God. *British Journal of Medical Psychology* 47, 83–99.

Robins, L.R. (1966). *Deviant Children Grown Up: A Sociological and Psychiatric Study of Sociopathic Personality*. Baltimore: Williams and Wilkins.

Rokeach, M. (1960). *The Open and Closed Mind. Investigations into the Nature of Belief Systems and Personality Systems*. New York: Basic Books.

Rosenthal, D., Wender, P.H., Ketty, S.S., Schulsinger, F., Welner, J. and Reiber, R.D. (1975). Parent–child relationships and psychopathological disorders in the child. *Archives of General Psychiatry* 32, 466–476.

Rouzic, L. (1927) *Le Père*. Paris: Téqui.

Rulla, L.M. (1971) *Depth Psychology and Vocation*. Chicago: Loyola University Press.

Russell, L. (1974). *Human Liberation in a Feminist-Perspective. A Theology*. Philadelphia: The Westminster Press.

Schodts, J. (1971). Godsbeeld en oudersymbool. Unpublished manuscript, University of Louvain.

Simon, A. and Ward, L.O. (1974). The performance on the Watson-Glaser Critical Thinking Appraisal of university students classified according to sex, type of course pursued, and personality score category. *Educational and Psychological Measurement* 34, 957–960.

Singer, M.T. and Wynne, L.C. (1965). Thought disorder and family relations of schizophrenics: IV. Results and implications. *Archives of General Psychiatry* 12, 201–212.

Sirjamaki, J. (1953). *The American Family in the Twentieth Century*. Cambridge, Mass.: Harvard University Press.

Smithers, A.G. and Child, D. (1974). Convergers and divergers: Different forms of neuroticism? *British Journal of Educational Psychology* 44, 304–306.

Sojit, C.M. (1969). Dyadic interaction in a double-bind situation. *Family Process* 8, 235–259.

– (1971). The double-bind hypothesis and the parents of schizophrenics. *Family Process* 10, 53–74.

Spilka, B., Armatas, P. and Nussbaum, J. (1964). The concept of God. A factor-analytic study. *Review of Religious Research* 6, 28–36.

Spiro, M.E. and D'Andrade, R.G. (1958). A cross-cultural study of some supernatural beliefs. *American Anthropologist* 60, 456–466.

Spitz, R. (1968). *De la naissance à la parole*. Paris: P.U.F.

Sprott, W.J.H. Jephcott, A.P. and Carter, M.P. (1955). *The Social Background of Delinquency*. Nottingham: University of Nottingham.

Stephens, W. (1963). *The Family in Cross-Cultural Perspective*. New York: Holt, Rinehart and Winston.

Strunk, D., Jr. (1959). Perceived relationships between parental and deity concepts. *Psychological Newsletter* 10, 222–226.

Sullivan, H.S. (1947). *Conceptions of Modern Psychiatry*. New York: Norton.

Szondi, L. (1952). *Triebpathologie*. Bern: Huber.

– (1972). *Lehrbuch der Experimentellen Triebdiagnostic*. Bern: Huber.

Tamayo, A. (1970). Structure psychologique des images parentales et leur symbolisme religieux. Etude interculturelle. Unpublished manuscript, University of Louvain.

Tamayo, A. and Desjardins, L. (1976). Belief systems and conceptual images of parents and God. *The Journal of Psychology* 92, 131–140.

Tamayo, A. and Dugas, A. (1977). Conceptual representation of mother, father and God according to sex and field of study. *The Journal of Psychology* 97, 79–84.

Tamayo, A. and Pasquali, L. (1967). Symbolization of the image of God by the parental images: Genetic and differential study. Unpublished manuscript, University of Louvain.

Tietze, T. (1949). A study of mothers of schizophrenic patients. *Psychiatry* 12, 55–65.

Tringer, L. (1975). Les troubles psychiatriques sous les aspects de la socialisation. *Annales Médico-Psychologiques* 133, 141–151.

Tucker, L.R. (1951). *A Method for Synthesis of Factor Analysis Studies. Personnel Research Section Report*, no. 984, Department of the Army, Washington, D.C.

Van Cottem, R. (1977). Religious attitudes of priests. *Lumen Vitae* 32, 434–464.

Van der Leeuw, G. (1948). *La religion dans son essence et ses manifestations.* Paris: Payot.

Van Mechelen, L. (1968). Waarde-oriëntering en godsvoorstelling. Unpublished manuscript, University of Louvain.

Vannesse, A. (1974). Testologie d'un groupe de 100 séminaristes. In *Szondiana* X (Proceedings of the International Congress of Fate Psychology), J. Schotte and W. Huth (eds.), 161–171. Bern: Huber.

– (1977a). Religious language and relation to the mother. *Lumen Vitae* 32, 423–433.

– (1977b). Relations entre langage religieux et structures pulsionnelles. Unpublished manuscript, University of Louvain.

Vercruysse, G. (1972). The meaning of God: A factoranalytic study. *Social Compass* 19, 347–364.

Vergote, A. (1969). *The Religious Man. A Psychological Study of Religious Attitude.* Dublin: Gill and Macmillan.

– (1978). *Dette et désir. Deux axes chrétiens et la dérive pathologique.* Paris: Seuil.

Vergote, A. and Aubert, C. (1972). Parental images and representation of God. *Social Compass* 19, 431–444.

Vergote, A., Tamayo, A., Pasquali, L., Bonami, M., Pattyn, M.R. and Custers, A. Concept of God and parental images. *Journal for the Scientific Study of Religion* 8, 79–87.

Virkkunen, M. (1976). Parental deprivation and recidivism in juvenile delinquents. *British Journal of Criminology* 16, 378–384.

Ware, R. and Harvey, O.J. (1967). A cognitive determinant of impression formation. *Journal of Personality and Social Psychology* 5, 38–44.

Warren, M.Q. and Palmer, T.B. (1965). *Community Treatment Project: An Evaluation of Community Treatment of Delinquents.* Sponsored by the California Youth Authority and the National Institute of Mental Health. C.T.P. Research Report no. 6.

Watzlawick, P. (1963). A review of the double bind theory. *Family Process* 2, 132–153.

Waxler, N.E. and Mishler, E.G. (1971). Parental interaction with schizophrenic children and well siblings. An experimental test of some etiological theories. *Archives of General Psychiatry* 25, 223–231.

Weber, M. (1930). *The Protestant Ethic and the Spirit of Capitalism*. New York: Scribner.

West, D.J. (1969). *Present Conduct and Future Delinquency*. London: Heinemann.

– (1973). *Who Becomes Delinquent?* London: Heinemann.

White, B.J. and Harvey, O.J. (1965). Effects of personality and own stand on judgement and production of statements about a central issue. *Journal of Experimental Social Psychology* 1, 334–347.

Wild, C.M., Shapiro, L.N. and Goldenberg, L. (1975). Transactional communication disturbances in families of male schizophrenics. *Family Process* 14, 131–160.

Williamson, R.C. (1966). *Marriage and Family Relations*. New York: Wiley.

Winch, R.F., McGinis, R. and Barringer, H.R. (eds.) (1962). *Selected Studies in Marriage and the Family*. New York: Holt, Rinehart, and Winston.

Winnicott, D.W. (1965). *The Maturational Processes and the Facilitating Environment*. New York: International Universities Press.

Winter, D.A. (1975). Some characteristics of schizophrenics and their parents. *British Journal of Social and Clinical Psychology* 14, 279–290.

Wynne, L.C. and Singer, M.T. (1963a). Thought disorder and family relations of schizophrenics: I. A research strategy. *Archives of General Psychiatry* 9, 191–198.

– (1963b). Thought disorder and family relations of schizophrenics: II. A classification of forms of thinking. *Archives of General Psychiatry* 9, 199–206.

Zazzo, R. (1974). L'attachement. In *L'attachement*, R. Zazzo (ed.), Neuchâtel: Delachaux et Niestlé.

Author Index

Ainsworth, M.D., 147
Alanen, Y.O., 149, 150
Allport, G., 2, 19
Alter, R.D., 109
Anzieu, D., 9
Ariès, Ph., 9
Arieti, S., 149
Armatas, P., 125

Bachelard, G., 234
Bachofen, J.J., 234
Bales, R.F., 196·
Balestrieri, I., 46
Bandura, A., 146
Barringer, H.R., 169
Barton, K., 103
Bateson, G., 150, 151, 167
Baur, F., 234
Beakel, N.G., 151
Beavers, W.R., 151
Benedict, R., 1
Berger, A., 151
Bergounioux, F.M., 201
Bernardi, G., 26, 47, 107
Bettelheim, B., 12
Beverly, G.D., 108, 109
Bitter, W., 234
Blumberg, S., 151
Boll, E.S., 169
Bonami, M., 26, 44, 99, 107
Bopp, L., 234
Bossard, J.H.S., 169
Boston, H., 147
Bovet, P., 2, 234
Bowen, M.A., 151, 152, 166

Bowlby, J., 146, 147, 186
Brenton, M., 169
Buytendijk, F.J.J., 234

Carter, M.P., 146
Cassiers, L., 166, 167
Cattell, H., 103
Cheek, F.E., 150, 152
Child, D., 103
Christensen, H.T., 169
Clausen, J.A., 152, 166
Cleckley, H., 146, 166, 167
Cooley, W.W., 127
Corin, E., 8, 21
Cornelison, A., 166
Craig, M.M., 146
Crutchfield, R.S., 9
Custers, A., 26, 43

Daly, M., 220
D'Andrade, R.G., 2, 5
Davies, M., 147
De Beauvoir, S., 234
Debesse, M., 234
Deconchy, J.P., 201
De Meester, P., 234
Denman, S.B., 147
Deri, S., 142
de Saussure, F., 6
Desjardins, L., 99
Despert, J.L., 149
Deutsch, H., 234
Distler, L., 196
Dolto, F., 1, 7
Douglas, M., 221

Dugas, A., 99, 167
Dumoulin, A., 200

Eliade, M., 2, 21, 201, 208, 234
Erikson, E.H., 1, 142
Evans-Pritchard, E.E., 2, 221

Farber, B., 169
Faunce, E., 146
Fleck, S., 166
Florence, J., 17
Fluegel, J.C., 169, 234
Fodor, E.M., 147
Freud, S., 2, 18, 187, 223, 224, 235
Friedan, B., 169
Friedman, A.S., 148, 149
Friedman, C., 148, 149
Friedman, S., 147
Fromm, E., 2, 186
Fromm-Reichmann, F., 149

Geertz, C., 6, 10
Geist, W., 235
Gelber, L., 235
George, R.L., 103
Gerard, D.L., 150
Gijsen, M., 235
Ginott, H.G., 169
Girgensohn, K., 2
Glick, S.J., 146
Glueck, E.T., 146
Glueck, S., 146
Godin, A., 5, 10, 18, 136, 143, 235
Goetz, J., 201
Goldenberg, L., 149
Goldman, R.D., 103
Gray, M., 169
Gregory, I., 147
Groeger, G.N., 235
Gruba, F.P., 167

Haendler, O., 235

Haley, J., 150, 151, 167
Hallez, M., 5, 10, 18
Hameline, D., 10
Handel, G., 169
Harding, M.E., 169
Hare, R.O., 166
Harman, H.H., 74, 157
Hart de Ruyter, Th., 235
Harvey, O.J., 108, 109, 110
Hauser, R., 9
Henry, G.W., 169
Hermann, I., 186
Hesse, H., 235
Hoemann, V.H., 103
Hoffmeister, J.K., 109
Hollenbach, J.M., 235
Hudson, H., 103
Hunt, D.E., 109
Hutsebaut, D., 125, 211

Jackson, D.D., 150, 151, 167
Jacob, T., 146
Jaspard, J.-M., 200
Jephcott, A.P., 146
Jeremias, J., 213
Johnson, J.E., 167
Jones, E., 2
Jones, E.M., 18
Jones, J.E., 148
Jung, C.G., 2, 4, 235

Kafka, F., 236
Kant, E., 4, 222
Kaplan, R.M., 103
Kardiner, A., 5, 236
Karon, B.P., 150
Ken, H., 169
Kennedy, T., 151
Kephart, W.M., 169
Ketty, S.S., 146
Kinget, M., 236
Kirk, R.E., 100, 117, 156

Kirkland, J., 103
Kirkpatrick, G., 169
Kittel, G., 236
Klein, M., 1
Kline, P., 103
Koeberle, D.A., 236
Kohn, M.L., 152, 166
Krech, D., 9
Kriekemans, A., 236

Lacan, J., 187
Lamb, M.E., 1, 17
Lang, A., 22
Laplanche, J., 187
Leach, E., 21
Legrand, M., 142
Lemay, M., 147
Lévi-Strauss, Cl., 6, 21
Lewis, H., 147
Lidz, R.W., 150
Lidz, T., 150, 152
Linton, R., 5
Little, A., 147
Lohnes, P.R., 127
Lord, F.M., 31
Lu, Y.C., 148

MacKinnon, D.W., 196
Malinowski, B., 21, 236
Marcel, G., 236
Marchel, W., 213
Marshall, J.C., 103
Masserman, J., 1
Maurois, A., 236
McCord, J., 146
McCord, W., 146
McGinis, R., 169
Mead, M., 169, 190, 236
Mehrabian, A., 151
Meyer, R.C., 150
Michel, E., 14, 236
Milebamane, B.M.M., 147

Minkevich, G., 103
Mishler, E.G., 146, 149
Mitchell, K.M., 150
Mitscherlich, A., 9
Morgan, C.D., 236
Murdock, G.P., 236
Murray, H.A., 236
Mussen, P.H., 196

Naess, S., 147
Nagel, E., 7
Needham, R., 221
Neff, T., 142, 199, 212
Nelson, M.O., 5, 18
Neumann, E., 236
Newman, G., 147
Novick, M.R., 31
Nunnally, J.C., 36
Nussbaum, J., 125

Olaerts, R., 44, 107
Olson, D.H., 151
Oltman, J., 147
Oraison, M., 236
Osgood, C.E., 25, 56, 75, 100

Palmer, T.B., 147
Parsons, T., 14, 196
Pasquali, L., 26, 46, 100, 107, 202,
    216
Passingham, R.E., 147
Pattyn, M.R., 26, 43
Perrin, A., 236
Platt, B.B., 103
Pohier, J., 22
Porot, M., 236
Potvin, R., 136, 143
Prather, M.S., 109
Prout, C.T., 150

Radcliffe-Brown, A.R., 8
Rank, B., 149

Ranke, B., 236
Reiber, R.D., 146
Reichard, S., 150
Ricoeur, P., 22
Ringuette, E.L., 151
Riskin, J., 146
Rizzuto, A.M., 1
Robins, L.R., 147
Rogers, C.R., 236
Rokeach, M., 9
Romaeus, P., 235
Rosenberg, A., 237
Rosenbuth, M.D., 147
Rosenthal, D., 146
Rouzic, L., 14, 237
Rulla, L.M., 143
Russell, L., 220
Rustoew, A., 237

Schodts, J., 44, 107
Schroder, H.M., 109
Schulsinger, F., 146
Shapiro, L.N., 149
Siegel, J., 150
Simon, A., 103
Sinclair, I., 147
Singer, M.T., 149
Sirjamaki, J., 169
Smithers, A.G., 103
Sojit, C.M., 151
Speck, O., 237
Spilka, B., 125
Spiro, M.E., 2, 5
Spitz, R., 186
Sprott, W.J.H., 146
Stephens, W., 1
Strunk, D., jr., 5, 18
Suci, G.J., 25, 56, 75, 100
Sullivan, H.S., 149
Suziedelis, A., 136, 143
Szondi, L., 142, 186, 199, 213

Tamayo, A., 26, 46, 99, 100, 107, 167
Tannenbaum, P.H., 25, 56, 75, 100
Tietze, T., 150
Tillman, C., 150
Timken, K.R., 151
Trier, J., 237
Trilles, H., 237
Tringer, L., 148
Tucker, L.R., 74, 100, 104, 111, 118, 157, 172

Van Benthem Jutting, W., 237
Van Cottem, R., 213
Van den Berg, J.H., 237
Van der Kerken, L., 237
Van der Leeuw, G., 2, 237
Van de Woestijne, K., 237
Van Mechelen, L., 43
Vannesse, A., 142, 199, 212
Vercruysse, G., 208, 212, 219
Vergote, A., 205, 212, 237
Virkkunen, M., 147
Von Le Fort, G., 237

Walters, R.H., 146
Ward, L.O., 103
Ware, R., 109
Warren, M.Q., 147
Watzlawick, P., 150
Waxler, N.E., 146, 149
Weakland, J., 150, 151, 167
Weber, M., 203
Weiner, M.F., 151
Welner, J., 146
Wender, P.H., 146
West, D.J., 146
Westermarck, E., 237
White, B.J., 109
White, M.A., 150
Wiechert, E., 237

Wild, C.M., 149
Williamson, R.C., 169
Winch, R.F., 169
Winnicott, D.W., 1

Winter, D.A., 148
Wynne, L.C., 149

Zazzo, R., 186